W9-DDT-846

THE FAMILY TREE
HISTORICAL
NEWSPAPERS GUIDE

DISCARD

WEST GA REG LIB SYS
Neva Lomason
Memorial Library

AMERICAN TELEGRAPH

PUBLISHED EVERY AFTERNOON,
(EXCEPT SUNDAY,)
ON THE 4t., opposite Odd-Fellows' Hall,
BY CONNOLLY, WIMER & McGILL,
3t TWO CENTS a Week, or
TWELVE CENTS A SINGLE COPY.

To subscribers served by the carriers, the paper will be furnished regularly for ten cents per week, payable weekly...

CIRCULATED SIMULTANEOUSLY
IN WASHINGTON, GEORGETOWN,
AND ALEXANDRIA.

CASH TERMS OF ADVERTISING.

IRISH EMIGRANT SOCIETY.

Office, No. 1 Reade Street, New York.

AMERICAN TELEGRAPH

For the American Telegraph.
THE BANNER OF LIGHT.
A NATIONAL SONG.
BY T. K. YOUNG.

All hail to the beautiful Land of the Free.

MUSIC

LITERATURE OF THE CENSUS.

THE TRUE LADY.
By the Editor of the Telegraph.

THE FAMILY TREE
HISTORICAL
NEWSPAPERS GUIDE

HOW TO FIND YOUR ANCESTORS IN ARCHIVED NEWSPAPERS

JAMES M. BEIDLER

FAMILY
TREE
BOOKS

CINCINNATI, OHIO
familytreemagazine.com/store

CONTENTS

PART ONE · LEARNING THE BASICS

CHAPTER 1
Learn how the most widely used print medium has affected society. This chapter will discuss the history of newspapers and why they're significant when researching your family tree.

CHAPTER 2
Jump-start your newspaper research! This chapter will give you a crash course in the various resources newspapers offer, from news articles to editorials to classifieds to social columns.

CHAPTER 3
Read all about your ancestors' major life events. This chapter will discuss how newspapers can clue you in to a community's births, marriages, divorces, deaths, and other milestones.

CHAPTER 4
Build your family tree using obituaries (the most widely known newspaper record) and other death notices in print.

CHAPTER 5
Track down papers from your ancestor's time. This chapter will discuss how newspapers were recorded throughout time, plus the formats they appear in today.

PART TWO · ACCESSING DIGITIZED NEWSPAPERS

CHAPTER 6
Explore the free resources that hold digitized newspapers (such as Chronicling America) with this wrap-up of websites for genealogists on a budget.

CHAPTER 7
See what you can find on Newspapers.com, the sister site of genealogy giant Ancestry.com.

CHAPTER 8
Uncover your ancestors in Genealogy-Bank's digitized collection of newspapers, obituaries, government documents, and more.

CHAPTER 9
Broaden your research with these smaller for-pay resources, such as NewspaperArchive, FindMyPast, and more.

CHAPTER 10
Locate individual newspapers with digital catalogs, such as the US Newspaper Directory and WorldCat. This chapter will show you how.

PART THREE · DIVING DEEPER INTO NEWSPAPERS

FRY IN YOUR OWN FAT

——If You Wish——

If you'd better however to go to

John Irwin's

White Front!

And Invest in

Cool Garments!

Now that you can buy at such

LOW PRICES.

——All kinds of——

Summer Goods

AT LESS THAN COST.

P. O. Block.

HENRY BROS.'
BREAD AND CAKE
BAKERY

S. E. Cor. Old Square, Decatur, Ill.

Best Lunch Counter
in Decatur.

Every Prohibition Club

Should be supplied with

Gen. Hudson's

Prohibition

War Songs.

Price 10c each or $1.00
Per Dozen.

Order of the SENTINEL.

The Popular Campaign
Song,

Prohibition's Coming,

Takes well Everywhere

In sheet music, Price 25 cents

Order of the SENTINEL.

Hotel Brunswick,

Opposite Court House.

Northwest corner Wood and Water stree
DECATUR, ILL.

Pleasant Rooms
Patronage Pleased,
Popular Prices.
J. F. CURRY, Prop.

Rates $1.50 and $2.00 per Day

STOP AT THE BRUNSWICK

THE GREAT PARADE.

At Columbus, Ohio, on Prohibition Day, October 11, 1888.

The great Prohibition party that will parade at Columbus, Ohio, on October 11, will consist of three divisions.

First, the "Veteran Division," composed of members of the army of the Blue and Gray, and all old soldiers of both North and South who will enlist for the present war against the Nation's greatest foe - the saloon.

Second, the "Uniformed Division," composed of all uniformed clubs having at least one uniformed article of clothing, such as hats, caps, helmets, capes or the like.

Third, the "Civilian Division," composed of clubs of men who will march, but are without uniforms and do not belong to the first Division.

In case uniformed companies of "Veterans" can be organized, two brigades, a uniformed and a civilian brigade, will be made in the last Division.

The general and division commanders are as follows:

General commander-in-chief, Capt. Wilbur Colvin, Springfield, Ohio.

First Division, General R. E. Hudson, Alliance, Ohio, Grand Commander of the Army of the Blue and Gray.

Second Division, General Walter S. Payne, Fostoria, Ohio. Prohibition candidate for secretary of State of Ohio.

Third Division, Col. Geo. W. Bain, of Kentucky, --if he can be present.

Counties and cities in all directions within reasonable distance of Columbus should at once proceed to organize a company, a batalion, or a regiment. What a million a reasonable distance? A club is coming from Nebraska.

Organize a company or a batalion or a club and get the local benefit of it at once as a campaign club for home work before and after "Prohibition Day." It will be a splendid investment. Make one or more good home parades; they will do you good.

Wherever possible, organize a company for the "Veteran Division." If a full company cannot be organized, form a squad or platoon and prepare to unite with other squads or platoons to form a full company for the great parade. Wherever possible, uniform the companies or clubs. But if this is not practicable, organize and prepare to join the "Civilian Division." Twenty-five to fifty members are the limits in a company. Less than twenty-five form a squad or platoon. If you can get over fifty active, reliable members organize another company. Small organizations will be more efficient and more readily handled.

CALL A MEETING,

or take a few minutes at some meeting; secure all the names that will enlist, elect officers - a captain and a first and second lieutenant - to save the nucei of several companies can be formed all the better, start with a dozen members and let the officers recruit their companies to the limit as rapidly as possible.

Wherever possible, have the young men. First First Voters, men who this year cast their first presidential vote, and young men who will vote in or before 1892, organize separate companies, "Cadets." They will enter into the work with wonderful vim. Encourage the young men.

GO TO WORK RIGHT NOW.

When several companies are organized form a batalion, and elect regimental officers. Each county should form a regimental organization. It not otherwise provided for, let county executive officers take hold of the matter and appoint a commander to attend to the organization of a batalion in the county. Begin immediately.

When you have organized, drill. Prepare to make good appearance on parade; 5,000 well drilled men, keeping step, with ranks well formed and capable of being maneuvered in simple movements, will produce a greater impression than three times that number a straggling along like a mob. Drill, prepare to march like sober soldiers.

THIS MUST BE THE FINEST PARADE ever seen in the United States. The Prohibitionists are the men that can make it. Every man in it will be sober. "Will you be there?"

For a uniform the following is suggested: A white duck helmet with gilt spike, and white cape of enameled cloth with red border and red collar. It is very neat and costs only 80 cents. Meanwhile if you wish to look farther, drop a card to some campaign furnishing house for a circular.

The commander-in-chief desires to be in direct communication with each and every company. If you have organized, send word to

WILBER COLVIN, SPRINGFIELD, OHIO, giving names and addresses of officers. If you are contemplating organizing and what are pictures, address him.

Remember that while we are putting forth activity and energy in this matter, we are by this very work energizing, enthusing, and making a splendid campaign investment.

On to Columbus, 10,000 strong!

I. O. G. T. GRAND LODGE.

38TH SESSION OF THE ILLINOIS WORKERS MEETS AT ELGIN. SEPT. 11 TO 13.

126 New Lodges and a Gain of Nearly 1,800 Members.

A YEAR OF HARMONY, PROSPERITY AND PROGRESS.

ELGIN, ILL., Sept. 11, 1888.—Grand Lodge, I. O. G. T., of the state of Illinois, met in Grand Templars Hall and was called to order at 9 o'clock a. m., by Uriah Copp, Jr., in the chair, and opened with usual ceremonies in the G. L. degree.

The roll of officers was called and the following found present:

G. C. T., G. C., U. S. G. Treas., G. S. J. T., G. Chap., G. O. G., G. A. S.
Absent, G. V. T., G. M., G. I. G., G. D. M. and P. G. C. T.

Vacancies were filled as follows: G. V. T., Sister Frank E. Finch; G. M., Bro. Frank Walton; G. I. G., Malinda Barnes; ar.: G. D. M., E. O. VanOrsdand, ar.: P. G. C. T. Bro. C. G. Hayman.

Committee on Credentials reported. Report adopted.

The Grand Lodge degree was then conferred upon those entitled to it.

Bro. E. W. Chafin, of Wisconsin, was introduced and addressed the Grand Lodge.

1. Resolutions were passed requiring all resolutions to be in writing and placed on secretary's table before being considered.

2. That all resolutions requiring legislation be first submitted to the appropriate committee and resolution requiring expenditure be submitted to the finance committee.

3. That no member be permitted to speak on any question to exceed five minutes, unless permitted by Grand Lodge.

4. That election of officers be made the special order of business at 11 o'clock a. m., Wednesday.

5. That the sittings be made from 9 a. m. to 12 m., and 2 p. m. to 5:30 p. m., and from 7:30 to adjournment, except this evening. On motion election of officers was fixed at 10 a. m. Wednesday.

On motion the above resolutions were adopted.

Bro. C. H. Knight, of Wisconsin, was introduced to Grand Lodge.

On motion reading reports of officers was dispensed with, their reports being printed and distributed to all delegates and considered read.

The following were appointed committee on distribution: Bros. Griffith, Tuttle and Robey. On motion delegates reported condition of their lodges. On motion the grand lodge decided to meet 7:15 this evening and in a body in regalia, to attend the public meeting at the First Methodist church, to be addressed by Col. J. T. Long.

AFTERNOON.

Grand lodge met at 2 p. m., Bro. Copp in the chair. Opened by singing a song ode. Roll call showed P. G. C. T., G. M., G. L. G., G. D. M. and G. Mess. still absent. Minutes of forenoon session read and approved.

The Grand Lodge appointed Bro. R. C. Elliott of Argo Pora lodge, Chicago, as press reporter with a compensation of $16.

Vacancies on committees filled as follows:
State of the Order—Sister Mott.
Constitution—J. T. Long and H. Y. Kellar.
Temperance Literature—J. M. Bond and John Weller.
Juvenile Templars—Sisters Finch, Vanordstrand and Mills.

Committee on Distribution submitted report which was adopted.

Each officer's report was thus distributed in proper sections to the various committees for intelligent and decisive action.

A motion was carried that a committee of three be appointed on resolutions.

The reports of lodges was resumed and completed.

Bros. Chafin of Wisconsin asked permission and presented "The Western Good Templar" and its claims as a Good Templar paper.

Bro. W. E. Mann followed and presented the STATE SENTINEL as the oldest Prohibition paper in existence and which for 12 years had advocated Good Templary, and which now proposed to give Illinois Good Templars all the space they want as an Illinois Good Templar paper.

Juvenile Templar work was next considered and Bro. Chafin was called on and made a pointing speech showing the Wisconsin method of increasing their membership over 3,000 and at the same time organizing fifty Juvenile Temples with but little extra expense.

Bros. Elsworth, Long, Finch, and Sisters Vanordstrand, Hazlett and Morris also made remarks on the topic.

The committee on Memorial appointed was Rev. T. J. Wood, G. W. Basset and Eunice Hooper.

EVENING MEETING.

The Lodge met in a body and attended a meeting at the First M. E. church.

After the opening ode and a song by the choir, Rev. Wood, of Colchester, led in prayer. Chief Templar Copp then introduced Col. J. T. Long who spoke for nearly an hour.

Synopsis of

COL. J. T. LONG'S SPEECH.

LADIES AND GENTLEMEN:—Our great cause never brought the blush of shame to the cheek of any who advocate it.

We do not care where stood the cradle of any man who advocates the cause. If he loves our land, if he is loyal. If he comes with a desire to prevent anarchistic power or to destroy the laws we love, then the Good Templars wave the line of his fraternity. This traffic brings ignominy on the land and is protected by our law. It brings wail and woe to the homes of our land. In this contest we ask no favors—we give none. We demand that every man who loves the country shall stand till the foe goes down.

The prohibitionist is misunderstood. He does not demand no drink, but that the government shall not protect the crime.

The whiskyite says, "we cannot make men moral by law." We demand he shall cease making men immoral by law.

Liberty is the pretense to do as one please, so long as one does not endanger any other man's liberty. Some more demand more than either church or state.

We have tried regulation and license long enough, to our sorrow. If you oppose agitation you lack patriotism. You are a political traitor. You have no right to fall to put yourself on record. Your vote is your record. We are not to be appalled by the terrible enormity of the evil. A few years ago north of Mason and Dixon's line were the southern people bitter and independent. In the north was another sentiment said. Mr. Lincoln's position was "No territory for slavery." One half free! One half slave. Were you honest? The G. A. R. boys will tell you both sides were honest. Appomatox the stars and bars were stricken from them and trailed in the dust. Sad no one man in the south to-day has the faintest hope of recovery. Why? "The will of the people is law." The stain on our country's honor to-day is slavery to the Rum Power. The money of the enemy is already set apart for the fight. We can never accomplish our object without agitation. The I. O. G. T. is non-partisan institution. It is a believer in prohibition. [Applause.] I haven't much intellect, but no brewer or distiller has a mortgage on what little I have. The great need of the hour is men who knows the economy of the hour. Who fear no party lash. Men sell in Illinois law allows. Men don't, in Iowa law forbids. Men who know that to secure such reform political power born of the hours used is wanted.

"The concentrated patriotism and better wisdom of the sovereign voters of this county must demand a political party born of the hours needs. A party with courage enough to say the saloon must go."

"A party that thinks as much of a law-abiding American as it does of a God-defying, law-defying, Sabbath-breaking lager beer dutchman."

"A party that proclaims boldly in the ears of the world that every reason why a man should vote is a reason why a woman should vote too."

"A party that does not ask its candidates whether they were born in Fannul Hall, and reared on Bunker Hill or born under a palmetto tree and nursed in the lap of John C. Calhoun; that does not care whether they think God they have never been republicans or that they have never been democrats, but a party that does demand of its standard bearers that they shall have clean hands and clean hearts and hate the whisky traffic like the devil does holy water."

Wive's plead for such a party. It will grow. It is growing.

Let every man vote never if not right. Just as surely as God reigns to-night, you cause will win.

If I've said anything I'm sorry for I'm glad of it, and if you'll come forward and apologize I'll forgive you."

Col. Long was followed by G. C. T. Chafin of Wisconsin, and Bro. Geo. Christian of Chicago, each of whom made telling talks for the cause of the Home against the saloon.

SECOND DAY.

Minutes of last session read and approved.

Committee on Credentials made additional report.

A box of roses was presented to the Lodge with the compliments of the Elgin Rose Company. The same was accepted and distributed among the delegates. Grand Chief Templar Copp extended the thanks of the Grand Lodge to the company for their kind donation.

Committee on Appeals made a report which was adopted.

The next was the election of officers which resulted as follows:

G. Counselor, T. J. Wood, Colchester.

Sister R. V. Williams, of Galesburg, in request favored the Lodge with a recitation during the counting of the ballots.

AFTERNOON.

Election of officers continued:

Dr. Henrietta K. Morris, of Chicago, was elected G. V. T.

R. J. Hazlett, of Freeport, G. S.

Sister A. E. Wells, of Chicago. G. S

Juvenile Templars.

George P. Harrington, of Edinburg, G. Treas.

N. Juul, of Chicago, G. M.

On motion a resolution was adopted for the government of session. Moved and carried that a committee of three including G. C. T. Copp be appointed to arrangement and reception for the next session of the Right Worthy Grand Lodge in Chicago next May.

Election of representatives to the Right Worthy Grand Lodge resulted as follows: J. T. Long, T. J. Wood, R. J. Hazlett, Frances E. Finch, with alternates—Dr. Henrietta K. Morris, G. C. Christina, N. T. Allen and George M. Bassett.

A communication from Sister Eunice Hooper regarding the Finch Memorial Fund together with plans for action looking to the completion and dedication of a suitable monument to our lamented leader, John B. Finch, was read and referred to the Committee on Memorial.

WEDNESDAY EVENING.

The evening session was devoted to reports of the various committees and action upon them, after which the members enjoyed a social hour.

STATE OF THE ORDER.

The secretary's report showed an increase of nearly two thousand members, now a surplus on hand with which to commence work for another year. This is an encouraging state of affairs.

The campaign year with its political excitement has alway in the past proven a diversion from lodge work much to be dreaded.

And our present campaign is probably more to be feared by our order than any previous because of our fact that temperance principles are sought to be kept out of sight in the political workings of to-day. While the spirit of excitement and rum claims antiquated right to the soil.

1. But the principles of our noble Order—total abstinence for the Individual and the entire abolition of the traffic in State and Nation—must not be lost sight of by the Good Templars as it is a part of his life-long obligation and necessary accompanies him in all his life relations.

2. We regret the loss by suspension of nearly five thousand members during the last year. We earnestly desire to stop if possible this loss to our order, therefore we recommend that each lodge procure a roll-book and that the roll be called each evening and that a list of absentees be given to the committee on absent members.

3. We also recommend that a book of notice in arrears be sent out with lodge supplies.

4. We recommend the adoption of the "New Ritual" that there be uniformity in our work.

5. We recommend that the resolution presented by Bro. Elsworth of Nunda 135 be laid on the table.

6. We recommend that a committee of three attend our next legislature and nominate Bros. Copp, Christian and Nichols and that the finance committee make provision for the necessary expenses of said committee.

7. We express our gratitude for the action of the U. S. Senate referred to by our Grand Chief Templar in the passage of a constitutional amendment for the submission of the question of the prohibition of the liquor traffic to the State and we hope for a ratification by the House of Representatives, and will not be satisfied until all our States are under Prohibition administration.

T. J. WOOD,
MRS. M. A. MOTT,
C. G. HAYMAN.

THURSDAY A. M.

A special hour was given to the memorial committee and devoted to brief addresses in memory of our fallen Chief Bro John B Finch. There were many and telling testimonials as evidence of the greatness of our fallen hero by those who best knew him.

The committee on constitution decided several questions.

The Ottawa decision as to ginger ale was sustained.

Badges are considered regalia.

Money should be distributed to the districts from the G. L. treasury.

The locating of the next session of the Grand Lodge brought warm invitation and spirited seconds showing up the special advantages and reasons for meeting at each of the following towns: Rockford, Moline, Galesburg, Decatur, Streator and Springfield.

REPORT ON TEMPERANCE LITE

TO THE OFFICERS AND
TO G. L.—Your committee on
literature in State of Illinois beg
call your attention to the inable
a lack of finance to vigorously
liberal dissemination of tempe
ature. We think that the comm
is now almost powerless, ought
a position to do effective work
quest that in the future this com
may be placed in a position to
can be at once value to the L
state than it is at present the
now constituting un")) in the au
of a report on which movemen
As it now is we can, only r
recommend to the order the sc
port of the various temperance
both own expense and urge thru
Templar support at least one
further, that each lodge app
spondent to furnish news dom
the lodges and also to the Th
XXI, and the Western Good Te
that representatives of the Wo
Templar and the STATE SE
diately commence correspondin
lodges for said purpose.

J. K. WELLER,
N. JUUL,
JAMES M. BOND

GRAND LODGE OFFIC
P. G. C. T.—J. W. Nichols, Dc
G. C. T., Uriah Copp, Jr., Lo
G. C., Rev. T. J. Wood, Colch
G. V. T., Mrs. H. K. Morris,
Chicago.
G. S. J. T.—Mrs. A. E. Wells, C
G. A. S., G. M. Bassett, Ode
G. S., R. J. Hazlett, Freepor
G. T., Geo. P. Harrington, Ed
G. Chap., Rev. J. K. Holstein,
D. M., Mrs. Emma A. Turner,
G. M. N. Juul, Chicago.
G. Mess., Oscar Ocelle..., Ch
G. G., Lizzie Stoll, Forsythe
G. Sen., J. B. Perry, Streator

COMMITTEES

Committee Elected—State du
N. T. Allen, Cornelius Darbi
Wells.
Appeals—C. G. Haymar
Hooper.
Temperance Literature—J
Finch, R. C. Elliott, Br. N. Ju
Juvenile Temple.—Sister
Sister McDuff, A. E. Mills, F.
Constitution.—J. W. Nicho
Long, A. F. Smith.

Other reports will be given
After the adoption of the t
perance literature, the Grai
journed with the usual ceremon

NOTES.

No more ginger ale.

The badge is regalia in Illin

The problem is "How to redu
ber of suspensions?"

Right Worthy Grand Lodge
Chicago next May.

Streator is happy. Grand
does next year.

Bro. Christian is funny. B
Jolly. Bro. Juul is forgiving,
patient. Bro. Hazlett is fa
Morris is pleasantly dignified.
impresses all of the importance
Sister Williams is eloquent. S
earnest. Sisters Vanordstrand
like our G. S.—faithful, and
and love the cause.

St. John at Batte

It was our pleasure to
John rally at Battery D, Chic
The immense auditorium whi
was completely filled and w
people were standing. The a
especially cared for the prese
only about one in five being
dress. The opening prayer
tinctly heard at the entrance
nature of the audience. T
address while there were often
applause. There was intens
a manifest desire to catch
of the speaker. Mr. St. Johi
lent trim and gave the peop
best and most forcible speech
His "Protection for Muscle
Foreign Labor." They've a
and "Arraignment of the old
all pointers for voters to car
consider. He was followed t
Gougar who also for an hour
words for redletion. A bet
marked after hearing her, Ho
to hear her and Ellen Foster
bate," to which another repl
safe in offering it for you will
J. Ellen will never accept, w
busy with other workers.
After Mrs. Gougar had sp
clock marked 10, Rolls Kir
chalk taler held the vast aud
an hour longer, sketching th
growth of prohibition," "the
dicament" and "Betsey and

INTRODUCTION

My first full-time job was as a newspaper copy editor. And the first professional job of my *genealogy* career was doing a search for newspaper death notices for another genealogist. This book, therefore, has been marinating a long time. It's being published long after that first career ended. It's being published at a time when the traditional print editions of today's newspapers are becoming scarcer and scarcer. To paraphrase and recast a remark attributed to German Chancellor Otto von Bismarck (who once said the public should not see how either laws or sausages are made): I have seen how the sausage is made.

But despite whatever flaws there have been in producing newspapers under deadline, no type of record group available to genealogists has the same potential to offer insight on virtually every ancestor—as well as the times in which those ancestors lived. We'll see how valuable this powerful contextual background can be in examples throughout the book, from both professional and hobbyist genealogists.

As you will learn throughout this book, historical newspapers have become the hottest "new" group of "old" records in genealogy thanks to search technology and reproductions of newspaper pages from days gone by. And the continuing arc of digitization is the *leading* cause of increased access to and awareness about historical newspapers. Resources relating to newspapers—from published and unpublished abstracts to genealogical newsletters to indexed online databases—offer genealogists a multipronged approached to documenting their ancestors, most of whom were the "common people." These same materials can help any sort of historical researcher get a much clearer on-the-ground view of social history than from more "official" records.

If you haven't found your ancestors in newspapers, you simply haven't searched enough newspapers—yet! Keep reading to find out how.

James M. Beidler
January 2018
Leesport, Pennsylvania

PART 1

LEARNING THE BASICS

The Historical Role of Newspapers

With all the genealogical resources available to you, why should you take the time to research newspapers? As we discussed in the introduction, newspapers can provide information that no other record type can, presenting you with unique opportunities to breathe life into your family's story. And since newspapers were the social media of their time, they document the everyday lives of your ancestors and their communities.

This chapter will discuss the historical role of newspapers, giving you some foundations of how more than three centuries of newspaper publishing have played out in America. We'll also discuss how time and place affect your genealogy research, plus how you can make your way through the rest of this book.

RESEARCHING TIME AND PLACE

Anyone working on family history needs to be familiar with genealogy's first principles, such as researching specific questions (to keep research from being scattershot), working backward in time (instead of assuming a distant person with the same surname is automatically an ancestor, only to waste time and effort), and practicing "whole family" genealogy (studying records relating to siblings of direct-line ancestors for the information it can add).

WHAT IS A NEWSPAPER?

In a book about historical newspapers, there's probably no more basic concept than "What is a newspaper?" As it turns out, answering that question is more difficult than you might think. The US Newspaper Program, the nationwide effort that preserved thousands of crumbling newspapers on microfilm began in the 1980s (and which will be referenced later in this chapter as well as chapter 10), laid down three "attributes" for a newspaper:

1. A serial publication designed to be a **primary source of written information on current events connected with public affairs**, whether local, national, or international in scope. It contains a broad range of news on all subjects and activities and is not limited to any specific subject matter.

2. Newspapers are **intended for the general public**. The general public may be further qualified and/or limited by 1) geographic location (e.g., local community) and/or 2) ethnic, cultural, racial, political, or national group.

3. A newspaper usually has some **defining formatting characteristics**. It is originally printed on newsprint, has a masthead (but not a cover), and is formatted in no fewer than four columns per page.

A few of the phrases in these "attributes" require a little more explanation. The project said a newspaper had to be a "serial" publication, meaning it was differentiated from newsprint fliers or handbills that were usually "one-shot" pieces. Rather, newspapers were published at particular or ongoing intervals (daily, weekly, monthly, etc.), and (unlike magazines) they do not have an illustrated "cover" that advertises its content.

While newspapers' audiences varied, they were intended for a "general public" as opposed to only scholars in a certain field (like an academic journal).

Please note that I say *a* general public to stress that some newspapers will have a more narrow appeal than "every" person in a specific geographic area. This book talks, for example, about foreign-language newspapers, which have an obvious appeal to speakers of the language in question. Likewise, some newspapers targeted African Americans, specific religious groups, and members of particular labor unions, and in this chapter's history section, we'll talk about how many nineteenth-century newspapers were explicitly tied to political parties. The point is that these newspapers all had *a* general public of readership if not *the* general public of everyone in a community.

But probably the paramount principle when starting a newspaper search is grounding yourself in the proper "time and place" of the people or events you are searching. Just as the history of newspapers in this chapter will help inoculate you from "presentism," using time and place—the date or era in which you are searching and the geographic (or, in some cases, ethnographic) area being researched—will keep you right on target in your genealogical and historical research. Knowing when and where an event took place is essential to finding records of it, and an event's time and place form a sort of crosshairs that allow you to target genealogy resources. Without historical context about the time era and geographic place you are researching, you won't know what records are available or when they began, causing you to miss out on records or waste time researching records that were never created.

The time and place you're researching will be narrow or broad, depending on what you're searching for. Time might refer to just one day or possibly a whole decade, while place could range from a borough in a large city to a whole country.

Let's take a look at the genealogical time-and-place intersect in action. Keep in mind the historical realities of the time and place you're researching in. If your research goal is a "California state birth certificate from 1879," you are likely to be disappointed, as the state did not begin registration of births and deaths until July 1905. Changing the goal to a "Record showing birth in California in 1879," on the other hand, opens up possibilities such as births written down by county recorders and church registers of infant baptisms— as well as mentions of births in newspapers.

But what if you want to look at "Documents from Edgar County, Illinois, in 1820"? Well, my research tells me Edgar County wasn't created until 1823. As a result, any records relating to those who became Edgar County residents will likely be in its parent, Clark County. Likewise, if you want to look for a Clark County, Illinois, ancestor's land in 1820 and later, be prepared for a lot of searching. A dozen-plus counties were later cut from Clark County's original territory (basically the whole northeastern portion of the state!), so you'll have a lot more land to search than just today's relatively compact Clark County. The description of the property in that pre-1820 Clark County deed likely will be helpful in determining in which modern county the property is located.

By "aiming" the crosshairs, you can hopefully avoid the aforementioned presentism, and you will have to re-aim with every ancestor. Often, you'll have to recalibrate in different parts of one ancestor's life. You have to know your history to aim those crosshairs correctly!

So how does this apply to newspaper research? You need to recalibrate your genealogy crosshairs for each new ancestor or family you're researching, as newspaper coverage and availability varied from place to place and across time. One important way this manifests itself today is that newspapers that are large and influential in a community now may not have always been that way, as the pre-eminent news source in a community will not necessarily have had the same role during the era being researched. That current news-paper might not have even existed during that earlier time, or it may have been an upstart afterthought versus a then-dominant-but-now-defunct title. Or you may have to do some research on the newspaper's own "genealogy" if it has gone through multiple titles or mergers or owners.

Looking at things from the "place" end of the crosshairs, what is now a substantial community previously might have been served by a geographically zoned "edition" of another town's newspaper (or just even a "column" in that other town's newspaper). The small community of your ancestor could have been part of the "territory" of the newspaper published in its county seat ... or even a paper in a different county, often dependent upon proximity (both in terms of actual mileage as well as connections through valleys in some areas).

HISTORY OF NEWSPAPERS

Print media have been a forceful tool since Johannes Gutenberg introduced the printing press to the European continent more than half a millennium ago, with books (especially religious works such as the Bible), one-page broadsheets, magazines, templates for personal documents, educational materials, sheet music, comic books, and more having a huge impact. But it's hard to overstate the ubiquity of newspapers, in particular, as the chief source of information around the world (not to mention their utility in birdcages and as bedding for farm animals). No other category of printed matter has reached more people, more often since the first attempts at newspapers were made in Europe in the early 1600s. This is especially true in America, where so many communities founded daily newspapers beginning in the mid-1800s. Even today, as the newspaper audience becomes increasingly digital, tens of millions of Americans—and hundreds of millions of people around the world—continue to read just print editions.

In this section, I'll share a brief history of newspapers in the United States.

COLONIAL TIMES

The first known print publication in the Colonies was a single issue of a Boston newspaper published (and, shortly after, suppressed) in 1690, and weeklies were being published in the major cities of half the colonies by the 1740s. One of the most prominent was *The Pennsylvania Gazette*, the Philadelphia newspaper considered the "newspaper of record" and owned by Benjamin Franklin for most of its run from 1728 to 1800. Multiple newspapers were being published in New York, Philadelphia, and Boston by the time of American independence in 1776. The first foreign-language newspapers were printed in German in the Philadelphia area beginning in 1739, in a nod to the region's ethnic diversity.

The news content of these Colonial newspapers reflected the publications' target audiences, often the merchant class who yearned to be kept abreast of happenings from farther

---

Research Tip: DEFINE "NEWSPAPER OF RECORD"
Declaring something to be a "newspaper of record" is somewhat subjective. Normally, such a publication covers news of its chosen market objectively and thoroughly.

Early newspapers, like this 1798 issue of the *Gazette of the United States and Philadelphia Daily Advertiser*, combined ads and news on their front pages.

away, especially in Europe. (Most people knew what was happening in their immediate communities.) However, advertisements in these publications often had notations of local interest, including lands for sale; runaway servants, enslaved people, or animals; and names of importers and their goods for sale (image A). You can also find articles on the politics of the day, travelogues from around the world, and documentation about the comings and goings of ships.

For those with Colonial ancestry or seeking information about the history of these times, it's useful to know a couple of things. First, nearly every surviving newspaper from Colonial times has been digitized by one or another service (which we'll discuss in chapters 6 through 9). Secondly, because American newspapers started first in large cities, their coverage of the "hinterlands" will be limited (but not nonexistent). Newspapers are worth a look through, as you are likely to find mentions of an ancestral area or someone in an ancestor's larger circle, what eminent genealogist Elizabeth Shown Mills calls the "FAN Club" of "friends, associates, and neighbors."

NINETEENTH-CENTURY BOOM

At the beginning of the 1800s, several hundred newspapers were in publication—including a handful publishing daily—but that was a faint preview of what was to come as the nineteenth century unfolded. More "average" people became newspaper readers, adding to the amount of space newspapers devoted to news versus advertising. Just as political parties sprang up in the new American republic, many newspapers in the early 1800s were partisan in their selections and presentation of news (with these political leanings often apparent in nameplates, which featured words like *Democrat*, *Republican*, and *Whig*).

By the 1830s, more than a thousand newspapers existed in America, and a few were now published west of the Mississippi River. Several technologies in the succeeding decades pushed the numbers to more than fifteen thousand publications by the dawn of the twentieth century, a time when virtually every county seat had at least one publication. Using telegraph wires to transmit stories—tested during the Mexican-American War in the 1840s and evolving into "wire service" like the Associated Press—made it possible to publish news in a shorter time frame. Steam presses enabled newspapers to print more copies with more pages to an edition, and railroads facilitated quick distribution of newspapers to ever-larger geographic areas.

These technological improvements advanced the mass-market "penny press" papers that appeared during the same time period. Newspaper publishing—which had previously profited mostly by selling other products—became a lucrative activity through advertising and a modest cover price (charged to buyers of subscriptions and single copies), plus requirements for the government to fund "legal notices" of government activities in newspapers.

Beginning in the second half of the 1800s and extending past the end of World War II, newspapers were the number-one source of information for most Americans. Understanding this to be the case, most newspapers made it their business to expand their news coverage to include the minutiae of the community's everyday life. Many publications attempted to have correspondents in even the smallest hamlets so all kinds of happenings made their way into print, such as visits from relatives, someone being approved for a military pension, or the closing of a local business.

In addition, many features that are still staples of newspaper articles—for example, obituaries of common people (see chapter 4), crime reports, and courthouse activity—became common in this "golden age of newspapers," during which profits were high, newsprint costs low, and virtually no other media challenged them as a source of news or advertising. Even when radio broadcasting (first viewed as a threat) came along in the 1920s, newspapers formed cross-ownerships with the burgeoning radio stations that

---

Research Tip: DISTINGUISH BETWEEN "HISTORIC" AND "HISTORICAL"
You'll note that we talk about "historical" (meaning "of past events") newspapers as opposed to "historic" (meaning "famous or important in history") newspapers. Some of them may be "historic," but they are all "historical."

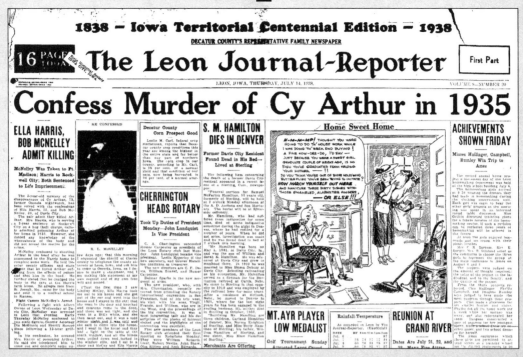

B

1838 – Iowa Territorial Centennial Edition – 1938

DECATUR COUNTY'S REPRESENTATIVE FAMILY NEWSPAPER

16 PAGE TODAY **The Leon Journal-Reporter** First Part

LEON, IOWA, THURSDAY, JULY 14, 1938. VOLUME 9 – NUMBER 30

Confess Murder of Cy Arthur in 1935

ELLA HARRIS, BOB MCNELLEY ADMIT KILLING

McNelley Was Taken to Ft. Madison; Harris to Rockwell City; Both Sentenced to Life Imprisonment.

Decatur County Corn Prospect Good

S. M. HAMILTON DIES IN DENVER

Former Davis City Resident Found Dead in His Bed— Lived at Sterling

Home Sweet Home

ACHIEVEMENTS SHOWN FRIDAY

Misses Hullinger, Campbell, Rumley Win Trip to Ames

CHERRINGTON HEADS ROTARY

Took Up Duties of President Monday—John Lundquist Is Vice President

MT. AYR PLAYER LOW MEDALIST

Golf Tournament Sunday

Rainfall Temperature

REUNION AT GRAND RIVER

Dates Are July 21, 22, and

Merchants Are Offering

By the twentieth century, newspapers (like this 1938 issue of *The Leon Journal-Reporter* in Leon, Iowa) began to feature more images.

allowed both media to benefit in ways the Federal Communications Commission rules would later prohibit.

Newspapers that focused on a specific ethnic group flourished during this time period. A few African American newspapers appeared during the pre-Civil War period to advocate for the abolition of slavery; more black-oriented publications emerged in major cities during the latter part of the nineteenth century. The German-language press—which peaked at almost six hundred newspapers in 1910 before a sharp decline as a result of anti-German feeling during and after World War I—was joined by a wide variety of other ethnic newspapers: Norwegian, French, Spanish, Polish, Portuguese, Jewish, and more. It was during this time period that some religious denominations published their own newspapers, and labor unions got into the act as well. As we will advise again in chapters 11 and 12 on specialized newspapers, those papers are often indispensable choices when researching African Americans, immigrant ethnic groups, and members of labor unions.

This golden age is probably the most difficult one for researchers to mine effectively, however. Many towns had multiple newspapers, providing a smorgasbord of opportunities to learn about a particular time period (image B)—but also extra work for researchers.

Researchers face additional challenges when studying newspapers from this era. First, changes in the names of newspapers (especially, but not exclusively, every time ownership shifted) can make trying to account for "all" newspapers of a time and place a trying experience. And, frustratingly, some newspapers have been "lost to history" either entirely or such that only scattered issues have survived.

TV-AGE CHANGES

The conditions that enabled newspapers' golden age began to change in the decades after World War II. Television competed with newspapers for advertising dollars and breaking news alerts—as well as for people's time. A fair number of individuals who might have read more than one newspaper every day now felt challenged to tackle even one, especially when TV news could be packed into a half-hour program and consumed without the effort of reading.

As a result, many newspapers allocated less space for national and international news, leaving that for the TV networks to cover. Instead, they tried to cover more locally based news and run longer, more in-depth articles for those readers still willing to invest the time. But many "minutiae" features began to die out when the price of newsprint began spiking in the 1970s, especially in midsized daily papers. The replacement of "hot type" technology (in which lead-cast lines of type were difficult to redo in a timely fashion) with "cold type" (essentially filmstrips with words and photos to be "pasted up" on boards in preparation for a photographic plate of the page to be made) created a focus on reader-friendly newspaper design instead of items being more randomly placed.

Newspapers were still overwhelmingly profitable, and publications in some cities stayed alive by forming Joint Operating Agreements, in which the production aspects of the newspapers were handled together (eliminating duplicated costs of separate printing, circulation, and advertising departments) while two editorial "voices" were preserved. In other cases, publishers developed "chains" of newspapers in different cities, many of which merged over time. Because some of these mergers were "leveraged buyouts" (in which the sale was financed with future profits), a significant number of newspapers began to fail in the 2000s when falling profit margins could not cover debt service and other operating expenses.

During this time period, officials and historians began to recognize the historical value of newspapers and started a number of different preservation efforts. The US Newspaper Program, put into place by the National Endowment for the Humanities with assistance from the Library of Congress in the early 1980s, took on the goal "to locate, catalog, and preserve on microfilm" the nation's newspapers, especially those deemed "newspapers of record" for their communities. With many newspapers printed on acidic paper, especially between 1850 and 1950 (often nicknamed the "Era of Bad Paper"), these publications were literally crumbling into dust. In addition, editorial offices began entering the electronic (not quite digital) age, producing digitized content that could be saved into a searchable electronic library in addition to being used in a print edition. Publishers themselves also began to understand the importance of microfilming their "back files" instead of just putting them together in unwieldy volumes that bound together issues from a certain time period.

THE INTERNET COMETH

While television ended the newspaper's golden age, the Internet turned the industry upside down. The business model for nearly two centuries had been for advertising to bring in the lion's share of the revenue (with most newspapers also charging a cover price that made up between 10 percent and 25 percent of income), enough to pay for the cost of newsgathering as well as ensure a profitable venture. But when advertising cratered in the Great Recession in 2008, newspapers were mostly caught flatfooted. While nearly all newspapers had a web presence, the profit from Internet advertising was tiny compared to what newspapers lost in display (with many advertisers going to direct mail) and classified (which found great audiences in classified-like websites such as Craigslist ads <www.craigslist.org>). Some newspapers began placing their content behind a paywall (which required users to purchase credits or have a paid subscription to view articles online), but this had limited success.

As a result, newspapers shrank in size (both in the number of pages as well as physical dimensions). Some reduced frequencies from daily to three days a week or even went "digital only" (image C). Nearly all publications slashed the number of employees in their editorial departments. Newspapers attempted to monetize features that were previously free (such as obituaries, which we'll discuss in chapter 4).

In today's world, the "package" of the newspaper has changed from printed material to "information delivered digitally or in print form." Editorial workers at

As the Internet Age dawned, newspapers began to digitize their archives as well as new content. This site hosts eight formerly daily printed newspapers from Michigan.

newspapers and other "legacy" media publications produce content, which is often plucked away by so-called "news aggregator" websites that republish it and add relatively little to the original articles.

Even so, American newspapers today have remarkable diversity. Fewer, for sure, are in the largest metropolitan areas, but many midsized papers remain in some combination of print and digital form across the country. And small weekly papers continue to have a micro-niche, serving mostly suburban and rural communities with local details that were spiked long ago from larger newspapers.

But what newspapers are now and will be in the future is an issue separate from our book: We're dealing with "historical newspapers"—whose influence and panoramic view of history during the three previous centuries is undeniable.

GETTING THE MOST OUT OF THIS BOOK

If you want to know what was "trending" in the eighteenth, nineteenth, or twentieth centuries, newspapers are the place to find out. This book is designed to help you find this "social media" of earlier times by using the full range of newspaper resources, whether you are a genealogist looking for ancestors, a historian seeking information about a specific event, or an academic researching a topic from a time gone by.

This book has several mantras, but the most important at this stage is: "There are more historical newspaper resources than you think—and they're easier to organize than you know." There are plenty of shortcuts you can take to get right into newspaper research (our flowchart in the appendix A is a good place to start if you wish to go that route), but you'll be better versed in the whole gamut of newspaper resources if you spend at least some time going through this book chapter by chapter. In addition to the text and examples, all chapters also have contain a summary and some have worksheets to help you organize your research.

As you've seen, this chapter discusses the basics of genealogy as it applies to newspaper research, plus a history of newspapers. The next three chapters are all about the types of information you may find in newspapers, from the resources with the broadest application to the narrowest. Just as traditional journalism articles are written in the "inverted pyramid" style (with information flow going from general at an article's beginning to specific at its end), the rest of this book's Part One examines general records in newspapers and ends with the more-specific (though more popular) obituaries:

- Chapter 2 surveys the whole landscape of items that might mention your ancestor, as well as those that might not mention your ancestor by name, but instead can be used to create historical context for your project.

- Chapter 3 emphasizes how newspapers have reported vital records and life events and (importantly) how chronologies of an ancestor or topic will help suggest to you some targeted time periods to research (especially handy if computer-searchable digitized newspapers don't yield the information you seek).

- Chapter 4, simply put, discusses death—and not just obituaries, but many types of newspaper items that may mention death and include data relevant to a search.

Having laid some groundwork on the breadth of what can be found in newspaper research, we turn in chapter 5 to the many different media in which newspapers appear. In addition to the newspapers themselves (which may be found in original paper, on microfilm, as digital images, or as online editions or databases), newspaper abstracts were published in books, repository clipping files, and journals.

Part Two moves into specific databases where you can find historical newspapers, and the explosion of newspaper digitization has merited four full chapters about these websites. Out of respect for readers' pocketbooks, we start with free sites (chapter 6), then graduate to separate chapters on two of the heaviest hitters, Newspapers.com (chapter 7) and GenealogyBank (chapter 8). We'll then survey other prominent for-pay sites (chapter 9). In all cases, we'll talk about each site's strengths and weaknesses, demonstrate searches, and try to project where they are headed as a constellation in the online newspaper universe. Chapter 10 gives you tools to find all those newspapers by creating your own chronology of the newspapers in a specific geographic region.

While exposure to all the different online sites will hopefully result in some finds, you'll still have some things to learn. Part Three discusses some more-advanced newspaper resources and techniques. Chapters 11 and 12 home in on newspapers with specific audiences—African Americans, those speaking a foreign language or adhering to a particular religion—as well as what's available as far as international newspapers. (Except for this broad overview of newspapers internationally, most of the information included in the book will target US publications.) Chapter 13 discusses other aspects of newspaper research: Collection and preservation of newspapers are talked about, as well as the importance of correctly citing these resources (especially given the different media and types of resources). Finally, chapter 14 shares some cases studies that put this book's strategies into practice, and a flowchart, bibliography, and chronology template in the appendixes will help you locate the best resources for your research.

KEYS TO SUCCESS

★ A newspaper is a serial publication designed for a general public.

★ Using the concept of "time and place" to avoid thinking of newspapers from a present-day perspective is crucial.

★ Newspapers are the most widely used printed materials in the half millennium since Gutenberg.

★ During the peak period of newspapers from roughly 1850 to 1950, they were the leading "social media."

★ This book focuses primarily on American newspapers, but also touches on publications around the world.

Records in Newspapers

The vast amount of content in historical newspapers can be beautifully abstract or (for the more Type A of us) frustratingly messy. And yet, genealogists, historians, and everyday researchers can pull from this seeming disorganization crucial information about the past. We often turn to newspapers for articles about people, but the details there show a much broader context for those people's lives: trends/fads, conformity or nonconformity to social norms, historical realities, and cultural priorities. And sometimes newspapers don't focus on people at all, instead focusing on the "scenery": fog-of-war reports about conflicts and disasters, advertisements hocking goods or publishing wages. Newspaper articles can tell us about the organization of a new country's government in either real time or via a longer view.

When you get to chapter 3 (vital records) and chapter 4 (obituaries and other death records), you'll be up to your eyeballs in newspaper elements focusing on people (including, hopefully, your ancestors). From this, you'll learn about putting together chronological portraits of individuals, with data gleaned primarily (if not exclusively) from newspapers. But before we get to that heavy lifting, this chapter will take a look at the many types of historical newspaper items you should look for in your research.

NEWS ARTICLES

All historical newspapers took pride in providing their readers with local, national, and global news. And since most people would have been involved in some kind of public event at some point in their lives (be it their "fifteen minutes of fame" or run-of-the-mill proceedings in civil, probate, or criminal courts), newspapers document large portions of a community's members. Much like a mention in an editorial section of a paper, these write-ups can go a long way towards sketching out an ancestor's personality and social life.

Finding your ancestor in a story detailing an arrest or criminal court action may not be the most glorious find, but these stories document what was *really* going on at the time (as opposed to the stories that may have been passed down through generations). One man's descendants, for example, may have romanticized his arrest for a fist fight that same weekend by recounting he was defending his honor against a woman's rival courter.

On slow news days (or perhaps as part of a regular series), editors would sometimes fill space in their newspapers with sketches or profiles of local people. These articles could sometimes be even more informative than obituaries, as they detail the way someone was perceived by their peers *during* (rather than after) his lifetime.

New Store Opens Today.

People's China Store Opens With Line of China, Crockery, Etc., A. B. Overholt, Manager.

Arthur B. Overholt announces the opening of a new venture for Kalamazoo today. He said to a reporter yesterday, "I have for some time contemplated the move which I have made, because I have felt the growing demand for some time of an exclusive China and crockery store of this kind. By the word exclusive I don't mean 'high price,' but a stock comprised of China and crockery the price of which being within the reach of all.

"I also added a fine line of tin, granite ware and kitchen utensils in order to satisfy the numerous demands for a store of this kind.

"We'll strive to please all the people all the time."

Newspapers carried even the most seemingly mundane of news, like the opening of a new store.

Research Tip: WATCH FOR REPRINTS

Newspapers have more information to sift through than perhaps any other record type—much of it redundant. An old adage in the news business says "there are no new stories, only new reporters writing about them," and as a result many articles from across time may discuss the same events or concepts. Some of these repeats may look like cut-and-paste jobs from earlier articles, while "facts" in these pieces may have evolved over time. Keep this in mind as you make your way through newspapers, and keep track of any conflicting information that appears across issues or publications.

☛ Jill Morelli found an Iowa newspaper item headlined "Family Reunion at Home of Chris Jacobsons" that (in just eleven lines of text) contains the names of twelve of her ancestors, plus a location in Wisconsin. According to the article from a 1929 issue of the *Britt (Iowa) News Tribune*, no meal could beat this family's pheasant dinner to honor relatives visiting from out of town on the verge of the Great Depression.

☛ For Kathryn Doyle of California, a newspaper article provided a "macro" genealogical chunk about her fifth great-grandfather and Revolutionary War soldier William Waters and his family. Doyle found the 1907 front-page article in the *Mount Union Times* (Huntingdon County, Pennsylvania), an out-of-the-way paper that's unlikely to be digitized, only by visiting the State Library of Pennsylvania in person. After stumbling across the borrowed microfilm at her local library in Oakland, California, Doyle made the trek across the country to access the Pennsylvania library's more advanced equipment. Her travel was rewarding, producing a reporter-created four-generation chart that was never published elsewhere and served as an "amazing guidepost" for further research. "Read the newspapers of your ancestors—you never know what you will find," Doyle said.

☛ Michael John Neill shares great advice on his *Genealogy Tip of the Day* blog <genealogytipoftheday.com>, which frequently focuses on newspapers. In one post, he discussed how he found a classified advertisement in an Albuquerque, New Mexico, newspaper that showed a man selling lilac bouquets there in 1913. Neill had previously only known that the man moved from New Mexico to Illinois between 1910 and 1920, so this find lopped a few years off the potential timing of that move. Another of his posts asked the intriguing question, "Did that event warrant newspaper coverage?" He knew from court records that an ancestral acquaintance was convicted of manslaughter in 1858 and pardoned a few years later. "I thought to look for a newspaper account of the trial, but should have looked for mention of the pardon as well," Neill wrote.

Similarly, articles covering the opening or closing of businesses can provide clues to an ancestor's ups or downs in commerce. Arthur B. Overholt and the city of Kalamazoo, Michigan, were undoubtedly delighted that he was opening a "People's China" store that stocked affordable quality china and crockery in May of 1910 (image **A**).

Along the same lines as obituaries (but with an added dramatic flair) are news stories that cover deaths by accident or homicide. They would often not only mention the decedents and their families, but also people suspected to be involved with the event; writers of these stories certainly were not above speculation in the court of public opinion. If you find someone whose cause of death is listed as "homicide," search contemporary issues of the local newspaper to attempt to glean additional details about the event. For example, according to a news article, Isaiah L. Weaver of New York City decided to lean his head out of the window of the rear car of a passenger train at the wrong time on the morning of

Thursday, September 12, 1878. The car derailed and rolled down a twenty-foot embankment, killing Weaver and wounding several others, including Weaver's brother. In a more sinister story, Roy Lauman made a grisly discovery along the side of the road in Normandy, Missouri, in the fall of 1903; his mother Kate Lauman had been robbed and murdered. The writer speculated that Frederick Seymour Barrington was the culprit, as the bullet wound Mrs. Lauman had in her left temple resembled one in a murder in which Barrington was suspected of committing four months earlier (image **B**).

Newspapers also carried coverage of current military conflicts. The United States entered World War I in 1917, and casualty lists soon started arriving from Europe and were reprinted across the country. Newspapers would also profile soldiers who had been wounded or killed in action, usually mentioning (or even profiling) the fallen's parents as well, including names, residences, and (if known) military unit. For example, Thomas J. McGann, William R. Cubberley, and Benjamin Cook were residents of Trenton, New Jersey, who went overseas to serve their country, and an article about them (image **C**) included the fact that William Cubberley's family had moved away from Trenton since he went to Europe. Casualties from later wars would have been handled in much the same manner, while newspapers covering earlier wars like the Revolutionary and Civil Wars would generally just report casualty totals by rank with estimates of the number of the enemy killed.

Other, non-man-made tragedies such as epidemics may have also been worthy of press coverage. Two of the more notable outbreaks of influenza (sometimes contemporarily called "grip" or "grippe") were in 1889–1890 and 1918–1920, so widespread in their destruction that they are now known as pandemics. The latter generated a 1918 article (image **D**) detailing the closure of schools, the deaths of four people,

B

SON FINDS BODY OF MURDERED MOTHER

Woman is Murdered and Robbed in St. Louis County, Mo.

BULLET FIRED INTO HER BRAIN

Mrs. William Lauman Meets Death in a Lonely Spot While on Her Way Home From St. Louis— No Clew to Mystery.

St. Louis, Oct. 16.—Mrs. Kate Lauman, wife of William E. Lauman, of Normandy, St. Louis county, was murdered and robbed by an an unidentified person or persons Wednesday night while on her way home from a visit to St. Louis.

The murderer used a revolver, and the bullet penetrated the temple just above the left eye.

The crime was committed some time after 6:30 o'clock, but the exact time has not been determined, as the circumstances surrounding it are as mysterious as any with which the city police or county authorities have ever had to work.

The body was found Thursday afternoon at 3:30 o'clock by Roy Lauman, a son of the murdered woman, as he was driving home from a business trip to St. Louis.

It was lying on the east side of the Lucas and Hunt road, in a clump of bushes. That there was a struggle before Mrs. Lauman died there is little doubt. Her chatelaine bag, in which she carried her money, had been forcibly torn from her belt. Clutched tightly in her right hand between her index and middle fingers was a small wig that she is supposed to have gotten in the brush on the side of the road while grappling with her assailant.

She wore a black silk glove, which was torn in a jagged manner in several places, which could have been used from brush.

You may find mention of your ancestors in a newspaper's account of a heinous crime, such as murder.

THREE LOCAL BOYS ON CASUALTY LIST

William R. Cubberley Killed.

McGann and Cook Wounded

in Action

The names of three more Trenton boys appear on today's casualty list. Thomas J. McGann, son of Mr. and Mrs. Patrick McGann, of 33 Kelsey Avenue, is reported as being wounded in action, degree undetermined. He was a member of the 309th Machine Gun Battalion of the 78th Division, and received his training at Camp Dix. He was called to the colors in April and was sent overseas six weeks later. Prior to entering military service he was employed in the plant of the Empire Rubber Company.

William R. Cubberley, son of Mrs. Lydia Cubberley, formerly of 636 Centre Street, city, is reported as being killed in action. He entered military service shortly after the outbreak of the war, and since then his family has removed from Trenton.

War casualties, like these three from Trenton, New Jersey, may have been mentioned in newspapers.

FLU CASES TOTAL 81 IN CITY; FOUR DEATHS

Epidemic in Wilkes-Barre and Valley Becomes More Serious as List of Patients Continues to Grow—More Than One Hundred Cases of Influenza in Glen Lyon —Public and Parochial Schools Are Closed

The influenza epidemic in the city and valley is becoming more serious every day. In the city 81 cases have been reported to the bureau of health since Wednesday of last week, when the disease first manifested itself. There were 11 new cases reported since Saturday afternoon at 4 o'clock. There was a death in the city today, two deaths at Glen Lyon yesterday and another at Sheatown, near Nanticoke. Over 100 cases have developed in Glen Lyon and the people of that neighborhood are greatly alarmed over the situation.

Late Saturday afternoon the local school board decided to close the public schools and following this step the city health department notified the private schools, with the result that all of the schools of the city were closed today, while some of the suburban towns have taken the same step.

Many Cases Reported.

The following is a list of the new cases that were reported in the city since Saturday afternoon at 4 o'clock:

Mrs. Mortimer B. Goldsmith, 430 South Franklin, contracted in New York.

Mr. and Mrs. Thomas Frank, 91 North Franklin street.

Mrs. G. L. Coleman and son, Lewis, 127 North Franklin street, contracted in West Virginia.

Carl Kemmerer, 17 South Pennsylvania avenue.

Benjamin Rifkin, 397 South River, contracted in Pottsville.

John Cart, 55 Prospect.

Mrs. Fred Sauer, 195 Carlisle street.

Mrs. R. Dunkum, 139 Waller.

William Ibach, 8 Maple street.

Thomas Jones, 33 Mill street.

Joseph Yamico, 175 East Market street.

Mrs. John Dugan, 87 Hillside street.

Nell McMananion, 491 North Pennsylvania avenue.

Charles Kelly, 512 Hazle street.

Fred Klipple, 195 West River.

(Continued On Page Three.)

Influenza outbreaks sometimes devastated communities, and newspapers would report on the growing epidemics.

and a list of people who had contracted the disease. Articles like these dotted the landscape of the country and even the world.

Significant weather events also made newspaper headlines. Dangerous enough in modern times, disasters like tornados, hurricanes, and floods were even more dangerous further back in history. Articles about them can give us depressing (yet enlightening) insight into what an ancestor would have dealt with if he were involved in an event like this, even if he was not on the casualty list. A devastating F4 tornado swept through St. Louis and East St. Louis in 1896, and one newspaper compiled and reported deaths and injuries, as well as what damage had been done to the cities. As it turned out, the newspaper's figures were only half the eventual confirmed deaths, but those it did report included names, ages, and addresses of the dead and injured.

ADVERTISEMENTS

Newspapers had a business side as well as a personal and social side. As we discussed in chapter 1, advertisements have evolved over the years. Early on, they were written more like notices, some of which were paid for with currency and some with political influence. As business ethics evolved, the practice of giving free space in a paper to friends and subscribers may have tapered, but that didn't slow the creation of content designed to sell.

Note that what were paid advertisements versus "notices" has changed over time. Subscribers/friends of publishers in olden days might have received notices for free that others were charged for.

DISPLAY ADS

Companies and individuals with larger budgets would often take out display ads on pages that editors expected to be heavily read. If your ancestor was a farmer or merchant, you might find him advertising goods on the pages of the local paper. Lawyers, doctors, and other service-based professionals would make sure their names were well known in the area by consistently displaying them in the newspaper. While not every individual was a proprietor, seeing an advertisement for the companies for which your ancestor worked can give clues to the "personalities" of those companies and the people who worked for them, like Critz Chevrolet in Little Rock, Arkansas, who wanted to make sure their company was perceived as supporting the local police force (image **E**). An advertorial might also detail an anecdotal experience with a product, person, or company, or be more of an essay-style advertisement like image **F**, written by the Association of Railway Executives.

E

A Tribute--
To Our Policeman!

The uniformed man who walks his beat, every day to combat lurking danger, is an officer of the city, working for you. All through the stillness of the night . . . when homes are dark and stealth is on the prowl . . . your watchful Policeman is going his rounds. Smiling, rosy-cheeked, a mountain of security clad in blue, he shepherds the little children across the street. He is their friend, their protector, their laughing pal, on occasion . . . and who of us would have it any other way! So let's be considerate and really warm-hearted toward our fine Policemen. The Cop, please remember, is one of our most dependable citizens!

CRITZ
Chevrolet Co.
300 W. Broadway, NLR
Phone 9204

SUPER CHEVROLET SERVICE

We Salute Our Town!

Some companies took out newspaper ads to support popular, honorable causes—in this case, Critz Chevrolet wanted to show its support for the local police department.

ASK any doughboy who was "over there" and he will tell you that American railroads are the best in the world.

He saw the foreign roads—in England and France, the best in Europe—and in other Continental countries—and he knows.

The part railroads have played in the development of the United States is beyond measure.

American railroads have achieved high standards of public service by far-sighted and courageous investment of capital, and by the constant striving of managers and men for rewards for work well done.

We have the best railroads in the world —we must continue to have the best.

But they must grow.

To the $20,000,000,000 now invested in our railroads, there will have to be added in the next few years, to keep pace with the nation's business, billions more for additional tracks, stations and terminals, cars and engines, electric power houses and trains, automatic signals, safety devices, the elimination of grade crossings—and for reconstruction and engineering economies that will reduce the cost of transportation.

Some newspaper ads, like this impressive one created by the Association of Railway Executives, were written in essay style.

CLASSIFIEDS AND LEGALS

Classifieds were not designed to sell a commercial product or service; rather, the notice may have been soliciting the private sale of an item or making the public aware of a specific event or situation. Sometimes, the person or organization paying for the classified ad would have done so in its own interest, while other times the advertisement was legally required (sometimes called Legals).

An exhaustive account of the many different types of classifieds is beyond the scope of this book, but let's look at a few examples of classified-type pages throughout American history to get a general idea of what one might find when reading through them. In a May 1754 issue of Benjamin Franklin's *Pennsylvania Gazette* (image **G**), we find numerous classified-type notices intermixed with reports from the various North American theatres of the French and Indian War (which had just begun). You'll notice a wide variety of notices and advertisements:

- no fewer than seventy-five unclaimed letters being held at the Third Street Post Office, plus the names and addresses of the intended recipients

- a list of current local goods prices

- a register of incoming and outgoing ships, including their origins and destinations at the US custom house in Philadelphia

- a sample of the inventory of the general store of Bourne and Jones near the Market Street wharf

- information about tradesmen: goldsmith Bancroft Woodcock, whipmaker Israel Morris, and storeowners Zacharias Nieman and Daniel Rundle

- an unsettling advertisement for the sale of a fourteen-year-old "Negroe" boy by William Jackson of Walnut Street

- Richard Walker (who seems to have been some sort of government official) advertising to the creditors of Edward Gilland (who had abandoned his "usual place of abode" in Bucks County without paying his debts) that they should assemble on June 17 to show proof of the debt owed to them

- notices of real estate sales: a 180-acre tract by Alexander McDowell and a 48-acre plot in Kingsess Township by Daniel Richard

- wanted ads for two runaway "Irish servant men," James Murphey and William McAnalty, who fled their masters (Often, such listings would be the only mention of immigrant indentured servants in any kind of document, and they can give very colorful details about them. James Murphey, for example, spoke French and was "a very proud fellow, love[d] drink, and when drunk [was] very impudent and talkative, pretend[ed] much, and [knew] little" in the opinion of his master.)

PHILADELPHIA, May 30.

Captain Rees, from Barbados, advises, that the Rebecca, Captain Lowther (who we lately mention'd to have been boarded by a French Guard de Coast off of Guadaloupe) is carried into Martinico: That Capt. Bowes, of and from this Port, was safe arriv'd in Barbados: That Capt. Codwise, for New-York, was to sail a few Days after him: That two Days after he left the Island, he spoke with a Ship from Piscataqua, bound in there: And that on this Coast he also spoke with a Sloop for Rhode-Island from Jamaica.

From Halifax we have Advice, that Capt. Condy, belonging here, was arrived there, after a very stormy Passage: Also a Brigantine belonging to Rhode-Island from St. Christophers: And that Hoffman, the Ringleader of the Mutiny at Lunenburg last Winter, had been tried, and brought in guilty of high Crimes and Misdemeanours, but had not received Sentence: He behaved very insolently on his Trial.

Saturday last the notorious John Crow (who a few Years ago was repriev'd here under the Gallows, and had been several Times in Danger of being hang'd since) and one Chester, were executed at Trenton for House-breaking.

We hear from Sadsbury, that one Daniel Kerr was kill'd there on Friday last by the Falling of a large Tree, occasion'd by a violent Gust of Wind.

The Myrtilla, Capt. Marsden, will sail, it is said, To-morrow; and the Carolina, Capt. Mesnard, certainly sails on Saturday, both for London.

A List of LETTERS at the Post-Office, in Third-street, Philadelphia (not before advertised) viz.

A
Israel Aerelius, Christina
Benjamin Armitage, Phil.
Henry Abbot, ditto.
John Amonnet, ditto.
John Anderson, ditto.

B
Edward Broadfield, ditto.
Sarah Bound, ditto.
Andrew Boon, Chest. Co.
James Batten, ditto.
Rev. Adam Boyd, ditto.

C
James Cowpland, ditto.
John Carver, 2, Biberry.
William Clark, New Cast. Co.
John Clary, Dover.

D
John Dockray, Phil.
David Dewar, ditto.
John Doyle, ditto.

E
Oswell Eve, ditto.
D. Eat, Germantown.

F
William Fox, Phil.

G
John Gaas, ditto.
Robert Guthry, Amwell.
Timothy Griffith, N. Cast. Co.
Nathaniel Grubb, Chest. Co.

H
Thomas Howell, Phil.
John Hutchinson, ditto.
William Hamilton, ditto.

J
Samuel Jones, ditto.
Robert Jackson, ditto.
Charles Jenkins, ditto.
Michael Jeffery, ditto.
Robert Johnston, Chest. Co.

L
Robert Lawrence, Phil.
Capt. Thomas Lauderdale, ditto.
Anthony Lawrence, ditto.
Philip Lenhear, Lancast.
Joseph Leech, Frankford.

L (col 2)
James Lea, Wilming.

M
William Morris, ditto.
Moses Minshal, ditto.
Andrew Morton, Phil.
William Martin, ditto.
John Moore, ditto.
Samuel Means, ditto.
Mary Moledor, ditto.
Patrick M'Fall, ditto.
Ann Munrow, ditto.
John More, ditto.
Thomas Martell, ditto.
Patrick Malone, ditto.
Thomas Marshall, ditto.
Thomas Mitchell, Bucks.
John Mathers, Chester.

N
Christopher Newton, Phil.

O
George Orr, ditto.

P
Joseph Pattison, ditto.
James Philips, ditto.
Robert Patterson, ditto.
Joseph Powell, Sadsbury.

Q
Thomas Quan, N. Cast. Co.

R
Rev. ------ Reed, ditto.
Richard Richardson, Wilming.
James Reynolds, Phil.

S
John Sage, ditto.
Anthony Smith, ditto.
Christopher Sinnott, ditto.
Michael Steward, ditto.
John Stuckley, N. Hanover.
Michael Square, Northamp.

W
James Wonderom, Phil.
William Williams, ditto.
George Wescott, ditto.
Dorothy Wire, ditto.
Samuel Weston, Reedy I.
Elizabeth Way, Wilming.

SERIOUS CONSIDERATIONS on the PRESENT STATE of the AFFAIRS of the NORTHERN COLONIES.

BANCROFT WOODCOCK, Goldsmith,

HEREBY informs the publick, that he has set up his business in Wilmington, near the upper market house, where all persons that please to favour him with their custom, may be supplied with all sorts of gold and silver work, after the neatest and newest fashions.

N. B. Said Woodcock gives the full value for old gold and silver.

ISRAEL MORRIS Whip-maker,

STILL continues to make and repair horse-whips, at the house of Joseph Saul, chair and spinning-wheel maker, in Market-street, opposite the lower end of the Jersey market, after the best and neatest manner, as usual; and has now made by him, for wholesale or retail, a neat assortment of the following whips, viz. Whole hunters, half hunters, silver and white mounted ditto, large and small silver mounted switches, white mounted ditto, crop whips, jockey, silver mounted, and white mounted ditto, thongs and lashes, womens best tortoise-shell handle whips, bone, horn, vellum, and wire handle womens ditto, &c.

N. B. The said Morris sells no whips but his own make; he has lately got a large well-struck with the buck, and his name round the border, which he puts in all his mens whips, that are large enough to take so large a nail; and on the lesser forts cuts the first letters of his name, I M. 5s. 7bc. 3 m.

THIS is to give notice, That Zacharias Nieman, in Almond-street, on Society-hill, has taken a commodious piece of ground, situated between Captain Attwood's and Mr. Davey's wharff, whereon he intends to land and wharff for merchants, and others, pipe staves at eighteenpence a thousand; hogshead ditto, at Fifteenpence a thousand; and barrel ditto, at Tenpence a thousand. Twenty inch and two foot shingles, at Sixpence a thousand; and three foot ditto, at Eightpence a thousand, for every month; and so in proportion for piling, delivering, &c. where due attendance will be given.

To be sold by said Zacharias Nieman, at his store on Capt. Attwood's wharff, a choice parcel of salt mackrel, with sundry other goods.

To be sold by DANIEL RUNDLE,

At his store in Water-street, a little below Walnut-street,

THE rigging, sails, and iron-work of a brigantine; 4, 6, 8, 10, 12 and 20d nails, steel, turpentine and pitch by the barrel, or larger quantities.

N. B. He hath also to dispose of, the service of sundry Germans, a taylor, smith, butcher, weaver and farmer, a woman, one boy, and two girls. 7betf.

To be SOLD,

A LIKELY Negroe boy, about fourteen years of age. Enquire of William Jackson, in Walnut-street.

NOTICE is hereby given, that Edward Gilland, of Warwick, in Bucks county, has absconded from his usual place of abode, and not paid his just debts, and that his goods are attached: Therefore all his creditors are desir'd to be and appear at my house the 27th of June next, to make proof of their respective debts. Given under my hand the 21st of May, 1754.
RICHARD WALKER.

To be SOLD,

A PLANTATION, lying about a mile from Little Elk Meeting-house, 12 from Christiana Bridge, and 11 from Charlestown, containing about 180 acres, a good dwelling-house, and other office-houses, a bearing orchard, a parcel of good meadow made, and more may be clear'd, all easily waterable. The title is indisputable, and all quitrents, yet due, are paid. It is a good place, the land rich, and about one half woods. Any person inclining to purchase, may enquire at the subscriber...

Classifieds in eighteenth-century newspapers were incredibly detailed, such as this excerpt from the Classifieds in the *Pennsylvania Gazette*.

Jumping forward about fifty years, we find the article in image **H** from the January 18, 1800, issue of the *Mirror of the Times, and General Advertiser*, published in Wilmington, Delaware, by James Wilson. In it, Major J. Cass of the Third Infantry Regiment warns local tavernkeepers and retailers of "spiritous liquors" not to serve noncommissioned officers and privates alcohol, as he had observed that "too many of his recruits have discovered such a propensity to intoxication." The rest of the newspaper (not pictured) listed the letters being held at the Christiana Post Office in a similar manner to the article from 1754, and the paper features real estate notices as well as an ad for a missing/stolen trunk full of personal items. John Martin hadn't yet named the gentleman who returned his pocketbook but had taken some papers out of it; he threatened that if the papers were not returned, he would be "addressed in plainer terms" in a coming issue of the newspaper. Robert Sawyer needed two "well grown lads, about 16 years of age" as apprentices in his blacksmithing business. More business and real estate ads dot the second column as well as a notice of public "vendue" (auction) of the real estate of Gideon Guyer, who, it seems, had died with more debt than assets. The third and fourth columns are mainly populated by ads for various stores, but also requests for the return of a stolen horse and runaway black servant Joseph Carty.

You might get a kick out of some classifieds that were published as notices. In this one from 1800, a major in the U.S. Army implores local taverns not to serve his soldiers, who were getting drunk too often.

In the same issue of the *Charleston Mercury* that reported on the Convention of the People of South Carolina as it seceded from the United States, we find more mundane classified proceedings, reminding us that routine daily business goes on even during the most significant historical events. In it, we see a full enumeration of the comings and goings of ships, goods, and passengers on the city's docks. R.A. Pringle advertised his shoe store, and Bluffton and Grahamville detailed a horse they had for sale (named Young Black Hawk), complete with pictures of their products (a feature that would have been rarely, if ever, seen in 1754 or 1800). O.H. Ott, the owner of a 1,434-acre tract of swampland some thirty miles away from Charleston, was making known his intention to sell the property, and William Minter, who perhaps foresaw the demise of slavery and the Confederacy, was selling his 2,100-acre cotton plantation six hundred miles west of Charleston in Yalobusha County, Mississippi.

Research Tip: LEARN A LITTLE LATIN

Newspaper articles often use *ult.* and *inst.* as abbreviations for *ultimo* (meaning "previous month") and "instant" (meaning "current month"), respectively, along with dates. Don't let this shorthand (one of which involves Latin) throw you off!

By the time the United States entered World War I on April 6, 1917, classified advertising had become much more organized, with a formal section and header dedicated to the activity. In the same issue of the *Pueblo Chieftain* that sported the headline "America at War; House Resolution Passes" was the Classified Advertising section of the paper on page 9. Males and females wanted for various tasks were requested; furnished and unfurnished rooms, houses, and apartments were made available; ranches, real estate, livestock, and automobiles were offered for sale. Business chances were advertised and items lost or found were made public. Under legal notices, the Primrose Coal Company printed a notice of a special stockholders' meeting at which shareholders would decide on the lease of a large mine; the Bessemer Irrigating Ditch Company was also having a stockholders' meeting in ten days.

Classified notices and advertisements, whether in 1754 or 1917, can provide insight into the daily lives of everyday men and women. Whether selling a piece of land or sounding the alarm about a fugitive servant on the run, these often short but sweet articles can sometimes best answer the question, "What was my ancestor's life really like?"

EDITORIALS

Despite the paper's need and desire to make money, not all advertisements or advertorials had to have a commercial interest. Rather, the staff often included content that would advance the editorial staff's political philosophy and/or agenda. In earlier papers, some of the most prominent space in each edition was used to advocate for or against political parties and issues of the day, while more modern papers generally moved these editorial sections to later parts of the edition and reserved front-page space for important local, national, and global news.

These opinions (called "editorials," not to be confused with editorial content) were often one-sided and biased, but they can still give you perspective about the time and place being researched. One such opinion is a scathing profile of Denver and the Colorado Territory published by L.L. Bedell, editor of the *Cheyenne Daily Argus*, on November 14, 1867. At the time, authorities were considering letting the Colorado Territory annex the Cheyenne region from the Dakota Territory, and Bedell did not mince words in his vehement opposition to the idea.

In addition to these more bias-driven features, editors of earlier papers would often publish letters written to the newspaper from out of town, and the writers of these letters functioned almost as a correspondent. These letters may go into detail about a specific person, business deal, court case, or other noteworthy event/topic that took place outside of a newspaper's readership. Take, for example, the letter in image , which does all three of these things. It was written by

[Correspondence of the Alabama Journal.]

Gossip.—No. 12.

Columbus; Sam. Flournoy; Columbus Factories; The Georgia and Alabama Case of Ingersoll, vs. Howard; Heavy damages.

COLUMBUS, GEORGIA,
April 11th, 1849.

Gentlemen: For several days, I have been in this city and its vicinity, but fail to pick up anything of interest to transmit you. The business season is over, and the dust and heat add to the dullness of the place. The river is low too, boats being only able to come up light—so that, really, I see Columbus at great disadvantage.

Instinctively, I found my way, soon after my arrival, to the "Enquirer" office, where I was very cordially greeted by the gentlemen who conduct the paper. I had long desired to know our friend Flournoy, personally, being fully advised beforehand, that I should find him a "very proper man." I was in no wise disappointed. Imagine a sedate-looking gentleman, somewhere between forty and fifty, of rather small size, with regular features, and you have something of an outline of "Old Sam." The quietness of his manners contrasts strongly with the vivacity of his editorials: and it is only after you have studied his gentle face for some minutes, that you begin to discover the "latent devil" in the corners of his mouth, and in his liquid eye. At a mere glance, you would set him down as a clergyman, little less than precise in his dress but the illusion soon vanishes; and you find, instead of a person abstracted from the consideration of all temporal things, a man of keen perception and delightful humor. Mr. Flournoy

Letters from out-of-town correspondents were frequently featured in newspapers.

Dear Editor:

It seems to us that the city has enough to handle without trying to hog any more territory. Talk about the benefits we will gain, when the city cannot even take care of the people you have in the City.

You talk about the advantages to the city of Fairbanks, that is just what it will amount to when you consider there is 10,000 people in the city at present, and there is about 20,000 in the so called bedroom areas. We all know where the tax money will go. It seems odd that last summer when we wanted some road work on Badger Road, we were just a secondary community, but when you need more tax money, we are promoted to first class citizens at once. You say if it wasn't for Fairbanks we wouldn't be here. You should say, "If it wasn't for Ladd and Eielson Fields that Fairbanks wouldn't be here." We know of several familys that have moved out in this bedroom area to get away from your so-called advantages of living in Fairbanks.

PAUL W. WHITE

Clear, Alaska
January 3, 1960

Letters from the editor can help you learn about the contentious issues of the day—and what the public thought about them.

"J.J.H." of Columbus, Georgia on April 11, 1849, and published in the Saturday morning edition of the Montgomery, Alabama-based *Daily Alabama Journal* three days later. The writer profiles "Old Sam" Flournoy (who published the *Columbus Enquirer*) and discusses the writer's opinion of Columbus, Georgia: slow at the moment, but capable of having more business. J.J.H. also summarizes a local business dispute that had made its way into the courts.

While in later years a paper's paid staff likely covered events in other places, most editors devoted a separate section of the newspaper to letters that had been written to them by local citizens, appropriately called "letters to the editor." Anyone concerned about a specific issue or the way in which the newspaper might be covering events could write in and express their opinions. These "voices from the past" show a range of everyday folks' opinions about issues of the day, as well as present their unique writing styles (which, in turn, can go a long way toward painting their personalities). Paul W. White, a resident in an area on the outskirts of Fairbanks, Alaska, was not happy about the idea of his area being annexed into the city (image **J**). In his January 1960 letter to the editor, he talked about how the city couldn't even handle the residents it currently had within its borders, plus how the city had previously been reluctant to improve its existing infrastructure.

Collecting names, dates, and places from our ancestors' lives is an important step in understanding the time and place in which they lived, but no profile would be complete without details about their social and commercial dealings. Content in editorials, ads, and advertorials won't be based around a specific event in your ancestors' lives, but it can go a long way toward painting a picture of what they were like personally. In addition, these pieces can show you the world in which they lived: their priorities, the contemporary issues they would have debated—even if only at the family or neighborhood level.

FEATURES AND SOCIAL COLUMNS

News briefs from a century ago detailing social goings-on in an area (now called a "Life" or "Living" section) are treasure troves of information about the people who came before us. For instance, the article excerpted in image **K** has a paragraph on each of fifteen events going on that week in Springfield, Massachusetts. Descendants of members of the African Methodist Episcopal Church, the Loring Street Methodist Church, the Memorial Church, Wesley Church, and Hope Church (among others) would be wise to take note. If you find the names of local clubs and organizations

LOCAL CHURCH MATTERS.

Ask for Pastor's Return.

Rev J. P. Sampson, presiding elder of this district of the African Methodist Episcopal church, last evening conducted the fourth quarterly conference of the Loring-street Methodist church. A unanimous vote was passed asking that the pastor, Rev C. H. Yearwood, be returned next year, and this sentiment was very much in sympathy with that of Rev Mr Yearwood. The reports for the past quarter of the secretary and treasurer were read and accepted and a general retrospect was given of the past three months' work.

The young women's class of Memorial church will give a reception to-morrow evening at 8 o'clock to their teacher, Mr Laudenslager, who graduated this month from the training school and closes his work with the class. A final union lawn fete will be held Saturday afternoon and evening on the church lawn. A sale of ice-cream, candy, aprons, etc., will be conducted from 3 to 10 p. m. Band music will probably be furnished by the Springfield musical club.

The Sunday-school of Wesley church will have its annual picnic at Riverside grove Saturday. A long list of athletic events has been arranged for the day. A lawn party and supper will be held at the church to-morrow afternoon, beginning at 4. At 8 in the evening a reception will be given to Rev Dr. C. F. Rice, pastor of the church.

The Cheerful Workers of Hope church will meet this afternoon at 4.30 with Miss Lillian Murphy on Homer street. A reception for members of the cradle roll and their mothers will be held at 123 Buckingham street Friday afternoon from 3 to 5. All children of the church under five years will be welcome.

Look for reports about social events in newspapers, as these can provide you with information about what your ancestors may have done in their free time.

in your ancestor's obituary, coverage of these groups in newspapers can be a vital proxy to understanding the daily lives of our ancestors.

If your ancestor was on the artistic side, you may find him in articles covering local arts and artists. Image **L** documents not only local Pawtucket artist James McCarthy, but also a recent portrait subject (Hughy Glancy), McCarthy's previous subjects (including Mayor Fitzgerald and other local officials), the location of his gallery, and the name of a local art dealer. Members of the Baptist Church in Grand Forks, North Dakota, were undoubtedly excited that local musician Louis U. Rowland had composed a Christmas cantata that would be performed by the choir two weeks later on Christmas Eve in 1911, as documented in image **M**. Along with detailing the work, the article mentions the object of the cantata composer's dedication, Mr. and Mrs. Paul B. Griffith; researchers of Rowland might want to look into how the Griffiths fit into his life.

Other social columns document local family reunions, genealogical gold for those lucky enough to find them. These articles would often lay out family relationships as well as (or even better) obituaries. A perfect example is "Reunion of the Manning Family on French Prairie, Marion County, Oregon," from the *Oregonian* published in Portland, the focal point of page 10 in the July 3, 1898, edition. Beneath a portrait of the family, the writer begins by mentioning who was absent, so we can see family relationships for people who did not even participate in the event. Two paragraphs detail the happenings and sleeping arrangements for the four-day reunion, followed by a brief biography of the heads of the family, Mr. and Mrs. Manning. The article finishes by listing the children of Mr. and Mrs. Manning who attended, as well as the living descendants of each of them who also made the trip. For frontier families like this one, vital records of births, marriages, and deaths might be few and far between, but an article like this can serve in their stead while also adding living color to what their lives were like—not to mention provide a picture!

HISTORICAL AND GENEALOGICAL ARTICLES AND COLUMNS

Genealogical research is becoming more and more accessible with the addition of records, newspapers, and other primary sources to the world-changing Internet. However, interest in family history isn't new, and researchers studying their ancestors one hundred or more years ago faced even more challenges than we do today.

To help curb the difficulty of genealogy research, many newspapers printed genealogy columns that profiled a local family historian's efforts or pondered a specific item up for debate. Although not contemporary sources, these types of articles can open new

L

HANDSOME PAINTING
OF HUGHY GLANCY.

The Creditable Production of a
Clever Local Artist.

James McCarthy, a resident of this city, is an artist of acknowledged ability, combining in every effort put forth — whether in response to private request or public order—the taste and skill of a true exponent of the possibilities of palette and brush. His latest production is a handsome portrait of Hughy Glancy, the well known local representative of the manly art, and it befittingly adorns the business place of Mr. Glancy's bringer-out and backer, Eddie Moore, corner of Dexter and Weeden streets, city. It is a solid pastel painting on oil canvas of the plucky pugilist as he appears in his corner in the ring, all accessories being faithfully reproduced, even to robe, towels, etc., just previous to battle. Life-size and of three-quarters length, he sits calm and cool, apparently, yet with that natural, pleasant and determined expression on his countenance denoting he is bent on victory, but will cheerfully abide by the result. Fastened by a belt is his sash of red, white and blue—the national colors—and the symmetrical proportion of physique and prowess is in consonance with the delicate, lifelike and effective coloring, as well as the suggestive surroundings. To Artist McCarthy's credit and to their satisfaction also, it should be said that he has finished the portraits of Mayor Fitzgerald and other public officials, as well as prominent citizens of Pawtucket, Providence and the state—aye, of all New England—and he has real and possibly greater reason to be equally, if not more, proud of this, his latest production.

At the same time, Mr. Moore, in securing such a superb addition to his art gallery—the portrait being encompassed by a magnificent gold frame, seven inches deep and of original design—is receiving from his host of friends deserved congratulations.

M

XMAS CANTATA
BY L. ROWLAND

Local Musician Has Composed Work Called "The
Light of the World."

Cantata Will Be Given by the Choir of the Baptist Church on Sunday, December 24—Owing to Its Nature. Cantata Is Suited to Church Service —Is Second Notable Composition by Rowland.

A Christmas cantana for solo voices and chorus called "The Light of the World," has just been composed by Louis U. Rowland, who last spring presented his song-cycle "In a Man's Life" at the annual festival of the oratorio society. The cantata is dedicated to Mr. and Mrs. Paul B. Griffith and will be given by the choir of the Baptist church on Christmas Sunday, Dec. 24. There are fourteen numbers including two well known hymns which are used in order that the congregation may take a part. Being comparatively short the work is suited to a church service and is of a well sustained musical interest throughout.

After an organ prelude, written in pastoral style, is the opening solo, "Arise Shine: For Thy Light Is Come," given to a baritone voice, the text taken from the prophecy of Isaiah. This is followed by the hymn "Joy to the World."

Artists and musicians may have had their works or performances mentioned in newspapers.

possibilities for research and spur on fresh thought about what may have happened during their lives. Image N documents the writer's experience with a family in Edmonson County who used a system of patronymics and matronymics to keep track of their family tree without having to put any pen to paper. In another article from 1915, when the Daughters of the American Revolution was in just its twenty-fifth year of existence, Grace Ward Calhoun wanted to make sure local chapters knew about the society's collection of published lineage books that came on the heels of newly discovered genealogies.

In one article from 1963, writer Kay King Kimbrough speculated as to whether or not the Lees of Bruce Township in Guilford County were a branch of the famous Lee family of Virginia. She starts in the early 1700s and follows a line of the family through the 1800s, even transcribing a letter written by one of the subjects, spelling errors and all.

The *Hartford Daily Courant*, the oldest newspaper still publishing at the time, was celebrating its 150th year of publishing in 1914, and the paper printed a multiple-page history of itself (image O) and its founder, Thomas Green. A complete reprint of the first issue was even included. Needless to say, an article that documents 150 years of history would be full of potentially important information to countless residents of

REMARKABLE LINEAGE

UNIQUE METHOD OF A KEN-TUCKY FAMILY TO PRESERVE GENEALOGY.

Louisville, Ky., May 5, 1901.
Editor Herald:

While walking through the wilderness of this world, I happened to find a family of people in Edmonson County, Kentucky, near Mammoth Cave, that had the strangest peculiarity of any family, even in that strange and peculiar county. Their dastinctive peculiarity is the method by which they preserve their genealogy—a method that is sui generis and without a paralel.

The name of the progenetor of this family was Meredith. This man had three sons—Pig, Jack and Sam. In the process of time there was born unto Pig Meredith a son whose name was Pete. Therefore, Pete, being a grandson of the original Meredith, was called Pete Pig Meredith, or, briefly, Pete Pig when ordinarily addressed. Pete has a son of the name of Toad. Now, for all practical purposes, Toad Pete answers for his name. But if he wishes to give his full name it is Toad Pete Pig Meredith. Jock has a son, Bill, who is called Bill Jock, etc. Thus the Christian name of the father becomes the surname of the son. Now it happens that Pete also has a son of the name of Pig. His name is Pig Pete, while his father is Pete Pig. Whether one finds a Toad Sam or a Sam Toad, the original name of Meredith is maintained.

Family historians have always been eager to share their research finds. This was even the case back in the day, when some researchers (like the one who wrote the column above) wrote in to newspapers to share their genealogical questions and discoveries.

History of "The Courant" During 150 Years Since It was Established by Thomas Green

Giving, from its Files, Sidelights upon the Development of the Town, City, Colony, State and Nation---A Record of the Progress of the Oldest Living Newspaper in America.

With Sketches of "The Courant's" Owners and Homes of the Paper

FIRST FIFTY YEARS
1764 to 1814

The *Hartford Daily Courant* published a history of itself upon its 150th anniversary, providing a detailed account of its founding and all of its owners.

Hartford and the surrounding area. Articles like these have filled America's newspapers for many years and can offer what was, at the time of printing, a modern perspective on historical events.

DUPLICATES OF DESTROYED RECORDS

Thanks to natural disasters, courthouse fires (either accidental or intentional), and office recordkeeping policies, whole groups of records may have been destroyed throughout the years. Fortunately for researchers, the events documented in those records may have also appeared in print in the local newspaper. And since newspaper archives were rarely stored alongside municipal archives, researchers can hold onto some hope that duplicate copies of information stored in destroyed records may live on in newspapers.

So what sort of events did newspapers cover? Local citizens having a milestone anniversary or birthday were often profiled, and newspapers often listed announcements of births and marriages in the area. The *Hobart Daily Republican* in Hobart, Oklahoma, reported on the golden wedding anniversary of Mr. and Mrs. W. H. Kemmerling in the

CELEBRATION OF
GOLDEN WEDDING

Mr. and Mrs. W. H. Kemmerling Celebrate Fiftieth Anniversary of Wedded Life --

---

Despite the downpour of rain, Mr. and Mrs. W. H. Kimmerling celebrated their Golden Wedding anniversary, Tuesday evening at their home on 422 South Hitchcock St., in the presence of a number of relatives and invited guests, some of whom came a long way to be present at this time.

Promptly at 7 o'clock the wedding march was played by Mr. and Mrs. Floyd Bradfield, on the piano and the violin, and the aged couple accompanied by their niece and nephew, Mr. and Mrs. Tad Shriner, took their places under the doubledoor which was beautifully decorated with large golden hearts, broad ribbons and chrysanthemums, forming the beautiful arch from the center of which was suspended a large golden bell.

The rooms were decorated with golden crepe paper running from the angles and corners forming cross sections over the electric lights in the center of each room.

Newspapers can serve as useful replacements for destroyed records. This article documents a couple's wedding anniversary, providing details about the original ceremony.

city on March 2, 1915 (image). Along with a detailed description of the decorations and gifts exchanged at the party, the article lists family members present and their relation to the couple, similar to an obituary or report on a family reunion. Likewise, the names, ages, and residences of ten couples who had recently obtained marriage licenses in Omaha, Nebraska, were printed in the *Omaha World-Herald* in 1898. Researchers of Oscar Ederburn could glean that he was born around 1863 and was living in Ainsworth, Nebraska, in 1898, and that his future bride Nettie Orth was born around 1869 and was living in Parnell City, Missouri, at the time.

Newspapers may have also published naturalizations as part of ongoing coverage of a court or to highlight the presence of a particular immigrant community for a geopolitical reason. The article in image **Q** would fit into the latter bucket; it was published on May 26, 1917, just as the United States was entering World War I against Germany and the Central Powers. Two of the Germans being naturalized were local to Pawtucket, and the court made sure to ask each man if he was aware that his new country was at war with his old, and whether he was loyal to the United States. One man went so far as to say he would be willing to join the armed forces and fight against his former country. The *Pawtucket Times* was most likely covering the event because of suspicion of German immigrants at the time.

GERMANS NATURALIZED IN PROVIDENCE TODAY

One, From Pawtucket, Has His Son as Witness.

PROVIDENCE, May 26.—One of the largest crowds ever seen in the Federal building to secure naturalization appeared in the United States Court today to secure their final citizenship papers. The court room was filled and two long lines stretched down the corridors when court opened at 10 o'clock.

Half a dozen Germans were among those naturalized. One was from Pawtucket. He is Henry Niebuhr, 56, of 182 Kenyon avenue. He told the court that he went back to Germany about 1900 and was gone for five years. When asked if he knew that this government was entirely opposed to Germany he replied that he did. He was asked further if he would be loyal to the United States and he answered in the affirmative. A son born in this country was one of his two witnesses.

Another German, Herman Konter of Prairie avenue this city said he had been in this country 14 years and that he would be willing to accept service in the military forces of the United States to fight Germany.

REAL ESTATE TRANSFERS.

Bucks County Properties That Were Sold Yesterday.

Special to THE INQUIRER.

DOYLESTOWN, Nov. 7.—J. Johnson Beans sold at his office, at the court house, this afternoon the following Bucks county properties:

Real estate of Henry Eisentrauger, in Hilltown township, containing about 31 acres and 157 perches, to John Romig for $100, debt, $4,100; real estate of Hiliary Shellenberger, in Hilltown township, containing about 5 acres, to William Bloom for $75, debt, $436; real estate of Aaron W. Haring, in Richland township, containing about 68 acres and 133 perches, to C. Hoff for $100, debt, $2,724.16; real estate of Samuel K. Swope in Tinicum township, containing about 40 acres and 114 perches, to William Good, for $800, debt, $1,700; real estate of Morgan Conard in New Britain township, two tracts, No. 1 containing about 10 acres and 31 perches and No. 2 about 2 acres and 10 perches, to Sarah J. Gill for $880, debt, $808; real estate of Edward H. Blaker in Warwick township, containing about 121 acres and 130 perches, to John and Rienza Worthington for $1,200, debt, $6,300.

Publications sometimes capitalized on the public's fears by reporting on immigration or naturalization trends, as it did in this WWI-era article on German-American naturalization.

Real estate transactions were sometimes covered in newspapers, providing an alternative to deed records.

Everyday men and women would have been mentioned in articles covering real estate transactions, even if the deeds from the county are no longer extant or (sometimes even more frustrating) exist but are not available online. Image **R** documents six real estate sales that occurred in Doylestown, the county seat of Bucks County, Pennsylvania, on the afternoon of November 8, 1891. The coverage about each transaction includes the grantor, the location of the property, the size of the property, the grantee, and the consideration for the property. Although not quite as descriptive as a land deed, this kind of article can serve in a deed's place when it's not available for research.

Actions in probate courts also would have garnered regular press coverage. Probate records can be some of the most insightful records in terms of both the existence and nature of family relationships. They describe how estates were distributed (e.g., by last will and testament or by intestate laws), the appointment of guardians for orphan minors, and other important legal proceedings. The article in image **S** starts off with coverage of a higher-profile estate disbursement for Frank H. Collier, then details actions on estates of lesser value, growing a family tree for the people involved in the span of a paragraph each. Here we not only see who is related to whom, but also which child might have received more money than the others, be it by birthright or personal preference of the decedent.

Hopefully, these examples are enough to convince you that research in historical newspapers is worthwhile for any number of reasons. And even if this chapter has convinced you that you only want to target your search on traditional records of a particular person or family, help is on its way.

Newspapers sometimes detailed how high-profile estates were settled.

But before changing to that focus, let's look at one more great example from Neill's *Genealogy Tip of the Day* blog <genealogytipoftheday.com>: a series of newspaper articles that he found from 1890 when a several-greats-uncle Theodore Trautvetter/ Troutvetter went missing from the streets of Warsaw, Illinois. An article in the *Courier-Journal* in nearby Louisville, Kentucky, was headlined "A Spirit Message" and recounted how "John Raymond, a local spiritualist of some note" reported a dream in which a voice told him to look for Troutevetter: "Look in the river. Drag the river. As the vine is full of grapes and matured leaves, so is the strong man full of years. The vine shall wither, the grapes and the lightest leaves fall; so hath the strong man fallen." Despite initial skepticism, authorities did drag (search) the Mississippi looking for Trautvetter, but no body was found. In fact, just a couple of weeks later, the *Warsaw Bulletin* reported "Theo. Troutvetter wholly dispelled the mystery surrounding his sudden disappearance by returning hime [sic] last Saturday, accompanied by John Heger, of Pitttsburgh, Kan., whither Troutvetter went." The short article went on to say that Trautvetter was in his right mind and that "no good can come of any criticism." When Neill was researching his relative, he first found the reference to Trautvetter's reappearance in Illinois after his "month away" in Kansas, which included enough clues to send him to other newspapers. While it turned out Trautvetter was alive and well just two states away, perhaps the spiritualist was painting a picture not of him just in this world ... but the next.

KEYS TO SUCCESS

★ Every section and type of item in a newspaper can provide historical details.

★ Pay particular attention to the "point of view" in evaluating a newspaper's content.

★ Remember that formats of newspapers differ from time to time and place to place.

★ Because newspapers often publish "look back" articles, be careful about limiting the time periods of your searches.

Vital Records and Life Events in Newspapers

You'll find that chapters 2 through 4 of this book are like a funnel that's wide at the top and narrow at the bottom. Chapter 2's wide "top" has many examples of the ways every column inch of historical newspapers can be helpful for research on the life and times of an area and its people, and chapter 4 is all about the narrow "bottom" of the funnel that for many people is their only exposure to newspapers: obituaries and other recordings of death. In this chapter's "sweet spot" middle of the funnel, we're going to look at a pair of other hidden newspaper gems: vital records about the people you are researching and personal chronologies of research subjects that document their major life milestones.

VITAL RECORDS

Genealogists especially worship the "big three" events of births, marriages, and deaths, and some researchers now consider them the "big four," including divorce because so many people experience that process. This section will arm you with some details to consider in your newspaper searches for these events. (Even though we're saving the bulk discussion on death records for chapter 4, we'll touch on them here to compare them to other vital records listings.)

We'll get started with one of the many newspaper finds that Eric "Rick" Bender of New Mexico has acquired about his Midwestern and mid-Atlantic kin over the years. Bender's a researcher who needs no one to tell him about how historical newspapers increase your understanding of the times in which your research subjects lived. "Part of the fun of old movies and old TV shows is they tell you about some of the attitudes and conditions of the times," Bender noted. "Old newspapers do that, too."

One of his favorite articles about a marriage comes from the *Daily Illinois State Journal* in Springfield on April 4, 1899, and was headlined: "ELOPED TO SPRINGFIELD. Bloomington Man and St. Louis Woman Brave the Anger of Parents." The reporting about the nuptials probably would be deemed "too much information" by today's newspaper standards, but it gives interesting details that only personal recollections might include.

The article leads off by saying the couple were "Anxious to be united in marriage in spite of the protestations of the bride's parents." The groom and bride are identified, including the names of their fathers and that "Both are of age." The article gives a short description of the marriage ceremony before a judge and details that the new wife was then heard saying "the only difficulty now would be to face [her] parents," from which the judge surmised that the couple had eloped.

The conclusion of the article states, "Both were well dressed, and the bride is good-looking. They will make their residence in Bloomington, and left for that place shortly after the ceremony was performed." As just about any genealogist would, Bender's always after more details, quipping, "Two newspapers noted how good-looking she was. Too bad they didn't include a picture."

BIRTHS

It was once common for newspapers to obtain lists of newborns from hospitals and run these listings on a fairly regular basis (image).
Medical privacy would make that impossible today, even if twenty-first-century newspapers would be interested in such granular information. Even before such lists faded away some twenty to thirty years ago, they had become considerably less informative, in many cases omitting the actual names of the newborns and merely indicating gender and the names of the parents. A time-honored "like clockwork" article for many newspapers would be to write about the last baby of the year born in the newspaper's circulation area as well as the first to be born in the new year. These articles continue to this day in some newspapers—as long as the parents agree to waive the privacy they're entitled to!

As we fight the never-ending battle against "presentism" (i.e., assuming things were always how they are now), it's useful to remember that hospital births were the exception rather than the rule before the

A

CITY NEWS

Relief Corps.
The Woman's relief corps will meet at the K. P. Hall Friday afternoon a 2:30 p. m.

At St. Alexius.
A boy was born to Mrs. Leo Jantolsky of Merricourt at the St. Alexius hospital today.

Births at Bismarck Hospital.
Mrs. Hagerman of Bismarck—a girl; Mrs. Gus Sayler, Underwood—a boy and Mrs. J. E. Holsti, Kintyre, a boy.

Luther League.
The Luther league of the Swedish Lutheran church will meet at the home of Mr. and Mrs. U. M. Danroot, 511 Seventh street this evening. The penny contest which has been carried on since the first of the year will be

Births were sometimes listed with other local city news, such as this column from the April 24, 1919, *Bismarck Daily Tribune* in North Dakota.

Patricia "Patti" Hobbs became somewhat of a newspaper junkie while following a family surnamed Van Hoesen (principally brothers Albertus Louis and Byron Wells) which was scattered from upstate New York through the Midwest and Plains states. Hobbs thinks newspapers helped her fill in details left sketchy by other records: "There are several things that came only through newspaper research."

According to Hobbs, Byron Wells Van Hoesen's wife, F.E. Van Hoesen, has only her initials and years of birth and death on her tombstone in Willow Springs, Missouri. Hobbs turned to the town's newspaper for help, and (despite the publication's archives extending only for a short period of time) discovered there that F.E.'s full name was Francis Ertle. Furthermore, the newspaper documented a case Francis Ertle brought against her adoptive father for sexual abuse and mismanagement of her biological father's pension. The case (from Butler County, Iowa, in 1878) was settled out of court, but Hobbs found that Francis placed an ad in the newspaper a few months later saying she had lost notes from her adoptive father. "That indicates he might have bought her off," Hobbs noted.

Hobbs said the newspapers are also the only other place where she learned that Byron Wells and Francis Van Hoesen had twins born in 1893. "The birth garnered attention by the newspaper in Luverne, Minnesota, when they were born, and the Clarksville, Iowa, paper noted when they came to visit family there," she said. "But one of the twins died before 1900 and never appeared in a census. As it is there was a tombstone in Willow Springs, but without knowing that there were twins, I would not know how he was related. Part of the tombstone is unreadable."

In addition to having info about Francis Ertle and her children, newspapers also contained a dearth of information about the death of Byron Wells Van Hoesen's father, Robert. Hobbs couldn't find Robert's probate records, deeds, or headstone in Howell County, Missouri, but his sister's New York probate record states he was living in Willow Springs by 1897. Only the newspaper in Clarksville, Butler County, could confirm Robert moved to Willow Springs a year earlier—and that same publication published a letter from Robert's son stating that Robert is buried in the city cemetery. The issue's date (along with his sister's probate record) even gave Hobbs a range for Robert's death date.

Newspapers also provided information on Hobbs' more-distant Van Hoesen relatives. "I also know more about the death of Albertus Van Hoesen's wife Carrie because of getting the newspaper where her sister lived in Iowa. It tells how she went to her sister's bedside in Willow Springs, but arrived too late," Hobbs said. "It also tells how she brought home to live with her for a while the youngest of Albertus and Carrie's sons." Hobbs said Albertus' father-in-law Hugh Finley Lucky Burton "also has a lot of newspapers," including a striking detail from an Iowa newspaper that states he was building a house around 1876. "By putting it into a timeline, I could more easily see that the house building occurred right after the final settling of his father's estate. So it made it more obvious that he had the money to build because of the estate settling," she noted.

At the time of her searches, none of the newspapers from various places (Luverne, Clarksville, and Willow Springs) were digitized, so Hobbs diligently worked through microfilms ordered through interlibrary loan (see chapters 5 and 10). "I went through the newspapers week by week on microfilm," Hobbs said.

twentieth century (and, in some areas, were still the exception well into 1900s). In this era—especially before civil registrations of births begin—births often will be remarked upon in the "social columns" and only may be reported upon sporadically if something out-of-the ordinary attached to the birth, such as a difficult birth, multiple births, or (as was unfortunately the all-too-frequent case longer ago) the death of the mother. It's also useful to remember that there may be references to births—at least the date of birth, if not more details—in other types of newspaper articles, from personality sketches to reporting on a trial (especially if paternity or inheritance was an issue) to offhanded mentions (like a reference to being the first or last baby delivered by a particular doctor).

MARRIAGES

As with births, simple listings of granted civil marriage licenses were once a staple of many newspapers. Back before most states instituted and enforced marriage license requirements in the nineteenth century, ministers often would report lists of couples wed by them to newspapers. But as history progressed, coverage of marriages in newspapers widely varied, both because of the differing policies of individual papers and the considerable divide between rural newspapers and their more metropolitan counterparts.

In the second half of the nineteenth and the first half of the twentieth centuries, coverage of weddings became full-on news articles (image **B**), running on for a column or more and sometimes including family historian delights such as the names of every guest at the ceremony (and sometimes even what gifts the couple received!). Beginning with the same 1970s "space crunch" that would also lead to highly stylized obituaries (see chapter 4), newspaper wedding (and engagement) notices

> SECRET marriages at Aberdeen are coming to light rather frequently of late. Several have heretofore been published in the EVENING BULLETIN. The latest one of these secret marriages to come to light was that of Deputy Collector Robert L. Baldwin and Miss Sallie V. Darnall. It is the sensation of the hour last evening. The groom is the youngest son of Colonel W. W. Baldwin, and the bride the eldest daughter of C. W. Darnall, of the firm of Hildreth & Darnall. The couple have been devoted to each other for the past year or so. The certificate of 'Squire Beasley shows that they were married at Aberdeen, on the 11th day of August, 1886. The couple will make their home for the present with the bride's parents on Fourth street.

Sometimes newspaper coverage of marriages included "investigative reporting," which can contain salacious details such as in this Maysville, Kentucky, paper.

Research Tip: PARTY AT LIBRARIES

Especially when dealing with obituaries in newspapers to which you don't have access, consider consulting the public libraries closest to the newspapers. They may have policies that allow you to do some limited research in the library's holdings, sometimes for a nominal fee.

became formulized. In newspapers that still run such items (now generally termed "announcements"), people submitting information actually have to fill out forms for newspaper staff, who rewrite the announcement in the paper's particular style (image). And because real-life pranks have been perpetrated (sending in fake announcement information featuring people who do not like each other, for example), some newspapers found the need to develop verification policies.

Because states differ as to whether they impose health testing or other impediments against immediate license-to-ceremony weddings, some couples would choose to elope and have a civil ceremony in another jurisdiction, such as the example from Rick Bender's research detailed earlier in the "Extra, Extra! Couple Elopes to Springfield" sidebar. This often will result in seemingly random publications to cover an event. It's also the case that—although marriage licenses are often issued at the county level—many states allow a license to be used anywhere in the state, no matter which particular county's marriage license office issued it.

And as was noted in the section on births in newspapers, reporting on court cases and any number of other types of later articles may reference a marriage later on. We'll take a look at the most likely of these (reporting anniversaries) in the milestone section later in this chapter.

Finally, newspaper reports of marriages are always secondhand information subject to the type of errors that such copying can introduce. In fact, in terms of the marriage license listings, they're also held captive by the accuracy of the original. If, for instance, the

C

MARRIAGE LICENSES

Following are marriage licenses issued during the last 48 hours by Probate Judge Ralph H. Gaw:

John A. Hammond, Emporia.....over 21
Lenora H. Lane, Topeka.......over 21
Walter A. Porter, Kansas City, Mo.over 21
Mabel H. Lyon, Topeka..........over 21
Edward Gilden, Bennington.........29
Edna Ostlander, Bennington.........35
Oscar Taylor, Kansas City, Mo........32
Roberta Dorsey, Kansas City, Mo......28

Marriage licenses recorded in a "just the facts" template (such as this one from *The Topeka State Journal* in 1920) became more popular in later decades.

Research Tip: **FIND OUT MRS. WHO**
You'll occasionally find married women hidden under their husband's names ("Mrs. Roger Danbury") in newspapers, rather than under their own first names. You'll then have to consult other resources, such as marriage documents or notices, to piece together the wife's first name.

marriage license clerk thought getting accurate addresses from both marital partners was a waste of time—as opposed to always listing the second party as "of the same address"—that's not an error that a newspaper will inevitably unearth and, in turn, it can lead to an error in your genealogy if not properly given an "according to" attribution.

DIVORCES

Before the post-WWII spike in America's divorce rate, the formal ending of marriage was fairly rare. State laws straitjacketed couples to make good their "until death do us part" vows in what was deemed the public interest. The flip side of this is that nineteenth-century and pre-1945 divorce proceedings were considered especially newsworthy, and divorce actions that went to trial often merited a good deal of newspaper coverage (image **D**). There was also occasional publication of divorce statistics, all the way back to when divorce was not regularized and literally required an act of the legislature!

Between the end of World War II and the 1970s, divorce became much more common and therefore less likely to be covered in newspapers, often being reduced to mere listings. During much or all of this time period, however, most state laws required there to be specific grounds for the marriage to be dissolved. Even couples who were both eager to end the marriage had to make one the plaintiff and the other the defendant and choose something from the state's list of grounds (such as desertion or adultery). As a result, newspaper lists that include specific grounds for the divorce from this time period should be taken with a grain of salt.

For the last several decades, "no fault" divorce has become the norm, and the frequency of divorces has continued to make it less newsworthy. In addition, attorneys in divorce cases often find a way to keep divorce proceedings sealed from the public (and therefore the media).

It's worth noting, too, that divorces may be a source of marriage information, since showing that a legal marriage had taken place is a necessary requirement for a divorce

D

Says Wife Kissed Him Only Once During 13 Years

One kiss in thirteen years of married life was all he received from his wife, according to the story told today to Judge James A. McClure by S. D. Woods, 126 Harrison street, during the second day of the contested divorce trial between Woods and his wife, Pearl Woods.

"While affection played no part in my wife's dealings with me," Woods said, "she wasted much time and attention on Harry Brady. In fact, after we had trouble and I left home I became suspicious and sent the police out to the house one night. There officers, after pounding at the door fifteen minutes, finally got my wife to open it and upon entering found Brady standing on the stairway in his shirt sleeves."

Mrs. Woods in her defense claimed that Brady was her sister's sweetheart. The sister, Phoebe Hunt, took the witness stand and swore that she and Brady were engaged. Brady's whereabouts at this time are not known.

Mrs. Woods claimed her husband was insanely jealous and cruel to her. Each wants a divorce and the custody of their two children. Mrs. Woods has another sister, who is the mother of Edna Dinsmore, the little girl strangled to death by Fred Bissell here several years ago. Bissell is serving a life sentence for the murder of the 11-year-old girl. Judge McClure took the divorce case under advisement.

Contested divorces provided interesting headlines. This article from 1920 documents one couple's relationship in *The Topeka State Journal*.

action. As a result, even the-least informative divorce listings can contain details about the marriage.

DEATHS

There are so many types of mentions of death in newspapers—probably because there are so many ways to die!—that they deserve a whole chapter of their own, and that's what chapter 4 will be about from beginning to end.

What we now call obituaries—a recounting of a person's life, with names of their relatives, the organizations to which they belonged, and details on any funeral services—evolved from much simpler "mentions" of a person's passing, as well as paid "death notices" that were like classified advertisements. Deaths from violence or accidents also merited newspaper coverage as articles. Many obituaries today appear online—with some only on the Internet and not in print at all.

But just as a teaser for the depth to come in chapter 4: Let's look at the story of Brian Hartzell from Perryville, Ohio, who used a newspaper item to learn about a relative of his wife who died young and might have been left unremembered otherwise. Emanuel Mathias Schamber, age 12, died in 1894 in Menno, South Dakota. Hartzell didn't find an obituary or death notice. The burial itself wasn't written up that he could find. The death apparently wasn't from violence or something else considered newsworthy. (From other circumstantial evidence, he's pretty convinced the boy died of appendicitis.)

Hartzell could find no birth or death records at all, not even in Zion Lutheran Church documents from nearby Scotland, South Dakota—but a newspaper did supply one slim lead: "There is a brief newspaper item in *The Northwest Blade* (Eureka, South Dakota) about the lad's two eldest brothers taking the train down to Scotland to attend the funeral."

That bare mention led Hartzell and his wife to a family plot in Scotland's Rose Hill Cemetery. "In September 2013, when we visited Scotland, there was no marker noting the child's burial there, but it was listed in cemetery records held by the village's sexton," he noted. Hartzell solicited donations to place a tombstone to the child's memory.

Research Tip: FIND PATTERNS

When "browsing" images of unindexed/unsearchable newspapers, look for consistent formats, such as marriages always being found on the second page.

Research Tip: HOLD YOUR RELATIVES 'NEAR'

If a newspaper article refers to "near" relatives, that could mean close by either geography or blood—don't assume one or the other! (This tip is just one of the great tidbits at Michael John Neill's *Genealogy Tip of the Day* <genealogytipoftheday.com>.)

Most references to death in newspapers will not be nearly as circumstantial as the one Hartzell encountered, and chapter 4 will run through them all, from obituaries to death notices to articles on deaths deemed newsworthy.

MILESTONES AND TRANSITIONS

Everyone has transition points in life worth celebrating. Together, these celebratory milestones and transition points account for a lot of newspaper copy that applies to individuals. However (because so many people experienced noteworthy events), newspaper coverage often was limited to individuals' names. Even so, references to milestones and transition points are likely to include previously unknown information.

With all these life events, you'll need to put together your ancestor's whole chronology: a timeline of major life events that will help you keep track of them. This is especially important in newspaper research, as newspapers at any stop along with way—whether your ancestor still lived in a community or was long gone—may report on former residents. Sometimes you'll need to do a "backwards chronology" from someone's obituary showing previous residences to use like a "trail of breadcrumbs" to show you the way to then make sense of the forward chronology.

A whole host of milestones can help you piece together these individual chronologies and are worth investigating. Newspapers cover each event/celebration in a different way and style (presenting research problems), but don't get jaded and think "Oh, the person I'm looking for will be just another name in a list"—you never know when it was that person's chance to shine. For example, a newspaper account of a high school graduation might list, not just the names of the graduates, but also those who won awards (e.g., an ancestor who took the "best history student" award even though he wasn't in his class' overall top ten) or was voted a "superlative" honor (e.g., "class clown").

Here are some of the types of milestones that might have merited newspaper attention:

- **Anniversary write-ups**: These apply to individuals, businesses, municipalities, churches, and pretty much any entity that can claim a founding date. Celebrating a certain number of years or months in business or in a marriage is a time-honored tradition, and was a popular space-filler in newspapers. Wedding anniversaries (usually starting with the so-called "silver anniversary" of twenty-five years and sometimes published in five-year increments afterwards) are a staple of the anniversary genre, often with details ranging from a description of the original wedding (including names of the wedding party and the minister who performed the ceremony) to names of family members attending an anniversary celebration if one was held (image **E**).

- **Birthday articles**: These are a sort of anniversary announcement, as they commemorate "anniversaries" of birth. Such articles are fairly common in newspapers, especially for individuals reaching ages that were uncommon at the time of publication. In the present day, with a goodly number of people living longer, the items about them sometimes follow a template with "just the facts," whereas older folks in years gone by often received the dignity of an actual article (if not front-page treatment in smaller newspapers).

- **Graduations**: High school and college graduations (and, less frequently, graduations from junior high school or trade certification programs) are other milestones that may appear in local newspapers. With a high-school diploma becoming the overwhelming norm after World War II, some newspapers would even publish special sections to list all the graduates' names, sometimes highlighting top-of-the-class individuals (such as valedictorians, salutatorians, and class presidents) with photos (image **F**).

- **Awards**: Who doesn't like awards? According to the papers, no one in America. If an award was given (whether the "tractor seller of the year" or "outstanding athlete of the county" or "top humanitarian"), a newspaper somewhere likely covered it.

- **Church events**: Because churches have played substantial roles in communities (especially during the newspaper heyday), events held at, by, and for those churches often received coverage. While some are mere calendar listings (or, in the case of fundraisers, a brief recap of results), church-related articles may list the names attached to the event in question—who chaired the social, what children received their first communions, etc.

- **Performances**: Theatrical and musical productions sponsored by local, school, or church groups fill up many column inches, especially in small-town newspapers. Sometimes coverage is limited to a photograph with several people involved in the production; other times there are actual reviews of the play or musical involved.

With all these kinds of records in mind, let's look at an example from Laurel Sanders of North Carolina. Her subjects of research, James Alpheus Askew and Mary (Bullock) Askew, lived in the Barton's Creek area of Wake County, North Carolina, during the 1880 US census. At the time, James' father owned a paper mill just north of Raleigh, North Carolina, which he had until his death in 1887. From further research, Sanders knows that James and his brother-in-law were active in the mill business until at least 1899. James and Mary appear in Durham, North Carolina, in the 1900 census and in Richmond, Virginia (where their son, Robert, was married in 1901) in the 1910 census.

A trio of newspaper articles suggested a new and unexpected place to look for records for this family:

- "Mr. J.A. Askew, formerly in charge of the paper mill at the Falls of Neuse, near Raleigh, has become manager of the Tiddy paper mills at Lincolnton." (*The Charlotte Democrat*, Charlotte, North Carolina, February 19, 1892, page 3)

- "Jim, the little son of Mr. J.A. Askew, left Tuesday for Raleigh to enter the Institute for the Deaf and Dumb." (*Lincoln Courier*, Lincolnton, North Carolina, September 22, 1893, page 3)

- "Mr. and Mrs. J.A. Askew wish to extend to the people of Lincolnton their kindest regards and feelings for the many expressions of regret of their moving away. They have found the people exceedingly kind, and made many warm friends from

E

MARRIED FIFTY YEARS

Mr. and Mrs. W. W. Miller Cele brate Their Golden Wedding Anniversary.

Mr. and Mrs. W. W. Miller celebrated their golden wedding anniversary at their home in the suburbs of Dallas Saturday. About eighty guests were present, and the entire day was devoted to the merry-making. A great forty-foot table was laid under a long tent on the lawn, and around this the guests were assembled at noon to partake of the sumptuous wedding dinner. After the banquet was ended a short time was devoted to speeches dealing with the life and influence of Mr. and Mrs. Miller. William Grant, W. P. Miller, Dr. T. V. B. Embree and Mrs. T. D. Phillips, in speeches of humorous or pathetic vein, paid many rare tributes to the aged couple.

Mr. Miller is 76 years old and Mrs. Miller 69. They were married in Adel, Iowa, in 1857, and came to Oregon in 1866. Three years later they returned to the East in disgust, only to come back to old Oregon in '71. Here they have lived in perfect content on their farm near Dallas through all the years since that time. Of their six children three are still living—W. P. Miller, Mrs. Lucretia Holman and Mrs. Chloe Butz.

Those who were present at this pleasant celebration were: H. S. Butz and family, J. F. Holman and family, W. P. Miller and family, Hardy Holman, Jr. and family, J. W. Miller and family, J. C. Morrison and family, of Independence, J. W. Morrison and family, Mr. and Mrs. Levi Miller, of Tacoma, Mr. and Mrs. Sylvester Miller, of Sodaville, Mr. and Mrs. William Grant, Mr. and Mrs. R. C. Craven, Mr. and Mrs. T. D. Phillips, Rev. and Mrs. A. C. Corbin,

The *Polk County Observer* carried this story about the Millers' fiftieth wedding anniversary.

The Denison Review published two classes' graduations on May 21, 1913, opening up opportunities for advertisements.

whom they regret to part." (*Lincoln Courier*, Lincolnton, North Carolina, October 6, 1893, page 3)

Sanders said the series of articles not only alerted her to a key transition point in the family's life—the unexpected relocation of this family—but also an enlightening detail about James (the younger).

KEYS TO SUCCESS

★ Newspaper references can be crucial in filling in details about peoples' lives.

★ Many vital statistics events such as births, marriages, divorces, and deaths appear in newspapers.

★ Milestone events covered by newspapers such as anniversaries and graduations may appear as lists of names only or have a more detailed angle to them.

★ Newspapers are often valuable in documenting "transition points" in the lives of individuals.

Obituaries and Other Death Notices

I t may seem that we've got the last couple of chapters "backwards," as many people researching newspapers go straight to obituaries. Many don't search any further once their search for an obituary ends—maybe not even trying to get more than one newspaper's obituary of the individual, let alone mining the newspaper for other recordings of the death. But armed with chapter 2's gamut of items that might be mentioned in newspapers—and chapter 3's roundup of other vital events and emphasis on building a chronology—you won't be that person who takes the easy way out and stops researching prematurely.

In this chapter, we'll dive into the most well-known kind of records in newspapers from any time period: obituaries.

A HISTORY OF OBITUARIES

Charles Darwin's theory of evolution about life on earth may spur some debates among researchers, but the evolution of obituaries over the past few centuries is much clearer. And the better you understand this evolution, the more you'll be attuned to what your obituary searches are likely to yield in any particular time period.

A note before we begin: Obituaries evolved in slightly different ways based on the papers that published them. One of the tips in chapter 3 was to look at a few full issues

EXTRA, EXTRA!
FAMILY MYSTERIOUSLY MOVES TO MICHIGAN

In chapter 3, we learned that a chronology puts you in the driver's seat in your quest to fill in the details of a person's life or an historical topic. Obituaries are crucial resources for these chronologies, as this story will tell you.

One researcher, Pamela Pracser Anderson from Chambersburg, Pennsylvania, used an obituary to determine why her great-grandmother Carrie McMaster Marquart (born 1875) was listed in census records as being born in Michigan even though her family had been tied to the town of Owego in upstate New York since the mid-1700s. "Then I found the obituary that explained it," Anderson said.

What she unearthed was that three or four years after they married, Carrie's parents Francis "Frank" and Mary McMaster moved to Michigan, circa 1874, as noted in one of Frank's obituaries from the *Owego Times* in 1899: "About 25 years ago, he went to Big Rapids, Mich., where he was engaged in lumbering and the liquor business two years. He afterward came to Owego where he spent the remainder of his life in farming and the liquor trade." Further research shows the family had returned to Owego three years later, in 1878.

Anderson said there is no indication why the McMaster family made the temporary move to Michigan, as she couldn't find any family members or other associates in the Michigan area. She thinks economic opportunities may have been the pull factor—perhaps Frank, a farmer, had tried his hand at farming and was attracted to larger tracts of land offered by a new state. She also observed that she finds that "older obituaries have a lot more detail than current ones"—though, as we'll see, the evolution of obituaries throughout the years has been complicated.

Anderson's example shows newspapers are invaluable for "snapshotting" short-time excursions that other types of records will miss—leaving "holes" in biographies between the once-a-decade US censuses or seemingly random transactional and tax records.

of a particular newspaper to get a good idea about that newspaper's format in that time period. This is true both in technical terms (Are obituaries always run on page 3?) as well as character (Does the newspaper have a consistent editorial tone throughout, and is that tone political or objective? Does it appear that only obituaries from a certain party are included?). Knowing about the paper (its format, its history, and its potential biases) will help you apply the general trends we'll outline in this section to the publication in your ancestor's hometown.

The history of obituaries in America, in some ways, begins with the history of America. Newspapers of the Colonial era didn't have obituaries per se, but rather "mentions of death." In keeping with the general trend of the times, in which most newspapers gave priority to national and international news, such mentions of death were mostly limited to people of some prominence or who died a "newsworthy" death. Such "newsworthiness" might

☞ We notice in the Laforche *Union*, the death of J. B. RODDY, of this city. Aged about 36 years.

Obituaries in the early 1800s were short—just a one- or two-sentence notice of a person's death.

George E. Hiersemann.

After four years of patient suffering, George E. Hiersemann passed away from the home, 1139 Twelfth avenue, at 3:15 yesterday afternoon. Tumor of the brain was cause of death.

Mr. Hiersemann was born in Buffalo, Iowa, Jan. 23, 1880, and came to this city in 1902, entering the livery business. He continued in this business until 1910, when he sold his establishment, owing to failing health.

He was married to Miss Theresa Free in Rock Island Sept. 18, 1907, and she, with one daughter, Elizabeth, survives him. He also leaves four sisters, Mrs. Frank Kautz of Moline, Mrs. William Cox and Mrs. O. Miller, of Rock Island, and Mrs. John Leyden of Goodland, Kas., and two brothers, Charles of Blue Grass, Iowa, and John of Buffalo, Iowa.

His long illness was marked by his patient and cheerful suffering, two operations being necessitated during that time, but through all his affliction Mr. Hiersemann bore up bravely and patiently. He was a devout member of St. Mary's church, Moline and of Leo Council No. 716, K. of C.

Obituaries evolved to be more detailed as newspapers grew in size and resources.

consist of a violent passing, or an individual who had an inordinately large number of descendants.

By the early 1800s, these mentions became more like what would later be dubbed "death notices." These prototype notices were usually just a sentence or two, and their content was not consistent from one death to another (image A). Coverage (in terms of the total number of deaths mentioned) increased from the Colonial period, but still involved only a minority of people. They were also still considered "editorial" matter as opposed to advertising and were run at the discretion of those in charge of editing the newspaper.

During the second half of the nineteenth century, two innovations affected the coverage of deaths in newspapers. First, as newspapers reached their competitive zenith and more greatly stressed local news, more and more deaths were mentioned in newspapers (image B)—even if some of them are oblique, like a mention of someone dying in an area workplace but not providing his name! In addition, newspapers began to monetize the death-notice process by offering paid death notices as a special sort of classified advertisement. In part, this was a way of ensuring the text the deceased's family wanted would see the light of day, although many of these early death notices were essentially advertisements for the funeral homes and highlighted service times and places.

The early 1900s into the 1970s, when newsprint was inexpensive and newspapers were riding high as an unrivaled advertising medium, might be called the "Great Age of Obituaries." They were often treated with the respect of news stories by reporters, made possible because newspapers of the time usually had little space constraints (paper was cheap, and loads of ads funded space for editorial content). As a result, any and every detail found its way into obituaries during these decades, including exhaustive lists of organizations to which the subject belonged and every one of his hobbies. It was also fairly common for newspapers to run an obituary announcing the death, then follow it up with an article reporting on the funeral (including such details as the names of the pallbearers).

That "great age" began to fade when newsprint prices soared in the late 1970s, causing publishers to look at newspaper space as a more precious commodity. Most began to look at obituaries, still often running for free as a service to readers, as an equivalent of the "box score" in baseball rather than as items worth reporting. A key part of this approach was a rigid style sheet that carefully delineated what circle of relatives' names would be published and what parts of the deceased's life were deemed relevant for publication. This resulted in a bit of uptick in paid classified death notices because you could put in anything you were willing to pay for in these small-print items.

Over these decades, newspapers continued to shrink in both the number of pages and (sometimes) in the size of the actual pages from fewer advertisements. As the WWII and Baby Boomer generations began dying in the late 1990s, the number of potential obituaries greatly increased the space required for them (even with a rigid style sheet). Some newspapers experimented with "editioning" their obituaries if they had geographic press runs, reporting only deaths that occurred within a smaller area within the paper's circulation area. This reader-unfriendly move counted on subscribers not being interested in deaths from the other end of town.

TIMELINE OF OBITUARY EVOLUTION

Colonial times	"Mentions of death" for prominent, violent, "newsworthy" people
Early 1800s	Proto-"death notices" of a couple sentences
Later 1800s	More deaths mentioned; paid classified "death notices" begin
1900s to 1970s	"Great Age of Obituaries"
1970s to 1990s	Strict style sheet limits obituary content
2000s to present	Paid obituaries proliferate; online obituaries debut

Research Tip: REMEMBER TO FACT-CHECK

While we're going to show a lot of ways obituaries and other records related to death can help with research, obituaries can often include incorrect information or omit data that might be considered embarrassing to the deceased or the survivors. Be sure to use obituaries in conjunction with other genealogy records to ensure the document is accurate.

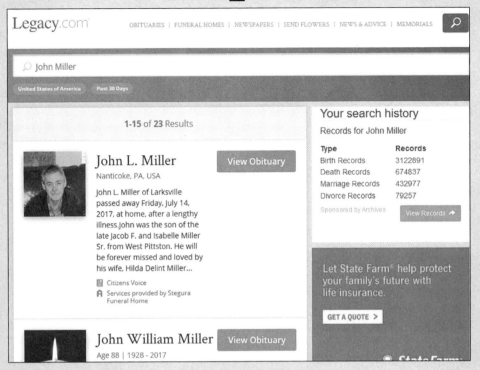

Many newspapers store their historical obituaries on websites like Legacy.com.

Finally, these events and experiments led newspapers to initiate a new way to monetize death: paid obituaries. Virtually every newspaper has adopted a paid model, which usually includes a per-line charge on top of just enough free linage to say that somebody died and when and where the services would be held. As with any change, it is not solely a bad idea: The mostly positive repercussion is that the rigid style sheet of the previous few decades disappears in this model, as newspapers will print as much detail as someone is willing to pay for. But therein lies the flip slide: What if no one cares that much to pay what is often several hundred dollars for a print obituary? And, with the rise of cremations and people simply not having funeral or burial services, more families see no need to submit any lines to a newspaper at all. For the first time in almost a century, significant numbers of peoples' deaths are unnoted in any newspaper.

Another innovation has been "online-only" obituaries, which newspapers have begun offering, often in conjunction with funeral homes or other online memorial services such as Legacy.com <www.legacy.com> in image . (We'll discuss these in more detail later in this chapter.) Print editions also continue to run paid death notices (sometimes simply a recitation of upcoming services and occasionally containing poetry), and small display advertisements on the anniversary of loved ones' deaths seem to be on the upswing.

What perhaps could become the final evolution of the obituary is what might be termed the "whimsical auto-obituary," in which the deceased has prewritten his or her own account of the individual's life and times, often in what's meant to be a humorous fashion. An upside to auto-obituaries is that they afford greater opportunity for the deceased's character to show through, while the downside that already applies to the accuracy of any family-written obituary might be amplified. Only a tiny minority of obituaries is done in this manner, so whether it's a trend will only be told by the future. What's for certain is that humor and good taste will continue to be "eye of the beholder" concepts.

OTHER TYPES OF 'DEATH RESOURCES'

While finding and using formal obituaries is a starting point for general research, obituaries aren't the only mentions of death you can find in newspapers. You have access to a whole gamut of other notices to search for that can supplement the information in the formal obituaries, be used as an alternative when no obituary can be found, or help us to find the obituary to begin with.

Specifically, deaths (as we discussed earlier) were historically often treated as news items rather than the "box scores" they became in more recent times. Newspapers have published human interest stories for a long time—and perhaps nothing's of more interest to humans than life-and-death stories. While these articles could be of any length—from a short anonymous blurb to full-blown, bylined pieces—the main takeaway is that articles reporting on deaths locally can be found anywhere in a newspaper, especially in the nineteenth century and first half of the twentieth century, when comprehensive local news was the norm.

Deaths involving a tragic dimension always have been especially worthy of column inches. In a genealogy journal (*The Palatine Immigrant*, Vol. XLI, No. 1: December 2015), Becky Thornton shared newspaper clippings about a family near Logan, Ohio, including one clipping headlined "AWFUL CALAMITY: A Young Man and His Wife Drowned in Scotts Creek." The account gave just a few names of blood relations of the drowned couple, but painted a detailed picture of the unfortunate demise of the two as well as its aftermath, including an analysis of the treacherous pool in which they drowned, a description of the macabre excitement generated in the town, and ending with a coroner's inquest and large funeral.

Reports involving death ordinarily would end with the burial of the individual. But a significant number of deaths were not "ordinary." Causes of death that were not obvious might require a coroner's inquest (or, at the very least, the release of a report for the

D

RECORD OF THE COURTS

Will of the Late Ananias P. Luse Presented to the Probate Court.

Administrators of the Estate of the Deceased A. J. Snell make a Report.

Stephen W. Gilman Sued for $50 000 for Alleged Fraud—Saratoga Hotel Suit.

WILL OF A. P. LUSE.

The will of Ananias P. Luse, late of the firm of Marder, Luse & Co., was admitted to probate yesterday, and letters testamentary were issued to John Marder, of Chicago, and Albert D. Anderson, of Crawfordsville, Ind., in bond of $300,000.

Mr. Luse left an estate estimated at $300,000 of which $50,000 is in realty and $250,000 is personal property. The only heir-at-law is Miss Alethea H. Luse, an adopted daughter. In June, 1873, Mr. Luse secured a decree in the County Court authorizing him to adopt Alethea Lee Hartmann, a girl of tender years and the daughter of David W. Hartmann, who gave his consent to the adoption. The girl's name was changed to Alethea H. Luse, and since then she has lived and has been cherished as a daughter by Mr. Luse.

Newspapers sometimes published wills and other legal documents, such as this one for Ananias P. Luse.

public record), which often would be reported on. And, of course, deaths suspected of occurring through foul play that might result in a trial (or other stages of adjudication) might appear in print for months or years after the actual death, as well as "anniversary" articles commemorating the date of the death.

Another thing to keep in mind is that most people did not keep their newspapers for long periods of time. By and large, newspapers were considered disposable after being read. As such, newspapers published "retrospective" pieces that sometimes included a summary of the deaths that had been reported in a year. This gives researchers another shot at seeing a mention of the death if the original obituary is either missing or no longer extant. For example, Debra A. Hoffman found an article titled "Chronik von Sterbefällen Deutscher in Baltimore, resp. Maryland, im Jahr 1897" ("Chronicle of German Deaths in Baltimore, Maryland, in the Year 1897") in the 1897 New Year's edition of the German-language newspaper *Der Deutsche Correspondent*.

Especially before today's era of everyone becoming "famous for fifteen minutes," newspapers looked upon someone having achieved a degree of fame as more worthy of coverage than some "Average Joe." People with fame beyond a local area might well end up with obituaries in many newspapers, particularly if a wire service wrote the obituary and disseminated it to its members or subscribers (in which case the wire-service obituary might be edited by the individual newspapers, a good reason not to settle for the first version of these widely reported events you see).

Even postmortem events such as an estate action might result in further recitation of death details. Some newspapers printed excerpts from probate proceedings on a weekly or other regular cycle; others were treated as standalone news stories. For example,

---

Research Tip: SEARCH FOR SECONDS

Don't stop with the first version of an obituary you find in any one newspaper. Obituaries may be "rerun" the next day to correct erroneous information included in the first version.

Loretta Luce Evans found a reading of her ancestor's will in a Chicago newspaper on GenealogyBank.com ("Will of the Late Ananias P. Luse Presented to the Probate Court," from the *Daily Inter Ocean*) that gave loads of details about family relations: heirs, married names of female relatives, and the addresses of those hearing the will. The Luse will (image **D**) even mentioned the deceased's siblings, half-brother, and nieces and nephews.

Another resource not to overlook is the result of a time-honored activity for historical and genealogical societies and researchers: abstracts of obituaries in newspapers. These excerpts are created to preserve historical publications and (in some cases) make them more widely available. These abstracts were often put into book or monograph form and published. In many cases, the abstracts have remained unpublished or in database form, sometimes only available at specific (local) repositories. In the same way that newspapers publishing yearly summaries of deaths gives the researcher a "second shot" to work around lost newspapers (or ones that are unsearchable due to scanning problems), these abstracts help fill in the gap, even including cases of newspapers that were available when the abstracts were done but perhaps never preserved through microfilming or digitization.

OBITUARY WEBSITES AND DATABASES

We'll look at websites that digitize and index whole newspapers in a few chapters, but website creators are recognizing the importance of obituaries by creating obituary-only sites and databases. Nearly all of these obituary-only assets are "digital first" creations, meaning (in most cases) they only feature relatively recent deaths (at most the last few decades, when newspapers began creating their editorial copy on computers). As a result, they do not show a print obituary as originally published, just the raw text of it.

The first stopping points for online obituaries are the newspapers' individual websites. Even newspapers that have adopted a "paywall model" (in which most content requires a digital subscription to see) will have their recent obituaries available for free. You can typically search obituaries by name.

While some newspapers host obituaries on their own sites, many US newspapers have affiliated with Legacy.com, which makes recent obituaries available for free and archives them on another site, ObitFinder.com **<www.obitfinder.com>**. Legacy.com charges a fee

---

Research Tip: READ MULTIPLE SOURCES

Don't stop with just one newspaper's version of an obituary. Especially during the nineteenth and early twentieth century, obituaries were treated as news items, with one reporter's version potentially being quite different than the story another reporter filed for a different newspaper.

---

for viewing archived obituaries on ObitFinder.com: $2.95 for a "24-hour restoration" and higher fees for a one-year or permanent sponsorship. The same newspaper obituaries are available through the subscription service ObitsArchive.com <www.obitsarchive.com>, with plans ranging from $2.95 to look at a single obituary to a years' unlimited service for $49.95.

You'll also find a number of other sites with lookalike names such as Obituary Central <www.obitcentral.com>, Obituary Depot <www.daddezio.com/obituary>, and ObituaryData.com <www.obituarydata.com>, some of which are free and worth a look if you haven't found a recent obituary elsewhere. RootsWeb <home.rootsweb.ancestry.com> still has a database called "Obituary Daily Times," where volunteers can add citations. NewspaperObituaries.net <www.newspaperobituaries.net> is a decent free "pointer site" that shows the way to thousands of databases of obituaries and other death records—new and old, including databases compiled from nineteenth century records—categorized by state, county, and city.

The larger genealogy websites, such as Ancestry.com <www.ancestry.com>, GenealogyBank <www.genealogybank.com>, and ProQuest <www.proquest.com>, also have collections of obituaries. We'll discuss these when we explore those services' other assets in later chapters.

For help in doing a general search of sites with obituaries, including the newspapers' sites, consult the Obituaries page of the venerable Cyndi's List <www.cyndislist.com> (a directory of thousands of genealogy websites). You may also wish to look at Find A Grave

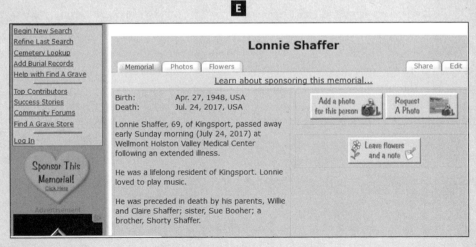

Although the site's focus is on headstones and inscriptions, some memorials on Find A Grave will have obituary information.

<www.findagrave.com> (an online database of tombstones and digital memorials to the deceased) since a fair number of people have taken to posting obituary "clippings" there. In fact, some Find A Grave entries will buck the site's original purpose and *only* have such a clipping, and not the burial and headstone information (image **E**).

KEYS TO SUCCESS

★ Newspaper obituaries have evolved, from short items to lengthy writeups and to paid articles.

★ You'll find many detailed articles from the "Great Age of Obituaries" from the early 1900s to the 1970s.

★ Other resources about deaths include: paid death notices, inquest or trial articles, retrospectives, and obituary abstracts.

★ Websites with obituaries include newspapers' own sites as well as Legacy.com and other commercial sites.

NEWSPAPER DEATH RECORD WORKSHEET

Use this worksheet to extract information from obituaries you find in your research. Download a printable, fillable version of this form online **<bit.ly/ft-newspapers-guide-downloads>**.

Obituary Extraction Worksheet

Deceased's name			
Source citation			
Repository/website			
Date accessed			
Date of death		Place of death	
Age at death		Cause of death	
Date of burial		Place of burial	
Date of birth		Place of birth	
Marital status		Spouse's name	
Surviving children's names			
Other surviving relatives' names			
Other deceased relatives' names			
Religious affiliation			
Community activities/hobbies			
Occupation/employment information			
Interesting biographical facts			
Funeral home or undertaker name/address			
Pallbearers			

Other death records

☐ Funeral report
☐ Paid death notice
☐ Coroner's report and/or inquest
☐ Articles about estate actions
☐ Retrospective articles
☐ "In Memory of" paid advertisements on anniversary
☐ Abstracts (both published and unpublished)

Understanding
Newspaper Media

It seems natural enough that versions of actual newspapers—in print, microfilm, or digital format—are "ground zero" for researching in historical publications. While these are certainly the most obvious forms in which they're preserved, newspapers are far from the only ones. As we mentioned in chapter 4, many other "newspaper resources" do not involve looking at any original newsprint or facsimile thereof. In this chapter, we're going explore the gamut of media in which original newspaper pages are found (both obvious and not) and also describe other resources from which newspaper information might be unearthed.

Before we tear into the different types of media, let's look at *The Carrolltonian*, the quarterly publication of the Carroll County Genealogical Society, as an example. In some ways, this newspaper is a model for how the different types of newspaper resources can benefit genealogists. In one year's worth of issues (September 2015 to June 2016), *The Carrolltonian* published the following types of newspaper information:

- A "necrology" in chart form taken from the late 1800s' end-of-the-year issues of the Westminster, Maryland, *Democratic Advocate* that listed the names, dates of death, age in years, and place of death for people age seventy and over

- Cover articles on "The Mills on Sam's Creek" that blended a few nuggets about the mills gleaned from newspapers (mostly advertisements) that round out the well-done articles written from a variety of primary sources including deeds, estates, historical maps and aerial photos, laws of Maryland, and tax assessments

- A listing from *The Sun* (Baltimore, Maryland) abstracting the names of men drawn for the Civil War draft in 1862

- A list from *The Democratic Advocate* of "A Sunday School of 1860—Names of the Boys and Girls of Fifty Years Ago" (which ran as a "look-back" feature in 1909)

- Several "Rural News from the Past" columns from *The American Sentinel* (Westminster, Maryland) and *The Democratic Advocate* that were roundups of items from countryside hamlets (all from a particular issue), including such tidbits as details of a hailstorm in Maidensville in the May 12, 1894, issue that concluded, "The rain washed cornfields so badly that those who had planted their corn are going to plant again" (which in turn tells you about the timing of planting corn in this area and time period!)

- A digital reproduction headlined "LIST OF LETTERS" at the Westminster Post Office in 1845, as published in *The Democrat and Carroll County Republican*

- Marriages and deaths relevant to Carroll County taken verbatim from *The Baltimore Sun* from the mid-1800s

The Carrolltonian showcases the variety of ways newspaper information might be found in places other than newspapers. Some of the publication excerpted newspaper data word for word while other sections are abstracts. And sometimes the info is just used as one of many sources for an article. Not every issue of the volume uses newspapers in the same way, and (despite all the newspaper resources) the publication included non-newspaper articles, too.

Many other genealogical and historical groups' newsletters and journals may provide such features, and the Carroll County organization's publication is just one of the many "non-newspaper" newspaper sources. We'll talk in this chapter about scrapbooks, clipping files, photo and text "morgues" (which have dead articles, rather than dead people!), and "electronic" and newspaper morgues. But before we get to that, we need to talk about the most popular media in which the full texts of historical newspapers are found: original print, microfilm, and digital images.

ORIGINAL PAPER COPIES

Yes, it's old school and now nicknamed "dead tree" journalism for all the pulp paper that has been used to print newspapers, but it was the only medium in which newspapers were found for centuries. (With one exception: Some newspapers had so-called "wallpaper editions" printed on wallpaper when the publisher ran out of newsprint, due to a flood, natural disaster, or—in some Southern states—the Civil War.)

Given that many thousands of individual titles were printed, it's not surprising that a substantial number have not survived. After all, this product—which often has a second life as fish wrap, birdcage lining, or animal-bedding in barns—hasn't historically been thought of as being "for the ages." Efforts to preserve newspapers are relatively recent. You'll learn more about the US Newspaper Program in chapters 10 and 13, but for now let me say that, until this project began in the 1980s, few felt the need to preserve newspapers for posterity—and even fewer considered how fragile newspapers from the so-called "Era of Bad Paper" from approximately 1850 to 1950 were becoming. Issues printed on the most highly acidic paper were literally crumbling; publishers eventually used paper with less acid and eventually switched to recycled newsprint in recent decades.

Given the lack of quality paper and a lack of foresight for their historical importance, some newspapers have only a few surviving print copies. Unfortunately, in many cases these so-called "orphan runs" (i.e., newspapers that have ceased publication without any successor and therefore no owner interested in preserving the previously published newspapers) are the least likely to be microfilmed. And since most digitization is done by microfilm-to-digital transfer, they are also the least likely to be digitized. In addition, even when a run of a title is more complete, it might have remained unmicrofilmed because the only copy was the publishers' own archive (called "back files"), often bound with other issues in volumes that are more difficult to microfilm.

All these factors conspire to make newspapers that exist only in paper form the most difficult to access. They might be found in public and college libraries' rare book facilities, publishers' vaults, or even in the hands of collectors.

They are worth seeking out, however, if they apply to the time and area in which you are researching. Even if they've been deemed as a lower priority for preservation, a single

---

Research Tip: COPY ME, PLEASE!

Pay attention to notes such as "please copy [city name]." It was one newspaper's way of letting others know that the item was of interest in another locality.

---

issue might have a gem that can color your historical search. And, as we'll discuss later in this chapter about microfilming and optical character recognition (OCR) digitization, you should try to consult original paper copies for a more accurate reading of the original text.

Duke University Libraries is in possession of a large collection of paper copies called the American Newspaper Repository <library.duke.edu/rubenstein/findingaids/americannewspaperrepository>, which was founded in 1999 by author Nicholson Baker. The collection has about five thousand bound newspaper volumes and several thousand unbound newspapers, including newspapers from major cities and some immigrant papers.

MICROFILMED IMAGES

Brown University in Providence, Rhode Island, has been a leader in the study of digital technology, and in the early 2000s I attended a weeklong seminar there titled "Born Digital." One of the best takeaways from that week was how the history of humanity's recordkeeping has been one in which the media we store documents in has a shorter and shorter lifespan. The instructors noted we still have cuneiform tablets from Babylon and papyrus from ancient Egypt—each dating back thousands of years—but find it more difficult to access information saved on technologies that now go obsolete in a decade or less.

At that time, microfilming all documents, including newspapers which had especially come into vogue with the US Newspaper Program in the 1980s, was considered the preservation gold standard. In fact, some people believe it *still* should be the gold standard even in the age of digitization. While there was once considerable concern about migration problems—changing data saved digitally from one format to another, such as eight-track tape decks; VHS, Beta, and other videocassette recorders; and floppy disks—it has become less of a hazard today.

Microfilm has been treasured because, under proper storage conditions, it can last hundreds of years. Materials used for microfilm before the 1980s—first a highly flammable nitrate base, then a base of cellulose acetate that allowed decay known as "vinegar syndrome"—have been replaced by a silver halide process that creates silver images on a polyester base. Having a microfilm as the format of choice also helped archivists create a stable, standardized system that could be used across the world. Specifically, archivists

---

Research Tip: SEARCH FOR ALTERNATE VERSIONS

Changes and corrections made to different editions of the same day's newspaper may not have been microfilmed (and therefore may also remain undigitized), so keep this in mind if you notice an error in a newspaper.

---

produced a first-generation "archive master" negative (known in the trade as "1N" and kept under the most rigorous of storage conditions), used only to produce one or more second-generation "print master" negative or positive films (called "2N" or "2P"). These second-generation films are, in turn, used to produce any number of third-generation "service copy" positives. The idea is to prevent wear-and-tear on the first generation, which is the best copy.

Microfilm's small size also allowed for more efficient storage. As mentioned earlier in this chapter, newspapers often kept print copies of their back issues in large binders. While this created problems for digitization efforts (volumes usually won't lie flat for a camera, and bent newspaper issues were hard to safely extract and flatten), publishers began to appreciate the smaller storage space required for microfilm and began microfilming security copies.

DIGITIZED IMAGES AND NEWSPAPERS

There's digitization ... then there's *digitization*. When discussing historical newspapers, we're generally talking about digital images of old newspaper pages originally produced on newsprint, which were preserved on microfilm then transferred to digital. But "digital" newspapers can also refer to the publications produced online in recent years, either for a website or as a collection of news/content published digitally before appearing in print (a "digital first" model). Let's take a quick moment and review digitization as it applies to newspapers.

The large file sizes of newspaper pages were initially the biggest problem facing digitizers in the early 2000s. Archivists largely overcame this challenge as computer technology marched on—the computer space for high-resolution scans became possible (and financially accessible).

Merely putting scans of newspaper pages on the Internet for browsing was not the full solution to the "accessibility" problem. While the scans often took away the need to go to a repository to look at microfilm, researchers still had to invest a huge amount of time and energy to research the individual scanned newspaper pages.

Research Tip: PARDON THE TYPO

For the record: Typographic errors in the nineteenth century often resulted because minor mistakes were difficult to correct in the "hot type" process because it meant either creating a new piece of leaden type or "chipping off" part of the existing lead. Twenty-first century typos probably come more from lack of copy editors—modern newspapers have no mechanical alibi!

ALL ABOUT OCR

No technology has been as crucial to newspaper research as optical character recognition (OCR). We'll spare you most of the technical details about OCR technology, focusing instead on common OCR pitfalls and ways to work around them.

OCR is defined as the mechanical or electronic conversion of images of typed, handwritten, or printed text into machine-encoded text, which is then able to be searched. Essentially, OCR makes a digitized newspaper page image a two-layer object—the image of the page and a hidden page of OCR text "underneath," the latter of which allows users to search using text keywords. The initial technology was designed to help create reading devices for the blind, and it had to be "taught" one font at a time, using images of each character. Nowadays, advanced systems are capable of producing a high degree of recognition accuracy for most fonts.

As noted earlier, conversion of the original newsprint pages presented problems stemming from bound volumes and folded pages. Spots, splotches, and other damage (even actual holes in pages!) on the only copies of historical newspapers also posed challenges for the new tech. Even printing presses that weren't inking properly might cause printed letters to look faded and unreadable. In addition, pages might have been microfilmed slightly askew (and, while careful digitization can correct for this, that correction doesn't always take place). All of these issues can make OCR go wrong.

OCR WORKAROUNDS

First and foremost, OCR can and does misread letters, so you should be flexible in how you interpret OCR text if you don't get the expected results. For example: A residence in a newspaper obituary should have read "Bern Township" but instead reads "Bem." A few of the more popular misreads are:

- Uppercase letters: *B* and *H*; *B* and *R*; *B* and *8*; *D* and *G*; *D* and *O*; *G* and *6*; *S* and *8*; *S* and *5*; *Z* and *2*

- Lowercase letters and combinations: *b* and *h*; *c* and *e*; *c* and *o*; *cl* and *d*; *h* and *k*; *h* and *n*; *i, l, 1, /, !* and (uppercase) *I*; *o* and *o* (zero); *n* and *ri*; *r* and *n*; *rn* and *m*; *v* and *y*

Because surnames usually have more spelling variants than common nouns (or other parts of speech, for that matter), you'll want to search for another word that might be associated with the individual, such as an occupation or address. You can also try searching for such a word along with an individual's first name, since given names generally have fewer spelling variants than surnames.

If you are including a surname in your search, be sure to work out all the potential phonetic spelling variants of that name, and try them relentlessly!

Sometimes printers "stretched out" words either to highlight them (such as a name) or merely to make the right-hand side of the type even ("justified," in newspaper talk). These "s t r e t c h e d" words may defy OCR searching. Your best bet will be to try a first name only in this case.

Note that OCR may not pick up words that are hyphenated, especially when hyphenated from one line to another. Keep your searches to syllables of words, if necessary, to get around this.

him upon the platform. He introduced him in a little speech, telling of Rickard's achievements as a promoter. Three cheers were given for Tex, but he modestly declined to respond to calls for a speech. Stakeholder Tim Sullivan followed Rickard in the ring and was introduced.

It is reported that a new purse division was brought out by Johnson's refusal to enter the ring unless agreed on.

Sullivan, Fitzsimmons and Gotch.

2:10 p. m.—John L. Sullivan was the next celebrity introduced by Jordan.

2:12 p. m.—in response to repeated calls, Bob Fitzsimmons left his seat in the crowd and came up to be introduced. Bob got a great hand.

Tom Sharkey was the next in order to be presented to the crowd. A performance that was quickly finished was the introduction of these men.

The wrestling profession was then recog-

Quiet Morning in Jeffries' Camp

State Doctors Examine the Pugilist and He Has a Shave and a Haircut.

JEFFRIES' CAMP, Reno, July 4.—Jeffries rose at 8:15 and said he was feeling fine. He went to breakfast and was then formally examined by Doctors Morrison and Hasher, in conformity with the state law. The doctors made no statement, but drove at once to the Johnson camp. All is quiet about this camp. Jeffries is lounging about the cottage, apparently in good humor.

Soon after the doctors departed Jeffries went out on the lawn, behind the cottage,

OCR allows you to keyword-search digitized newspapers, drastically cutting down your research time. This search for the word *Johnson* in a 1910 issue of the *Omaha Daily Bee* returned a few results.

Ein amerikanischer Geschäftsmann schreibt auß Buenos Ayres: Die hiesigen Geschäftsleute sind schwer zu bewegen, mit amerikanischen Firmen Handelsverbindungen anzuknüpfen, weil sie bei der Ausführung von Bestellungen sich so unwissend und

Either for emphasis or to fill a line in hot-type printing, words were sometimes "stretched out" with extra space between letters (as it was in this 1914 German newspaper from Cincinnati). This can affect how words are picked up by OCR.

Sometimes it's obvious why OCR doesn't pick up a paper's original copy. In addition to having a torn page, this issue of the *DeSoto County News* wasn't laid flat for microfilming.

But again, technology provided. Optical character recognition (OCR) technology allowed for whole documents to be scanned and indexed, making them keyword-searchable. Initially narrowing down only to the article level, OCR allowed researchers to drastically cut the amount of time needed to work through text-heavy resources. OCR originally only worked for "Roman"-type fonts, but within a few years became more dependable with other historical newspaper fonts, such as Fraktur (used by nearly all German-language newspapers in Europe and America). Most digital images of old newspapers are created through high-speed microfilm-to-digital transfer. (See the "All About OCR" sidebar for more.)

RESOURCES CREATED FROM NEWSPAPERS

In chapter 4, we discussed non-obituary recordings of deaths in newspapers because not all death pronouncements came in obituary format, but it bears repeating that newspaper data was published in a variety of forms. We've already shown how much some genealogical societies' publications mine newspapers for content, but those resources are just the beginning. In this section, we'll discuss some of the other resources that use data from archived newspapers.

NEWSPAPER MORGUES

"Newspaper morgue" is the term newspapers used to refer to their libraries. Up until just a generation or two ago, the average newspaper morgue consisted of paper clippings (snippets of newspapers cut from the large publication) organized by subject matter, sometimes including photographs and other times having a separate morgue for photos. This changed when newspaper articles began to be produced on computers, with articles stored in a database for retrieval by subject, date, or other parameters—an "electronic morgue."

While a digital archive was somewhat more stable than a physical one, the medium shift opens up the possibility for discrepancies between what was printed in the newspaper and what was stored in the electronic morgue. Granular corrections made between editions of newspapers published in a single day's cycle might not make it into the electronic morgue.

The old-style physical morgues still might be in the hands of publishers or may have been converted digitally in some way. Others may have been donated to historical societies or archives, most likely from the geographic area served by the newspaper. The morgue of the defunct *Philadelphia Bulletin*—once the dominant newspaper with the slogan "Nearly Everybody Reads the Bulletin"—is now held in Temple University Libraries' Urban Archives <library.temple.edu/scrc/urban-archives>. This morgue includes internal news-clipping files of helpful card indexes, approximately half a million pieces, and three million photographs. Thousands of *Bulletin* photographs have been scanned and are available online along with a limited sampling of clippings.

THIRD-PARTY VOLUMES

The newspapers themselves were not the only ones to keep clipping files. Some private individuals did, too, and a few even compiled them in some form by pasting them into volumes. The Sheppard scrapbooks <www.yatespast.org/genealogy/sheppards.html>, preserved by the Yates County (New York) History Center & Museums, are an example of this. George S. Sheppard began keeping copies of local newspapers in the early 1900s, and his son, Oliver, continued adding to the scrapbooks after his death. The final work has newspapers for more than half a century, from the early 1900s to the 1950s. The Sheppards even prepared a handwritten index, which was later photocopied and bound. The clippings include many Yates County-related births, marriages, deaths, and historical narratives and images. The original Sheppard scrapbooks and an index of them are available for research at the Research Center in Penn Yan, New York, but the center has also made them into searchable PDF images for the collection's more than two thousand pages.

While the Sheppard scrapbooks are an exceptional collection, many local and regional history and genealogy organizations could have clippings, sometimes organized into topical "vertical files" and left unindexed and undigitized.

EXTRACTS AND ABSTRACTS

Finally, we return to published and unpublished extracts and abstracts that may appear in publications (like *The Carrolltonian* example that began the chapter), in published form (primarily, but not limited only to, vital events), and in repositories.

In some cases, these unpublished abstracts might be used by a society to "hold information hostage," holding off the Internet and requiring users to physically visit the society for access. While this virtually never works in the long run, it does sometimes create a reason to visit a society. In many cases, at least a catalog for a society's repository will be online so potential users can better evaluate whether a trip to a library is worthwhile. Societies may also know of a clippings collection that still lives in private collection—another reason to connect with a local society.

KEYS TO SUCCESS

★ Original newspaper pages can be found in print or microfilm format, or as digitized images held either by individual repositories or large databases.

★ Today's "digital first" environment may make online content different from newspapers' print content.

★ Newspaper resources extend far beyond those original newspaper pages and include abstracts, clippings, and scrapbooks.

★ Abstracts of newspaper content can be found in published volumes as well as unpublished compilations, the latter often found in repositories.

★ Genealogical and historical society newsletters and journals may contain many types of newspaper resources.

NEWSPAPER RESOURCE TYPES

This worksheet can be helpful if you are compiling a list of newspaper resources, either at one particular repository or from a geographical area. Download a printable, fillable version online **<bit.ly/ft-newspapers-guide-downloads>**.

Type of newspaper resource	Newspaper title	Time frame included
Catalog of newspaper holdings		
Narrative about specific newspapers		
Original paper form		
Microfilm copies		
Digitized images		
Online electronic archive		
Published abstracts		
Unpublished abstracts		
Clipping scrapbooks		
Vertical file clippings		

PART 2

ACCESSING DIGITIZED NEWSPAPERS

6

Free Newspaper Websites

Are some newspapers available for free on the web? With a huge trove of newspapers at Google News Archive **<news.google.com/newspapers>** and millions of pages at both Chronicling America **<chroniclingamerica.loc.gov/newspapers>** and the idiosyncratically named Old Fulton New York Post Cards **<www.fultonhistory.com/ Fulton.html>**, the answer is an emphatic "yes." This is especially true when you consider the many free state sites that "add on" to the national Chronicling America project as well as public library sites that may have a local newspaper or two that they've digitized from their own holdings.

As we run through the free sites in this chapter, you'll see that, in some cases, the bells and whistles are limited. (This will become even more apparent once we talk about the more full-featured subscription sites in subsequent chapters.) But these free resources are still an excellent starting point.

Before we get to the free sites with actual newspaper pages, we'll first take a look at several search aggregator websites—the "search engine for search engines" that seemed necessary a decade ago before Google's superior searching ability lapped other engines. Then it will be onward to the free newspaper websites themselves, along with some notes on the copyright regulations and legal considerations for dealing with newspaper research, the terms and technology of newspaper searching, and even an app to make your searching mobile.

SEARCH AND LIST AGGREGATORS

My definition of search and list "aggregators" is somewhat broad. Some simply list online newspapers and the sites for their archival issues, while others will allow you to search the historical newspapers from other sites they've aggregated. These can be useful in a couple of contexts. First, if you're looking for a specific newspaper, these lists may bring you to it without your having to "turn down the noise" from something like a Google search. Secondly, these sites allow you to get your feet wet in newspaper research before having to pay for access or a subscription—though these sites may only *list* currently publishing print or electronic publications, and these may or may not have a searchable archive on their sites.

Here are some of the more useful aggregator websites.

ELEPHIND

The leading force on the search side of aggregators is Elephind.com <www.elephind.com>, which crawls across more than three thousand free historical newspaper sites around the world. In addition to the United States, the site scans newspapers from Mexico, Australia, New Zealand, and Singapore. A simple search box available on Elephind's home page allows you to enter a word or words. Click Advanced Search on the home page to limit the search in a number of ways:

- just the newspaper text, including user comments and searching online headlines
- range of dates
- particular country
- source of newspaper (e.g., the free site on which the newspaper resides, such as Chronicling America)

Once your search results come back, you can click a listing to go to the source of the digitized newspaper.

Research Tip: CHECK OUT FAMILYSEARCH

In talking about free sites, you might ask, "Well, what about FamilySearch?" While The Church of Jesus Christ of Latter-day Saints' system has a lot of material from newspapers (books with abstracts, etc.), it does not collect newspapers per se. FamilySearch does have an agreement with NewsBank, the parent of GenealogyBank <www.genealogybank.com> (the solo topic of chapter 8) to publish large volumes of newspaper content, mainly consisting of obituaries, birth, marriage, and death announcements.

On the site's home page are helpful tabs such as Getting Started and Search Tips, as well as an all-important "List of Titles." Searching the site is free, and registration is required only to bookmark pages you've viewed and comment on the site. Even without registration, you can submit your e-mail to join Elephind's mailing list and receive updates on what's added to the site.

ICON

The International Coalition on Newspapers (ICON) is administered by the Center for Research Libraries (more on them in chapter 10), and it's a clearinghouse of sorts for newspaper digitization projects, which it lists on its website <icon.crl.edu/digitization.php>. While its website mentions some individual newspapers being digitized, it's more useful as a descriptive hub for projects around the country (and, indeed, around the world; see chapter 12). ICON keeps track of newspaper digitization on both free and library-only subscription sites. In some cases, ICON gives descriptions of the collections, too.

WIKIPEDIA

You can find another listing aggregator at Wikipedia's "List of Online Newspaper Archives" <en.wikipedia.org/wiki/Wikipedia:List_of_online_newspaper_archives>. This listing gives more detail than ICON, often with newspaper-by-newspaper rundowns on what a particular digitized collection contains that include the date ranges of digitized newspapers. It does not list when a newspaper is part of a library-only subscription collection. Individual newspapers are listed as either Free or Pay to indicate the need (or lack thereof) for a subscription to access the site. The Wikipedia list is worldwide and breaks down US listings by state, with notations that explain whether these state papers are Multistate or National. In addition to links to and lists of actual newspapers, the page details some magazines as well as newspaper resources such as obituary indexes.

SMALL TOWN NEWSPAPERS AND BLOGS

Another listing site is Small Town Newspapers <www.smalltownpapers.com>, which is the hub for some 250 free newspaper archives across the country. For general searches, you'll want to use the Articles by Subject tab on the home page. You can browse both current editions of its member newspapers as well as whatever scanned archives the particular paper may have available. In many cases, the site has just a few years' worth. Small Town Newspapers notes in its terms of use that individual users may not use its materials for commercial purposes, though it offers Business User Licenses and Media User Licenses for these cases. (More on copyrights and terms of use coming up shortly.)

OTHER AGGREGATORS

Many newspaper sites are works in progress, such as one that bills itself as "The Online Historical Newspapers Site" **<sites.google.com/site/onlinenewspapersite>**, and many genealogy-related blogs offer insights on newspapers, including the well-known and long-running Eastman's Online Genealogy Newsletter **<blog.eogn.com>** (with Dick Eastman's Plus edition of the newsletter usually including at least one item on newspaper digitization each week). The Ancestor Hunt **<www.theancestorhunt.com>** has loads of historical newspapers on free sites (aggregating state-by-state searches of the free sites profiled in this chapter, such as Chronicling America, Old Fulton, and a variety of state sites).

CHRONICLING AMERICA

In barely a decade, the National Digital Newspaper Program, created by a partnership between the Library of Congress **<www.loc.gov>** and the National Endowment for the Humanities **<www.neh.gov>**, has placed millions of searchable pages of newspapers online at its website Chronicling America: Historic American Newspapers **<chroniclingamerica. loc.gov>**. The Library of Congress has been the leading collector of newspapers, both in paper form and microfilm (see chapter 10 for more).

The Chronicling America homepage has tabs that take you to other Library of Congress services (such as Ask a Librarian). Below the tabs is the simple interface for Chronicling America, with tabs for Search Pages (a basic search), Advanced Search (exactly as the name implies), and "All Digitized Newspapers 1789-1924," which is your entrée to a full list of the titles digitized on the site. If you click through to this list and select a newspaper's title, you'll see brief historical sketches about each of these newspapers. You'll also note a button "US Newspaper Directory, 1690–Present"; we'll get to that shortly.

The first option, Search Pages, only has three parameters: a dropdown list of states (the default is for "All states"); a pair of dropdowns to narrow the date range; and a box to enter one or more search words.

Advanced Search allows you to select a state or a particular newspaper title; choose date or year ranges; limit the search to front pages or page numbers specified; and restrict results to newspapers published in a particular language. You can also access several additional search boxes.

The Enter Search boxes can act as Boolean operators, described more fully in the "Smooth Operators and Search Terms" sidebar. The first box is labeled "with any of the words" (meaning at least one of the search terms will appear on a particular newspaper page, like Boolean *OR*). The second is "...with all of the words" (meaning all search terms will be on a page, like Boolean *AND*). The third box is "...with this phase," which means the

COPYRIGHT AND TERMS OF USE

Several Congressional revisions of US copyright laws have left us with a system in which copyright status is largely dependent on time period. Perhaps even more relevant to researchers of online newspapers is the difference between *ownership of the copyright* and *terms of use or service* that may be imposed upon by the websites hosting digital images. How free can a genealogist feel about using a clipping from a newspaper in a family history book, especially if they're getting that "clipping" from an electronic source?

Let's start with copyrights and how they relate to newspapers. Copyright law varies by the year in which newspapers were published:

Pre-1923: Everything published before 1923 is considered "public domain" and therefore is fair game (but see terms of use or service, below). Under current law, this "copyright freedom" date will begin to advance a year beginning in 2019.

1923-1963: Copyright may or may not apply to content created between the years 1923 and 1963 (inclusive). Contemporary law required copyright notices in very specific places of the newspaper (as well as applications for renewal of the copyrights), and research has shown that few newspapers did these things. However, syndicated or freelance content could have been copyrighted separately, which is more relevant to organizations that want to digitize the material than it is to an individual researcher republishing some locally produced content in a family history book.

1977-present: If the paper has no copyright notice, then you can extend your green light through the end of 1977. The laws are more complicated for newspapers published from 1978 through March 1, 1989, however, because publishers had extra windows to file for a copyright notice (and this was when copyright time periods were made very long). From March 1, 1989, copyright became automatic without registration, so seeking permission from the copyright holder is always wise.

Depending on the time period you're researching, copyright may be of little issue to you—but the terms of use of the site from which you're getting the newspaper will always matter. It's not unusual for researchers to confuse the foregoing information on copyright with the "terms of use" or "terms of service" imposed by a website—usually you are prompted to click a box before you subscribe to a service (often without reading, at your peril!). You can usually find a link recapping a site's terms of use/service at the bottom of a website's homepage in very small type.

The terms of use vary from site to site. For instance, a government-funded entity such as Chronicling America can impose no restrictions on use (and while it is diligent about only digitizing newspapers free from copyright, it puts the usual disclaimer that it's not making any representations to that effect). Google News Archive has no separate terms of use, but some of its newspaper images are from recent time periods that are clearly in copyright. The privately run Old Fulton NY Post Cards, on the other hand, appears to have only copyright-free newspapers and lists in its "Rules of the House" that, "If you have a reasonable need for something on this site, and you will not use it for commercial purposes (Make Someone Pay For it), I will give it to you." We'll briefly discuss terms of use for Newspapers.com and GenealogyBank in the respective chapters.

Best practice is to look at these terms before accessing the site, and consider looking at them periodically for any changes. It's also not a bad idea (and not just from the standpoint of newspaper research) to become a regular reader of Judy Russell's blog *The Legal Genealogist* <www.legalgenealogist.com>.

On Chronicling America, you can view and enhance newspaper pages.

search terms will appear in that order consecutively on a page. The final box is "...with the words," with a dropdown choice for the search terms to appear within five, ten, fifty, or a hundred words of each other on the same page. Once your search hits have been returned, you have a "Share/Save" option to put that search out on social media, e-mail it to others or save the URL of the search to your computer's "Favorites."

Let's look at a quick sample search. From the Chronicling America home page, I selected "Illinois" from the dropdown and entered *"Hiram Snyder"* (with quotes) in the search box. The site returns results with full thumbnails of pages with hits from the search. Click on either the page thumbnail or the underlined text below it (with title, date, and page).

On a newspaper's page (image ), you'll be able to work with the image in a number of ways using the controls on the gray bar at the top of the viewer. From left to right, these controls do the following: the plus and minus signs zoom in and zoom out, respectively; the home icon re-centers the image if you've moved around in the viewer; the next button expands the image to your full computer screen.

A series of buttons can help you with browsing:

- Image gives you a dropdown to choose any pages from the same issue
- Page lets you "page through" an issue with arrow keys or view thumbnails of "All pages" of an issue
- Issues lets you use arrow keys to jump to the earlier or later issue or use "All issues" to go to a calendar marking issue dates

Research Tip: REFINE YOUR SEARCHES

You'll sometimes wish to search for just a surname (perhaps with an occupation) rather than attaching a first name that's either common or frequently garbled. Likewise, if your search comes up dry for the ancestor you're really looking for, try the names of other people who might have been in the same newspaper—such as relatives or even business partners.

The right-hand portion of the gray bar has three important functions. First is Text, which shows a readout of how the optical character recognition (OCR) software interpreted the newspaper page (image). This is valuable when trying to translate foreign-language newspapers (e.g., making it available to cut-and-paste into Google Translate **<translate. google.com>**) or viewing misinterpretations made by the OCR to arm yourself for accounting for the same miscues in future searches. Next is PDF, which (unsurprisingly) generates a PDF file for downloading or physically printing. Likewise, the "JP2" key generates a JPEG file. Finally, you can click on the key with a "scissors" icon to generate a printable image that includes only whatever portion is visible in your computer window, so zoom in or

B

OCR Interpretation

Chicago daily tribune. (Chicago, Ill.) 1872-1963, February 02, 1876, Image 1

Image and text provided by Library of Congress, Washington, DC

Persistent link: http://chroniclingamerica.loc.gov/lccn/sn84031492/1876-02-02/ed-1/seq-1/

What is OCR?

at))* fimiu
VOLUME 29.
SHIRTS.
SHIRTS.
WILSON BEOS. 9
ORDER DEPARTMENTS
it MReoad J* gi I.
t2ocr doz. Bliirtn extmVf'UnffVaroaUaohed.
9 XS. r.inonf are made to onr order Id Ireland, and ara
,t]Lreel/eqn»led la elegance of appearance and la dara-
oar extraordinary eretem of adapting the gar
_ln(4 to the wearer, our anperlor workmanship In mann-
RitofeTaiid ear oxqaltite finith la laundrying, the eom-

Chronicling America allows you to view a text readout of the page's OCR text.

SMOOTH OPERATORS AND SEARCH TERMS

One of the best lines that writer and humorist Mark Twain stole (supposedly from a friend named Charles Dudley Warner) was, "Everyone complains about the weather, but nobody does anything about it." Well, Boolean search operators are kind of like that: Everyone talks about them, but few people know what they are.

First things first: Boolean search terms are named after nineteenth-century English mathematician George Boole, who was basically a computer geek before there were computers. The Boolean operators are the words *AND*, *OR*, and *NOT*, which are used between keywords to either narrow or expand the search:

- *AND* narrows a search because it instructs the database to look for both keywords/phrases (in the case of newspapers, in either the same article, page, or issue).

- *OR* broadens a search to bring back hits that include either phrase or keyword

- *NOT* narrows a search by looking for one keyword or phrase, but only if it's not accompanied by the other (again, in either the same article, page, or issue), useful for excluding irrelevant results

These Boolean operators are crucial in refining newspaper searches. For example, a name you're searching might also be a generic word, so you might search *Farmer NOT agriculture* to exclude results that are about the profession rather than a person. People sometimes have surnames of famous folks who merited much press attention and create many false hits—think using *Rogers NOT Roy* to find an ancestor named Rogers rather than famous actor Roy Rogers. Sometimes the subject being searched might have so many spelling variants that bigger search parameters are needed (e.g., *Machmer AND Machemer* to catch those spelling variations). Some of the sites you'll encounter (usually in searches marked "advanced") will give several search boxes to make Boolean and other searches easier.

You can expand or contract word searches in other ways, too. Check a website's help guide for special ways to manipulate searches. On many sites, you can use quotation marks to search for an exact name or phrase (for example, *"Henry Jacobson"* or *"four score and seven years ago"*).

Many sites also allow "wild card" symbols to take the place of a letter in a word. In some cases, a separate symbol is used to replace a single character, while a different symbol is used to replace multiple characters—a godsend when searching for names or places with a lot of similar spelling variants. An example: If an asterisk (*) replaces one letter and a question mark (?) replaces several, then *Sn*der* would yield variants such as "Snyder" and "Snider," but *Sn?er* yields those two plus "Sniter" and "Snyter."

For each of the major sites in this and the succeeding chapters on online sources, we'll outline the primary search capabilities. Chapter 5 cautioned about OCR pitfalls involving mismatching letters, but those aren't the only problems you may run into. It was not unusual for newspapers to use abbreviations (even for names) that might now seem idiosyncratic. Since most newspaper sites do not account for such variants or search phonetically (Fulton, as we'll see, is a welcome exception), you have to be on your toes for shortened forms such as "Saml." for Samuel, "Fredk." for Frederick, or "Jno." for John. A further complication can be if the final letter of an abbreviation (such as the *l* in "Saml." or the *k* in "Fredk.") is "superscripted," which can throw off the OCR.

Chicago daily tribune. (Chicago, Ill.) 1872-1963, February 02, 1876, Image 1

Image provided by Library of Congress, Washington, DC

Persistent link: http://chroniclingamerica.loc.gov/lccn/sn84031492/1876-02-02/ed-1/seq-1/

⎙ Print this image | ‡⊞ Download this image

153 LA SALLE-ST.

| 868. | —— | 1876 |

MPERIAL & NORTHERN INS. CO., Lon-
don. Assets.....................$25,000,0(
MERICAN CENTRAL INS. CO. Assets.. 1,60(),0(
|IAGARA FIRE INS. CO. Assets......... 1,500,0(
IRE AND MARINE INS. CO. Assets.... 600,0(
COTTISH COMMERCIAL INS. CO. As-
sets.................................. 10,000,0(
AMAR INS. CO. Assets.................. 408,0(
IANUFACTURERS' INS. CO. Assets.... 270,0(
IERCHANTS' INS. CO. Assets.......... 268,0(
TANDARD INS. CO. Assets.............. 400,0(

Forty Millions

Enough to cover half the losses paid by all Insu
nce Companies occasioned by the fire of 1871.
 DAVIS & REQUA have a record of TEN YEAR:
XPERIENCE in Insurance in Chicago, and ha'
lways represented Companies which paid 100 cents (
he dollar, even including the great fire of 1871. F(

You can select print or download only certain portions of a newspaper page by using the scissors tool on Chronicling America's toolbar.

out before you do this. The printout will include the newspaper title, the date, and what institution provided the image to Chronicling America (image C).

In addition to searching and browsing the selection of online newspaper pages, you can also use Chronicling America's other helpful features. The "US Newspaper Directory, 1690–Present" is as close to a master list of American newspapers that you'll find. (We'll dig into it in more detail in chapter 10, both in its native form on the Chronicling America site and also through a Stanford University-based interactive map.) Also on the site are a list of Recommended Topics, which are hundreds of subjects covered by newspapers—everything from "Anarchist Incidents" to comic strips—that give some background on the subject, a list of sample articles, and, most helpfully, keywords and research strategies for maximizing search results (which will help you search any database of newspaper images, not just Chronicling America).

Although the Chronicling America site is dwarfed by some of the for-pay sites (as well as the free Old Fulton site, profiled later in this chapter), its significance extends past the raw page count. For starters, the National Digital Newspaper Program has helped write standards used by other high-quality digitization efforts. In addition, the project has doled out grants to state projects, which use the money to digitize newspapers from all over the country—especially foreign-language papers and publications from counties overlooked by commercial sites. These state projects research the best available copies (usually microfilm copies) and prevent duplicate digitization efforts. The program also urged state projects to consider so-called "orphaned" publications (i.e., those no longer in existence and without any successor titles or an active successor company).

STATE AND LOCAL SITES

The National Digital Newspaper Program that has fed the Chronicling America website has also helped inspire state libraries or archives to found state-based websites and digitization projects. These state sites sometimes merely mirror the content on the national site, but other times include more newspapers. The standards for digitization that the program has established have also helped as digitization has spread to local public and college libraries in the last decade, and these repositories sometimes became the only ones to have a digitized version of a community's newspaper. We'll give a runthrough of some examples of state and local sites in this section. (See appendix B for more-detailed information on state-specific sites, many of which you can find on Elephind.com.)

The same sort of partnerships going on in the rest of the genealogy world apply to historical newspapers and you can potentially take advantage of these by contacting your state's library. For example, the Arkansas State Archives and the Central Arkansas Library System partnered with Newspapers.com to digitize some two dozen newspapers. In addition, the archives and library system brokered free access for its patrons.

The Wisconsin Historical Society, the national number-two newspaper repository, that continues to be a newspaper leader in the digital age, putting together the Archive of Wisconsin Newspapers (funded by the Wisconsin Department of Public Instruction). In collaboration with the Wisconsin Newspaper Association, it put together the BadgerLink website **<badgerlink.dpi.wi.gov>** that gives Wisconsin residents free access to a wide selection of the last decade of newspapers (which is kept up-to-date within three months of your date of search) and some historical newspapers through a partnership with NewspaperArchive.

On the regional and local level, community newspapers are swiftly being digitized as well. As noted earlier, you only need to read the Eastman newsletter on a weekly basis to realize many public libraries are doing their parts to preserve historical newspapers. Often assisted by community foundation grants, public libraries have been especially active in getting their community weekly papers digitized. Sometimes their efforts are pooled into existing state sites. But, in other cases, the digitized papers are only on the sponsoring library's website—or even only on computers in the physical library.

OLDNEWS USA

One of the biggest things to come from the 2017 RootsTech conference was a mobile application for searching newspapers that took the first prize at the Innovator Showdown. OldNews USA, from Revgenea Software, combines a simplified search with the data from the Chronicling America collection and serves it up on a smartphone <revgenea.com/announcing-oldnews-usa>.

When you open the app, you select whether you're searching for a person (with options to enter names, date ranges, and locations), a topic, or aren't sure. The app then serves up search results from a variety of sites. If you save a particular hit, OldNews automatically embeds a complete source citation at the bottom of the image.

Able to run on Android and Chromebook mobile platforms with a cross-platform version that would also support iOS (Apple products) and Windows in progress, OldNews USA costs a nominal fee. Revgenea <revgenea.com> offers a free trial that includes all features, "but once the user finds and saves a few pages, the app requires a one-time, in-app purchase for continued use," creator Bill Nelson said.

The app as of 2017 is designed to work with any newspaper website that uses the same backend server software as Chronicling America, Nelson said, which is currently the case with a few of the state sites. Those state sites may become OldNews USA-enabled once Nelson is marketing the cross-platform version.

OTHER MAJOR FREE SERVICES

The two remaining major free services couldn't be more different in their outlooks and features. One is a product of Google (the Information Age's most prominent corporate success story), and the other is the brainchild of a single person and a tremendous amount of effort—and, funnily enough, the site started by the individual is more searchable than Google's product. We'll look at the two services in turn.

GOOGLE NEWS ARCHIVE

Let's start with the corporate one: Google News Archive <news.google.com/newspapers> (image D), with more than two thousand titles from newspapers worldwide that are free to browse. Of course, the key word in that sentence is "browse." Google word search capabilities are limited, and its database is not fully searchable. Don't be misled by the search box and Search Archive button—you'll get results from it, but just a small number compared to what a fully searchable database could return. As a result, you're not able to drill down into title based on geographic area or time period—you just see newspaper titles and date ranges. You also can't print from the website; you'll have to rely on your device's screen capture or "print screen" option.

Google News Archive has millions of newspaper pages (many of them exclusive), though its search capabilities leave a lot to be desired.

Be that as it may, Google News Archive should not be ignored. Its scans are state of the art, and the site boasts newspapers you will not find on other major free or paid sites. When you have an individual newspaper page called up on your computer screen, you're able to zoom in, zoom out, and browse from page to page within a given issue of a newspaper.

OLD FULTON

Tom Tryniski's Old Fulton New York Post Cards <fultonhistory.com/Fulton.html> began as a postcard digitization project and has morphed into a large, free collection of upwards of forty million pages from digitized newspapers, mostly from New York State. The website is pretty much devoid of extraneous features, but in part makes up for it with its helpful search abilities. These assist in overcoming some OCR problems at the site, which Tryniski acknowledges may stem from the fact that many of the microfilms he used for digital conversion were third-generation copies (i.e., copies of copies of originals).

Pretty much everything about Old Fulton is idiosyncratic. There's a crawl across the bottom half of the page that includes click-on links such as "If You want to see what Newspaper Titles I have" and "NEW Here!!" However, this listing does not appear to be in a discernible order; a post called "Newspaper Research Links" on *The Ancestor Hunt* blog lists them by state **<www.theancestorhunt.com/newspaper-research-links.html>**. The "NEW here!! You might want to go First and read" link hosts a comprehensive FAQ for the site as a whole.

Old Fulton goes far beyond just Boolean operators. It allows "fuzzy" searching to account for misspellings—and allows the user to decide how much "fuzziness" they want on a scale of 1 to 10. Plus and minus signs can be used to include and exclude words. You can use notation of *w/[number]* between two words to indicate the number of interrupting words allowed between the two search words. You can also perform phonic, synonymic, and wild card searches.

Search results appear on the left-hand side of the page, and if you select one (by clicking on the underlined page title), the page will come up on the right-hand side of the screen as a PDF. This has the normal options for a PDF such as zooming in and out, printing, or downloading. To browse issues, it's probably easiest to go to the list of Fulton's papers at *The Ancestor Hunt* and click on the newspaper titles.

Finally, you want to remember that it's not just newspapers on Old Fulton—yes, there are post cards! Tryniski also has an extensive "photograph" collection, which includes thousands of documents such as city directories.

TIPS, CAVEATS, AND FORECASTS

Millions of newspapers are available for free in the digitized historical newspaper world: aggregators; full-featured national, state, and local sites (with Chronicling America at the centerpiece); and limited (but still useful) sites such as Google News Archive and Old Fulton.

None of these projects shows any sign of stopping. Chronicling America is set to expand its date parameters to the 1923-to-1963 period in which nearly all newspapers are out of copyright. As has been the case in other parts of the genealogy world, more collaborations between publicly run sites, subscription sites, and the newspapers themselves are likely to alter the landscape of the online historical newspaper world. The bottom line, however, will be a continued march toward more online availability of the newspapers from days gone by.

KEYS TO SUCCESS

★ Several websites, such as Elephind and Small Town Newspapers, are search engines that lead to other sites that have newspapers.

★ Copyrights and "terms of use" or "terms of service" vary from website to website and should be studied carefully. Remember that something may be out of copyright but still subject to a site's terms of use.

★ Chronicling America is a growing site with millions of free newspaper pages using a standardized technology protocol that's a model for many state sites.

★ Many state consortiums and even local public libraries are digitizing various newspapers.

★ Google News Archive is a free website with millions of newspaper pages, but it is not fully searchable.

★ Old Fulton New York Post Cards has millions of free newspaper pages.

Newspapers.com

When Ancestry.com <www.ancestry.com> rolled out a subsidiary called Newspapers.com in 2012, it had just returned to private ownership after years of being a publicly traded company. As part of an overall trend, Ancestry.com was integrating its holdings into just a couple of subscription packages, and its public member trees became a marquee item of the Ancestry.com community. (At the time, the company's most recent game-changing feature, DNA testing, was still more dream than reality.)

Ancestry.com's main subscriptions had already included collections that contained newspaper information, primarily obituaries. But Newspapers.com <www.newspapers.com> took advantage of the latest technologies—fast microfilm-to-digital conversion and every-word optical character recognition (OCR)—to quickly bring millions of searchable historical newspaper pages online for researchers. In addition, Newspapers.com subscribers now had the ability to connect with each other by "following" each other's research. Indeed, Ancestry.com has many properties to explore. In addition to Newspapers.com and the parent Ancestry.com site, Ancestry.com also owns Fold3 <www.fold3.com> (formerly Footnote), a site that hosts military records and some newspaper material, among other resources.

Ancestry.com's newspaper-centric subsidiary Newspapers.com has hundreds of millions of digitized pages, available to search.

Newspapers.com (available as part of an enhanced Ancestry.com subscription or as its own standalone service) has become one of the leading resources for digitized newspapers. In this chapter, we'll examine Newspapers.com in depth—its holdings, its search capabilities, and other features, including a look at "Publisher Extra" (the enhanced subscription)—as well as discuss what other Ancestry.com properties have to offer newspaper researchers.

SCOPE OF COLLECTION AND LOGISTICS

Though young, Newspapers.com (image **A**) has become a major player in the historical newspapers field. Its top selling-point is likely its number of pages, which surpassed 300 million in 2017 when considering the newspapers included in the "Basic" subscription and the "Publisher Extra" together. All told, more than five thousand titles are included, with publications from every US state. The best thing about Newspapers.com, according to its Director of Product Management Peter Drinkwater, is that it has "a large and fast-growing content set and a website that makes it easy to find and use what you are looking for."

While the Basic and Publisher Extra sections are often counted together (presumably to enhance the "Wow! Look at all we got!" effect), the two subscription levels are separate offerings, in part because the images exclusive to the Publisher Extra subscription are mostly still in copyright and licensed from publishers (see chapter 6). In addition to these titles, the Publisher Extra subscription includes all the digitized papers from the Basic package. A separate "library edition," vended through ProQuest **<www.proquest.com>**, includes a large portion of the newspapers in the Basic subscription.

New Jersey genealogist Shamele Jordon and her cousin Floyd M. Riley have taken full advantage of Newspapers.com's collaborative features as part of their research on the Toomer family. "It began as a search for the pride of this large African American family in a small black enclave of South Jersey," Jordon said. Specifically, Jordon and Riley wanted to research James Cecil Toomer, who owned the Tippin Inn, a bar and showroom in the town of East Berlin, New Jersey. The venue, a stop on the "Chitlin' Circuit" of bars in the 1950s and 1960s where black musicians performed for black audiences, attracted acts like B.B. King, Ike & Tina Turner, and Fats Domino.

Their goal was to use newspapers to document family stories of famous entertainers who played at the Tippin Inn. Paid advertisements of upcoming performances were easy to find, Jordon said, and African American newspapers based in Philadelphia provided more texture with articles and photographs. (We'll talk more about the value of African American newspapers and how to access them in chapter 11).

Newspapers.com has a long run of the daily newspaper *Courier-Post* in Camden, New Jersey, that Jordon and Riley used to their advantage—even though they had to account for racial bias in reporting from that newspaper. "There was a lack of balance beyond sensational news. The only articles written on the Tippin Inn in the local newspaper occurred when it was robbed and burned down," Jordon said. "Even with this, the *Courier-Post* is a great source of family information. Beyond obituaries, the articles paint a picture of a vibrant community. We learn about social events, achievement in sports and academia." The *Courier-Post* also reported on a few fires that family members called "activist" arsons. "As a way to encourage the township to add fire hydrants to the African American section of town, abandoned structures were set ablaze," Jordon noted.

The amount of family information was so enormous that Jordon and Riley were thankful to have the collaborative features of Newspapers.com. "This subscription website allows us to follow each other. I can see when he clips an article, which avoids duplication. Also, an e-mail digest is sent when he clips."

You're able to purchase either service by the month or in six-month increments. As of this book's publication, the subscriptions cost:

Subscription Level	One-Month Cost	Six-Month Cost
Basic	$7.95	$44.95
Publisher Extra	$19.90	$74.90

In addition to these à la carte options, you can bundle either subscription with a one-year Ancestry.com subscription for a steep discount.

Newspapers.com content continues to grow, particularly in the Publisher Extra category as newspaper giants like Tribune Media and Gannett are continually adding recent publications. Digitized papers include those from the Mid-Atlantic and Midwest along with populous states such as Florida, Texas, and California. (The emphasis on page counts, rather than titles or number of issues, is somewhat distorting, since many more pages of newspapers were printed in the twentieth century heyday—and a substantial portion of those pages consisted of full-page advertisements, many more than in the nineteenth century).

The Newspapers.com website is well designed, versatile, and user-friendly. You can perform virtually any function in a couple different ways. The home page offers a search (basic or advanced). Tabs on the home page include Search, Browse, Papers, and Clippings, all of which we'll detail in the next section of this chapter.

In the upper right-hand corner of the home page, you'll find the nuts-and-bolts items if you're a subscriber:

- **My Profile** identifies your state and gives you the chance to give a tweet's worth of information on your background. It's public to other Newspapers.com members by default, but can be made private by unclicking "You're allowing visitors to contact you."

- **Upgrade Subscription** allows you to upgrade to a Publisher Extra subscription.

- **Account Details** shows details such as your original subscription date and expiration.

- **My Clippings** shows what items you've "clipped" from newspapers online (described in the next section).

- **Recently Viewed** shows up to the last twenty pages viewed.

- **Help** brings you to a menu called the Help Center, which provides a great primer on the major features of the site.

- **Sign Out** logs you out of your account (especially important if you're working on a public computer).

Toward the bottom of the front page, you'll see recently added or updated newspapers for either the Basic or Publisher Extra subscription, as well as an historical headline from the day's date and access to video tutorials to help you get started. At the very bottom of the page, you'll find duplicate links to key areas of the site as well as a Contact link. Newspapers.com's phone support is generally of the "leave a message" sort, while its e-mail support promises a reply within one to two business days (and is usually even quicker than that). Newspapers.com's terms of use (also available at the bottom of the page) are consistent with those of other Ancestry.com products.

SEARCH, BROWSE, AND PRINT FUNCTIONS

Let's discuss how you'll be spending most of the time on Newspapers.com: searching for, browsing, clipping, saving, and printing all those digitized newspapers.

SEARCHING ON NEWSPAPERS.COM

The quickest way to start searching on Newspapers.com is to use the search box and enter a name or other keyword on the home page, but that's just the tip of the iceberg when it comes to the features for searching, clipping, and sharing—even for non-subscribers—your finds from the website. Let's go through all those features now.

As previously noted, the quick-and-dirty search is available right in the middle of Newspapers.com's home page. If you hit "Add more info" to the right of where you enter a keyword or name, you can enter two "advanced" search terms, "Paper Location" and "Date" (an exact day or range). Going to the Search tab on the home page basically gives the same options. You can use the Boolean search terms described in chapter 6 to help focus your searches—but things get interesting once you perform an actual search.

Once a search comes back with results, you'll see a list of matches on the right-hand side arranged in order of what the software's algorithm considers the "best match" (most recent, oldest, and last added to Newspapers.com can also be selected). Results include preview windows of the pages where the search terms appear, plus which hits are found.

The site also presents four ways to refine that search on the left-hand side:

- **Narrow by Date** allows you to change the default of no time limits via either sliders or a calendar to select a date or manually typing in a date range.

- **Narrow by Location** gives the user a US map of states to click as well as a list of states to check in or out of the search. This is the default—you can click on World to see Newspapers.com's international collection.

- **Narrow by Newspaper** allows you to perform a limited search to one or more newspapers and conveniently limits your choices of newspaper titles by any previously entered date or location.

- **Added in the Past** lets you to look at only search results that are in newspapers added after a certain point in time. "Any time" is the default, but you can also choose one, three, or six months or one year. This is especially useful for people who want to see what's new on the site rather than rehash already-searched-and-discarded "hits."

Let's take an in-depth look at how to search for names in digitized newspapers on Newspapers.com:

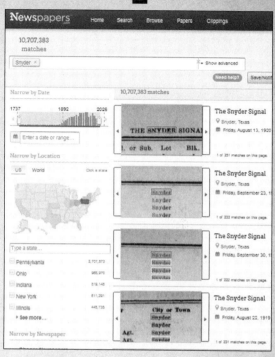

1 **Enter your search terms**. Again, you can access the search form either from the main page or by clicking the Search tab on the main toolbar. Here, I'm searching for Snyder. Once you've entered your term, click the magnifying glass.

2 **Review your results**. As you can see in the screenshot, my search returned more than ten million hits.

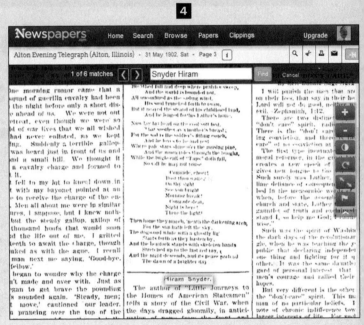

3 **Use filters on the left-hand side to narrow your search**. This will allow you to cut through the potentially millions of results to find the most relevant. I set Date to 1896 to 1898 and limited Location to Illinois, and this lowered my results to 448,000. I filtered again (this time by Name—Hiram) to get down to 9,715 results.

4 **Select a result**. The results page will show you a preview of your keyword in various newspapers, plus the name of the publication, its location, and the date of the issue and page number upon which it appears. I selected the second hit from the *Alton Evening Telegraph* by clicking on preview.

If there is more than one reference to your search on a particular page, "flippers" allow you to move through the hits on that page from the upper left to the lower right.

Another important feature of Newspapers.com is the Save/Notify button to the right of the terms used for a particular search. This does exactly what it says, "remembering" those search terms so you can perform an identical search later if you wish. This will then send you an e-mail if new content is added to Newspapers.com that matches your search.

Once you click on a search hit and bring up an image of a newspaper page, you have several options. You can change your search terms (box right above page image) on the fly to search for something different. In the upper right-hand side of the page image, you can use a series of controls to zoom in or out. Click the down arrow below the zoom controls to see (from top to bottom): adjust contrast and brightness, rotate clockwise in increments of 90 degrees, shift to full-screen view, and report a problem (anything from offensive content to a problem with the image).

A status bar below the main toolbar near the top of the screen gives the name of the newspaper, the date of the issue (including day of the week, a helpful feature!), and page being shown. The right half of the status bar has a series of controls:

- A magnifying glass icon that toggles the search box
- A scissors icon that sets in motion the "clipping"
- A printer icon that allows the image to be printed or saved as either a JPG or PDF image, with the latter including source information
- A mail icon brings up a Share menu allowing content to be saved, e-mailed to yourself or another interested person (who does not have to be a subscriber), or shared on social media
- A button allowing you to save a record to your family tree on Ancestry.com

---

Research Tip: KEEP IT PRIVATE

If for any reason you have a clipping that you don't want in the public pool, hover on your clip so an Edit/Share/View menu comes up; choose Edit; go to the gear that represents "Clipping settings" and click on it; and uncheck the box next to "Public" in the lower left-hand corner.

CLIPPING AND OTHER FEATURES

Newspapers.com looks upon research as a social activity in which the whole becomes greater than the sum of its parts, encouraging researchers to join together to help each other discover family history of common interest. The site benefited from Ancestry's acquisition of Fold3 in 2010, which (in its original incarnation as Footnote.com) pioneered transcribing and "annotating" its military-record-heavy databases with text, allowing users to collaborate.

This annotating feature seems to be the genesis of Newspapers.com's "clippings" functionality, which allows users to select segments of newspapers to share for later viewing. Once you've clipped the article, it's automatically saved to a file accessible any time you're logged in to Newspapers.com.

One great advantage of the clipping process is that clipping saves all the metadata information (name and date of newspaper, etc.) that you can use to cite or easily find newspapers. Clipping the article also draws a box around the clipping to highlight it for other users who come across that page and therefore potentially benefit from what details you've added to the clip.

Here's a quick step-by-step guide to clipping a portion of a newspaper article:

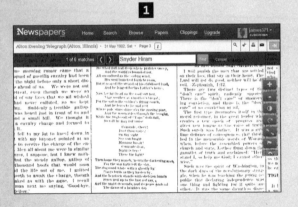

1 Select a newspaper page. I've used the same page as I did in the previous step-by-step.

2 Prep the page for clipping. Reposition the clip to show what you want to clip by dragging and using the zoom out (minus sign) or zoom in (plus sign) buttons. To remove keyword highlighting, click the Cancel button.

3

4

3 Select the area and add a description. Go to the scissors icon marked Clip in upper right. A box and highlighted area will come on the screen. Adjust this to suit your needs using the "flippers" (the description box moves helpfully out of the way). Be sure to also add a description to the box, as this will allow you to more easily find this clipping later on. Once you're finished, hit the Clip button.

4 Choose where you want the clipped article to go. You can add the clipping to your Ancestry family tree, save it to your desktop, e-mail it to yourself or someone, share it on social media, or generate a link to the clipping. Note: If you are e-mailing a clip to someone else, you can only e-mail one individual at a time.

When printing or saving an image, Newspapers.com gives you default options to either capture the "entire page" or "select portion of page." If you choose entire page, you are prompted to either print or save. If you choose print, you end up with a dialog box for the printer or printers linked to your device. If you choose save, you'll be prompted to choose either JPG or PDF format, with the latter including source information with the image. The process is the same for "select portion of page," except that a highlight box with corner flippers (like the one for clipping) comes up to define what part of the page you want printed or saved.

OTHER HOME PAGE TABS

In addition to keyword-searching through Newspaper.com's collection, you can also "page through" images of the newspapers from the Browse tab on the home page. When you click on Browse, you'll see one of two screens.

You may see a map of the entire world, with a marker indicating the number of papers for which Newspapers.com has content in each particular place. As we've briefly discussed, the collection is overwhelmingly concentrated on US newspapers, but the subscription service also has a couple hundred publications from Canada, a few dozen from the United Kingdom, and just a few from elsewhere in the world. A chronology slider allows you to cut down the time period of your browse, while a search box lets you switch to a search. If you want to browse on a more granular level, hit a marker tab and "drill down" to maps that include the number of papers in each state, then city. When you've drilled down further to the city level, you can see the names of papers that Newspapers.com has for that city. Clicking on the name of the paper lets you see the date range available, and if you click further, you're at the point of being able to select the dates of issues you want to browse.

You might also see the Browse Newspapers page, which presents you with a table featuring Country and (for the United States) State. Click each state to drill down further, and you can eventually select an individual newspaper. You can navigate back and forth between this page and the Newspaper Map by clicking "Papers by Location" in the top right (from the Browse Newspapers page) or by clicking List (from the Newspaper Map page).

Research Tip: WORKAROUNDS NEED APPLY!
Make sure to remember all your OCR workaround hints from chapter 5, as Newspapers.com does not have OCR-text representation as a backup.

The Papers tab goes at the browsing process from a different angle. On the left-hand side, you can look for papers by typing in bits of its title and narrow your paper search by date or location. The thousands of papers themselves are shown in alphabetical order on the right-hand side, along with the dates and number of pages that Newspapers.com has. Just as the Browse tab allows you to toggle the List format, the Papers tab has the word Map to toggle to the Browse tab's "drill-down" map of the world. Once you've selected an individual newspaper to browse by date, you can also "Follow" this newspaper to be notified anytime either new content from that title is added on Newspapers.com or if another user clips an article from it.

The Clippings tab gives the user direct access to clippings—either "My Clippings," showing the ones you've created from Newspapers.com papers, or "All Clippings," which shows every clipping done by any member of Newspapers.com that has been left public. There's also a search box to drill down the clippings to words of interest.

Once you see another user's clips, you can click on their username to see all of their clippings together and have the opportunity to e-mail that individual. The other user's e-mail is not revealed to you—but yours will be if you use this approach. You can also click Follow to be notified anytime the user adds another clipping.

NEWSPAPERS ON ANCESTRY.COM AND FOLD3

Before creating Newspapers.com, Ancestry.com already had quite a bit of newspaper data in what it called its Historical Newspapers Collection. While the subsidiary site adds historical newspaper images now, the pre-Newspapers.com collections have remained on the parent site. Many of these collections are searchable full-page images (in some cases, duplicating portions of Newspapers.com content, in other cases exclusive to Ancestry.com). In addition to digitized pages, some of the collections on Ancestry.com consist of information abstracted from newspapers (primarily vital events such as marriages and deaths).

The best way to find newspaper collections is by using Ancestry.com's Card Catalog (found under the Search dropdown list). You can start by using Filter By Collection and choosing Newspapers & Publications (which can be further filtered by selecting the subcollection of just Newspapers). Drill down further by using the Title and Keyword(s) fields in the Card Catalog. To successfully use the Title field, you must enter in the same words as appear in the title Ancestry.com has created for the collection, making the Title search somewhat limiting. The Keyword(s) field, on the other hand, doesn't require a match on the collection title, only that it's of the same theme. Using a city, county, or state name in the Keyword(s) is a good way to limit the collections you're searching.

Once you've found a particular collection, you can search and browse for names, dates, and sometimes other information. For more of the ins and outs of using Ancestry, see Nancy Hendrickson's *Unofficial Guide to Ancestry.com* (Family Tree Books, 2018) and *Unofficial Ancestry.com Workbook* (Family Tree Books, 2017).

As was noted earlier, Fold3 undoubtedly made a contribution to Newspapers.com by laying the foundation for the "clippings" feature with Fold3's "annotations," but Fold3 also has a limited amount of newspaper content. It has some runs of newspapers from Atlanta, Chicago, San Francisco, and Washington, DC, as well as the *Times* (London, England) and papers from the states of Indiana, Kentucky, and Virginia. As on Ancestry.com, the newspapers can be word searched or browsed.

TIPS, CAVEATS, AND FORECASTS

Ancestry.com's full-fledged foray into historical newspapers has largely been a success. Newspapers.com has a lot of functionality that goes beyond just "bells and whistles," and Product Manager Drinkwater said the service's top priority "is just that we plan to continue to add content at quick pace." He noted that, in concert with the growth in content, the other big projects underway are of the "infrastructure" variety. "As we add more users and more content to the site," Drinkwater said, "We need to add more servers and update the site so that it can support more use and more content and keep doing it quickly." Unfortunately, OCR text representation, similar to the functionality at the Library of Congress' Chronicling America **<chroniclingamerica.loc.gov>**, does not seem to be one of the forthcoming infrastructure improvements. "We've talked about it, but haven't decided what we think about it," Drinkwater noted.

The Basic and Publisher Extra products are likely to remain separate, although packaging with other Ancestry.com products seems possible, and, as stated earlier, there are discount "bundles" for subscribers of Ancestry.com and Fold3. Ancestry.com has gone through a number of "expand and contract" cycles (even as it has gone from privately owned to public to private again), so it's not impossible to think that a greater bundling might occur in the future.

Finally, it's not impossible to think that Ancestry.com might buy a competitor, especially the largely defunct database NewspaperArchive.com **<www.newspaperarchive.com>**, which has rights to a large cache of newspapers, or even the significant newspaper resources of GenealogyBank **<www.genealogybank.com>**, which will be put into the limelight in chapter 8.

KEYS TO SUCCESS

★ Newspapers.com was launched as a newspapers-centric subsidiary product of Ancestry.com.

★ Ancestry.com and fellow subsidiary Fold3 also have some newspaper content on them.

★ Newspapers.com has collaboration features that enable subscribers to notify each other of finds and avoid duplicating efforts.

★ In addition to its basic subscription, Newspapers.com has an add-on product called Publishers Extra that includes many more-recent editions of newspapers.

★ Newspapers.com continues to aggressively add content, and it has a feature for subscribers to be notified when new content matches previous searches.

NEWSPAPERS.COM WORKSHEET

Use this worksheet to record your Newspapers.com login information and a log of your search efforts. Download a printable, fillable version online **<bit.ly/ft-newspapers-guide-downloads>.**

Account login	
Username	
Password	

Time period(s) to research	Place(s) to research

Search results

	Newspaper 1	Newspaper 2	Newspaper 3
Title			
Time period searched			
Keywords/names searched			
Items found			
Notes			
Citations			

GenealogyBank

NewsBank Inc., debuted GenealogyBank <www.genealogybank.com> as a privately held subsidiary in 2006—and it pretty much became the biggest game in town because of the resources that parent NewsBank brought to the table. The full corporate history of NewsBank is a complicated family tree in and of itself. Suffice it to say that businessman and futurist John Naisbitt, who would later become a best-selling author with his first book *Megatrends* (Warner Books, 1984), founded the company in 1972. Ever since, the company has been a major player as databases have migrated from paper indexes (subject and personal indexes created from publications) to CD-ROMs to web-based computer searches, selling mostly to libraries. Much of GenealogyBank's firepower comes from NewsBank's 1980s acquisition of the Readex Microprint Corporation.

While GenealogyBank (image **A**) has many more assets than just newspapers, it continues to be an innovator in the historical newspapers field—including being the first to offer optical character recognition (OCR) searches of German-language newspapers in the Fraktur font. In this chapter, we'll discuss this and other facets of GenealogyBank, beginning with the basics (including a summary of its subscription packages), a profile of

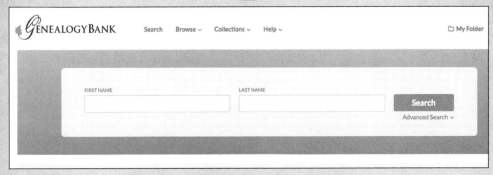

GenealogyBank, owned by media giant NewsBank, Inc., has thousands of newspaper titles in its database.

the site's holdings, and a nuts-and-bolts look at its search functions and capabilities. Then we'll take a quick review of the many non-newspaper resources on the site.

SCOPE OF COLLECTIONS AND LOGISTICS

One fact (newspaper availability) should stand out to researchers when deciding how many newspaper database subscriptions to maintain—and even whether or not to get any. Thomas Jay Kemp, NewsBank's director of genealogy products, says that 95 percent of the site's newspapers are not on any competitor's site. And he's quick to tick through what he considers some marquee items of GenealogyBank: "The largest collection of Hispanic American newspapers online. The largest collection of African American newspapers online. The largest collection of colonial period newspapers online." Indeed, the overall collections at GenealogyBank span more than eight thousand newspapers and have titles from all fifty states. (GenealogyBank does not track "pages" as a metric like Newspapers. com <www.newspapers.com> does, so we can't compare the two using that data point.)

The base-level GenealogyBank subscription comes with both a large newspaper database as well as one devoted strictly to obituaries. The second tier, called NewsLibrary, includes hundreds of millions of searchable articles from online newspaper and television station databases. As with Newspaper.com's Publisher Extra, NewsLibrary contains more-recent papers licensed from the copyright holders. (Note: GenealogyBank and NewsLibrary remain separate products.)

As of publication time, GenealogyBank carries a list price of $19.95 a month or $69.95 a year, which includes not just newspapers but many other materials that will be described later in this chapter. The company also frequently runs "thirty-day free trial promotions" in addition to discounted $9.95 monthly renewals. The NewsLibrary list price is advertised at $199 per year, but frequent discounts for GenealogyBank customers bring that down to

Researchers such as Elissa Powell and Terry Reigel have used newspapers on the GenealogyBank site to find family history details both big and small.

Powell followed a relative in a Seattle newspaper on GenealogyBank. The relative was a policeman, and Powell said, "His encounters in the papers have been interesting, including [him] being shot a year before he retired." But the real "money" examples added much extra information to a single line from his employment record: "7 June 1927 - Suspended 5 days - Returned 12 June 1927."

Powell kept rifling through newspapers to learn more. An article that explains the suspension appears in the *Seattle Daily Times*, Tuesday, June 7, 1927, page 11: "Mrs. M.A. Matthews Roiled; Traffic Slip Creates Furore; Traffic Patrolman Suspended for Five Days for Arguing with Wife of First Presbyterian Church Pastor." Another article from the *Seattle Daily Times* states he did not have the "temperament for downtown crossing duty." Yet another attests to his temperament, stating they would place him "patrolling a beat somewhere where he would learn to curb his temper." Powell couldn't believe the amount of unique information she was able to get from these resources.

Reigel, on the other hand, was researching someone who turned out to be on the other side of the law. He found the article "Bail Jumper in Auto Case is Captured in Detroit" (*The Sun*, Baltimore, Maryland, Feb 17, 1921, page 4). Reigel learned that the husband of a woman he was researching was not Taylor J. Wallace, as the man had led his wife to believe. Rather, the article listed two aliases, Clyde Fulerton and Clyde Larkins. *Fulerton* didn't seem to have any significance, but *Larkins* was the second married name of Taylor/Clyde's mother. Reigel used this to find the man in the 1920 census under yet another name (this time, his actual birth name): Clyde Culipher.

The total name change was apparently an attempt to escape a criminal record from his youth. "He didn't change his ways, though!" Reigel said. "Without this article, I would never have identified his true name nor his parents."

just $29.95. NewsLibrary also offers an à la carte price for articles ($2.95 per article) and a $19.95/month subscription plan.

When it comes to content, GenealogyBank continues to grow. Its fifty-state reach equals that of Newspapers.com, but GenealogyBank's by-state coverage is superior, with at least a dozen titles in each state. Of special interest are the 270 newspapers in its "African American Newspapers, 1827–1998" collection. In addition, the site has more than three hundred Spanish-language newspapers among its holdings, collected under "Hispanic American Newspapers, 1808–1980." It also has a collection of eight newspapers about Irish immigrants, starting in 1810.

The website design of GenealogyBank is fairly basic—and that's a strength in some ways. It has a clean design that takes you right to the action of searching. If you are not a subscriber, you can do an "all-in-one" search of all of the GenealogyBank materials and get "hit" counts in the various categories of newspaper and non-newspaper records. Not surprisingly, when you go to look at the content you are prompted to subscribe in some form, often including a thirty-day free trial.

When you're logged in as a subscriber, the home page centers on search boxes where you can enter your ancestor's first and last names. This is a global search of all GenealogyBank holdings, just like the one for non-subscribers. An Advanced Search uncovers options to make the name search "exact" (instead of phonetic) as well as Keywords to include or exclude (the latter is useful for names that are part of generic phrases; for example, excluding "left" and "right" when searching for someone with the surname Hand). You also have the capability to include a date/date range or location, plus filter your search by categories of record collections.

Tabs across the top of the home page include:

- **Browse** allows you to look for specific record collections by state, by title, or by newly updated.

- **Collections** directs you to specific popular records collections, including obituaries and the Social Security Death Index.

- **Help** provides a bevy of tips and answers to common questions.

- **My Folder** includes your Saved Articles, Saved Searches, and Recent Searches (the last several dozen, even if not performed recently).

The Learning Center, accessible under the Help menu, contains an archive of monthly e-newsletters that are sent to subscribers and offer a summary of content updates and articles by Kemp.

When you continue down the home page, you'll see quick links to Search by Collection (i.e., search within a specific records collection) and Browse Newspapers by State (with a clickable map of the United States).

Note that GenealogyBank's terms of service (as listed in a page linked to from the bottom of the home page) allow only personal use, so you'll need additional permission if you want to publish your images.

Let's move on to GenealogyBank's varied search capabilities.

SEARCH, BROWSE, AND PRINT FUNCTIONS

Searching is a little different for the two large newspaper-related groupings (newspapers and obituaries) on GenealogyBank, and NewsLibrary requires a separate search. The obituary collection is the simplest of the searches, so let's start with that.

OBITUARIES

While you can access the sixty-million-plus records in the obituaries collection as part of the one big search—with hits from this collection identified as such—you can search just the obituaries collection to help narrow your results. Under the Collections tab on the main toolbar, select either Historical or Recent under the Newspaper Obituaries subhead.

Here's how to research obituaries on GenealogyBank:

1 **Navigate to the search page.** Hover over the Collections tab, then click either Historical or Recent under the Newspaper Obituaries subheading.

2 **Enter your search information.** The search form will be similar to the one on GenealogyBank's main page. Click Advanced Search to access more options, including date range, keywords, and location.

Review your results. Once you enter search information and press Search, you'll see several newspaper thumbnails, with your search terms highlighted in newspapers' text. You'll also see the kind of item for each result (e.g., newspaper article), plus the date of publication, city/state, and newspaper title. The default settings list results by best match, but you can also sort them by newest or oldest. If your search brings back an unwieldy number of hits, you can use the left column to edit your search terms and/or filter your results. Notably, you can use a slider to indicate date/date range or narrow your results by location. The toolbar on top of the page allows you to further narrow your search to a particular section of the site/collection, such as Newspaper Archives or the Social Security Death Index.

Note that when you select an obituary from your results, what comes up may not be the actual obituary as formatted to appear in a print edition. Rather, it could be from an electronic morgue that (as talked about in chapter 5) contains millions of obituaries that have been contributed from a computer-indexing collaboration with FamilySearch.org <www.familysearch.org>, which also hosts obituary abstracts. The upside of this presentation is that the electronic readout more easily can be e-mailed, printed, or saved to My Folder without your having to go to the extra steps of highlighting text from a portion of a full-page image. The downside is that you're not seeing the obituary in its original print context.

HISTORICAL NEWSPAPERS

Now that we've looked at how to search a specific collection on GenealogyBank, let's learn how to search for records newspapers more generally. As previously noted, you can either search from the GenealogyBank home page, or from a specific Newspaper Archives page by hovering over the main menu's Collections tab and selecting Newspaper Archives.

1 **Navigate to the collection**. Go either to the GenealogyBank home page or to Newspaper Archive under the Collections tab.

2 **Enter your search terms**. Put in a name and other information to search. Limit your search to a certain state or states by selecting a state from the dropdown menu (under Advanced Search). Here, we're putting in the name *Hiram Snyder* and choosing to look at only Illinois.

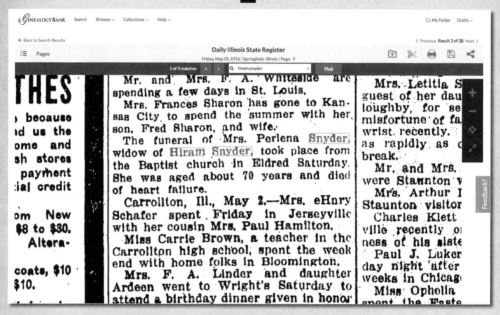

3 View your results. Click on an individual hit to view the article. In this case, I chose the third hit (from the Springfield, Ill., newspaper). The newspaper page that you then view can be read, saved, and/or printed. Use the menu above the page image to e-mail, print, save, or download the image.

Once you view an article or page image on GenealogyBank, you have several options for using and manipulating the image. From left to right, these "click to activate" buttons are:

- The Pages menu, where you can view a brief table of contents for this newspaper and jump to other pages
- Highlights, which enable you to re-search a page or turn off the highlighting of search hits
- A folder icon, which lets you save the article/image to your folder for later use, plus add a title and description
- A pair of scissors, which allows you to create a clipping of the site (similar to Newspapers.com) with a title and description
- A Print button, which allows you to draw a box around a portion of page to print or PDF (or print the whole page, as you wish)
- A floppy disk that allows you to download the image to your computer as either an image file or a PDF
- The "share" symbol allows you to e-mail the image to others
- A set of zoom in (+) or out (-) buttons
- A button that looks like a set of crosshairs to re-center the image
- A set of arrows pointing in different directions to stretch the image to full screen

SEARCH STRATEGIES

Need to narrow a search that brought back too many hits? Simply refine your results using the left column. You'll have the same parameters as the advanced search described in the last section (include and exclude keywords, date and date range, etc.). The lower left-hand side of the results page has a list of states with click-boxes. As with the home page, the option gives the number of titles that GenealogyBank has available for each state/locality.

In addition to the search parameters already named, you can focus searches in several different ways:

- The basic Boolean operators *AND* and *OR* (described in chapter 6)

- *NEAR* and *ADJ* (short for adjacent) followed by a number will bring back hits with terms that are the stated number of words apart. For *NEAR*, the two terms can fall in any order, while *ADJ* is order-specific.

- Wildcards can be used to help account for variants in spelling or faulty OCR. A question mark (?) takes the place of a single character while an asterisk (*) substitutes for up to five characters.

- Quotation marks around combinations of words limits the search to an exact match for those words, in that order.

When you choose a "hit" to look at, it will sometimes—especially from the 1700s and early 1800s newspapers—look like a single article, as if that article had been clipped from the original newspaper. (This is, in all likelihood, a throwback to parent company NewsBank's beginnings as a clipping service as well as the "article level" scanning technology that was employed, as touched upon in chapter 5.) To see the article in context, go to the left-hand side of the page and click on Pages. This will give you the opportunity to choose to see whole pages or other articles that appeared on the same page in the original publication.

You can browse newspapers on GenealogyBank in a similar way. Select Browse from the top menu to view a List of All Newspapers. First, drill down to the home page of the particular newspaper title (the service has separate home pages for every newspaper). You then can choose a state, sorted alphabetically by city of publication, and click on the publication's title. From the individual newspaper title's home page, you leave the search form blank except for the date or date range that you wish to browse. When the search results come up, choose to see the oldest results first instead of the default (most relevant search results first). Click on the first result. Then click the Pages tab at left to view all the pages in a particular issue.

NEWSLIBRARY

As with the GenealogyBank's Recent Newspaper Obituaries, NewsLibrary is a collection culled from electronic databases rather than images of print articles or full pages. The collection extends beyond newspapers, however, to include other types of publications as well as transcripts of stories presented by broadcast outlets. The number of sources totals more than six thousand and number of articles totaling around three hundred million.

You have several choices for searching NewsLibrary. Searching "by location" allows you to drill down from regional areas that include several states to single states. A list of national newswires and transcripts can also be searched individually or all at once. Searching "all at once" does just what it says—searching the whole gamut of titles at once. Finally, there's a "Build Your Own Search" function that allows you to customize and save a list (called "Tracked Searches") of sources you may want to search again in the future.

Regardless of how you search, you'll have many of the same options. At first, you'll see only one box to fill in, but hitting Advanced Search gives you several boxes to fill in with names or keywords and the Boolean *AND*, *OR*, or *NOT* operators to help focus searches. The searches also understand the "NEAR2" format talked about for the regular newspapers searches. The Advanced Search also gives you the opportunity to "limit by date," including both a specific day or date range.

OTHER FEATURES ON GENEALOGYBANK

As we've been alluding to, GenealogyBank's storehouse of records only begins with the huge newspaper collection. But you can access GenealogyBank's other great resources by selecting the Collections tab from the home page. Here are some of them:

- "Social Security Death Index" includes the publicly available portions of the "death master file" from the Social Security Administration, with an unfortunate privacy blackout on more-recent records. This collection includes some ninety-four million records.

- "Government Publications" has close to half a million records, including: the US Congressional Serial Sets (from 1817) and American State Papers (before 1817), which are committee reports related to bills and other matters; presidential communications to Congress; treaty materials; certain executive department publications; and certain non-governmental publications. Other documents in this collection include Revolutionary War burial records (often including a few lines of biography about the person) and other military and pension records.

- "Historical Books" includes more than just books. Here, you'll find family genealogies, local histories, and even collections of funeral sermons, as well as historical maps and directories. You can do the same type of searching in the books collection as you did in newspapers. You can also drill down to a list of the titles included in the collection and do a search of titles—but only titles, unlike the documents collection, in which both titles and text are searched. More than fourteen thousand documents are included in the collection.

TIPS, CAVEATS, AND FORECASTS

GenealogyBank continues to make its subscriptions more valuable by adding more content and gives users notice about that growth with its monthly newsletter; it estimates that an average of six million records are added each month. "We'll be adding millions of additional articles every month," Kemp said. "We are constantly adding new newspapers and filling in any missing issues as we locate a library that holds it—make arrangements to digitize it, etc." NewsLibrary, with its offerings based on digital-first content, is a major part of the expansion.

The search capabilities are also a selling point for GenealogyBank. The newspapers on GenealogyBank do not offer OCR text representation (retrofitting this functionality would require major money, according to Kemp), but the site's other features make up for it, such as the My Folder tab for saving articles and searches. Direct social collaboration for users would seem to be another logical step to take, augmenting the blog on the GenealogyBank site <blog.genealogybank.com> as well as the Facebook users group <www.facebook.com/GenealogyBank>, which features daily tips and historical news.

With parent NewsBank's library subscription collections, GenealogyBank has a big footprint in that market, and it continues to grow. As was the case with Newspapers.com, the NewspaperArchive.com database <www.newspaperarchive.com> is one site that would be an attractive acquisition.

GENEALOGYBANK UPDATES

At press time, GenealogyBank was preparing to implement several changes to its website, including to its home page and search interface. The screenshots in this book were taken from the beta version of that site, and (as a result) the screen you see in your search may be different from how it appears in this book.

KEYS TO SUCCESS

★ America's GenealogyBank, the individual subscription offered by NewsBank, Inc., has made newspaper content one of its priorities.

★ GenealogyBank has large collections of Hispanic and African American newspapers, plus the first searchable digitization of German-language newspapers in Fraktur font.

★ Like Newspapers.com's Publisher Extra, GenealogyBank has an add-on subscription called NewsLibrary that has more recent newspaper holdings.

★ GenealogyBank has databases of obituaries, historical books, and historical government documents, in addition to newspapers.

GENEALOGYBANK WORKSHEET

Use this worksheet to record your GenealogyBank login information and a log of your search efforts. Download a printable, fillable version online **<bit.ly/ft-newspapers-guide-downloads>**.

Account login	
Username	
Password	

Time period(s) to research	Place(s) to research

Search results

	Newspaper 1	Newspaper 2	Newspaper 3
Title			
Time period searched			
Keywords/names searched			
Items found			
Notes			
Citations			

Other Subscription Websites

We've profiled both major and statewide free sites and taken a detailed look at big kahunas Newspapers.com <www.newspapers.com> and GenealogyBank <www.genealogybank.com>, but we still have more for-pay players in the historical newspaper field to cover. Some make their databases available to individuals, while others are available only to libraries. All are worth a look and could be worth the price of admission or a trip to a subscribing library, depending on those ever-present factors of "time and place" in your historical search.

Whether or not you use the full gamut of online newspaper resources can make a difference between just finding the "usual suspects" (as far as newspaper titles) and enriching your database of documents with coverage and opinions from more obscure titles that may have been influential during the time period being researched. (Yes, once again we emphasize "time," "place," and "presentism.") The less-expansive "other" databases, Newspaper Archive (not to be confused with GenealogyBank's "Newspaper Archives") and Accessible Archives, are both good places to start, as are the three big databases we'll cover in this chapter that are only for subscribing libraries.

Let's start with the for-pay services that you can buy as an individual, though I recommend not buying them directly.

As part of the 150th anniversary of the Civil War, Trish Nicola of Washington state participated in a project designed by a public historian to increase understanding of Washington Territory's involvement in the conflict. "Although the Civil War did not take place in the territory physically, our first governor, Isaac Ingalls Stevens, headed the national campaign in 1860 for John Breckenridge and Oregon's Joseph Lane," Nicola stated. "Many Washington Territory residents went back east to fight for the North or South."

The project was dubbed the "Washington State Civil War Read-In" and was sponsored by the state historical society. Nicola, one of a few hundred volunteer readers, was assigned to read the *Daily Evening Bulletin* (San Francisco, CA) from October 1 to December 31, 1860. She used the Gale "Nineteenth Century U.S. Newspapers" database (a library-only subscription collection) through her local public library for her part in the project.

The read-in was part of the historical society's Civil War Pathways exhibition, and the volunteers' finds in newspapers became a portion of the documents still found on the exhibition's website **<pathways.omeka.net/items>**. The project won an award from the American Association for State and Local History, and the writeup about the award from the association confirms what Nicola said about the area's Civil War atmosphere: "Although the Washington Territory saw no battles during the war, the whole Northwest was awash in political intrigue, desertion, and divided loyalties." The report further noted, "Yet there is little in the way of published research examining this tumultuous period."

The volunteers of Civil War Pathways found more than two thousand documents to make up for this lack of research—many of them newspaper articles rich in details about the Civil War era and its aftermath. In just one example, the editor of the *Walla Walla Statesman* opined on June 9, 1865, that President Andrew Johnson was considering too wide an amnesty for former Confederates, ending with the sentence: "The Constitution defines treason, and under that definition it required no great acumen to ascertain who had been or who were traitors."

NEWSPAPERARCHIVE AND FINDMYPAST

NewspaperArchive <www.newspaperarchive.com> stems from Heritage Microfilm Inc., which in turn sprang from the microfilm division of a company named Information Technologies. Heritage Microfilm saw the coming transition from microfilm to digital and started co-branding digital sites with newspaper clients, launching NewspaperArchive in 1999. The site and its parent reached digitization deals with many of the parent company's newspaper microfilming clients, which gave some credence to it making the claim of having the "world's largest newspaper archive."

Along the way to the present, NewspaperArchive has been accused of less-than-ethical business practices. Users report subscription prices being changed without notice, while the

website's fine print green-lights user fees to be donated to the owner's private charity. In addition, its slogans, such as "Discover 410 Years of Newspaper Archives—1607 to Today!" aren't accurate, as the first newspaper wasn't even published in the United States until 1690 (1607 likely refers to the founding of Jamestown, Virginia). The customer service is also slow and inconsistent, with answers to media questions coming back garbled.

NewspaperArchive, once on the forefront of newspaper digitization, still has newspapers for researchers.

All of that aside, NewspaperArchive does have many valuable newspapers in its collections. And, because it anticipated the digitization wave, it has exclusive digital rights to some of its microfilm clients' newspapers. Happily, you can access the NewspaperArchive trove without dealing with the site directly. International subscription service MyHeritage <www.myheritage.com>, which has a few newspaper collections of its own and is working to acquire additional content in its never-ending-war with Ancestry.com for worldwide for-pay genealogy supremacy, had the NewspaperArchive newspaper databases as an on-loan item for several years. A subscription to British-based FindMyPast <www.findmypast. com> is also a "back-door" ticket to NewspaperArchive, as is a subscription to ProQuest (see the section on this later in the chapter).

For those wishing to subscribe directly to NewspaperArchive, seven-day trials are available for $6.95, and semi-annual subscriptions cost $49.95. By comparison, FindMyPast has a variety of subscription packages that include NewspaperArchive materials available from $9.95 a month ("US Starter") to $239.50 annually ("World Premium" package).

Initial searches, which bring back a preview window of results, are free. You can start a search by filling in a basic search form (first names and last names or keywords) or the advanced search form that allows you to use any or all the following parameters: "With All of the Words, "With the Exact Phase," "With at Least One of These Words" and "Without the Word(s)." You can also narrow initial searches by publication date and publication location. All this means that you can get a free feel for what the NewspaperArchive holdings, which include a significant number of international newspapers, may yield for you.

The home page of NewspaperArchive (image **A**) has a number of other tabs at the top of the page. Browse takes you to a number of ways to "drill down" to a particular state and city's newspapers. (After several steps, you'll finally see a specific title as well as dates covered.) The Historical Events tab has some of the same types of drilling down but adds click-ons to limit a search to a particular century. Obituaries limits the search to just that, while Clippings is a searchable collection of articles that have been saved by NewspaperArchive users. The Family Tree tab has subscribers' family trees, and Search gives you a direct link to the Advanced Search boxes.

To access the NewspaperArchive collection through FindMyPast, go to the FindMyPast's home page and look for "Newspaper records" in the list of records groups. This link brings you to a page to search just those records, with search boxes at the top for first name, last name, and keywords. You'll want to click on the "US & World newspapers" button, then narrow your research results, first by country, then by state, publication, and either exact dates, date ranges, or exact dates with a "plus or minus."

Here's a step-by-step for saving or printing newspapers (including those from NewspaperArchive) on FindMyPast:

1

1 Select your state. Picking up from the instruction above (on FindMyPast's "US & World newspapers" page), limit your search to focus on a particular state (e.g., Illinois) by going under "Narrow your search results" to the By State section and clicking Show filters. A list of states with radio buttons will come up; select the state you want and click "Apply filters."

2

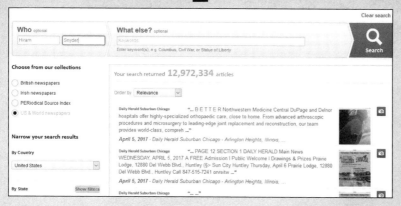

2 Enter your search terms. Next, return to the initial search page and fill in the Who boxes. Here, we'll search for *Hiram Snyder* as we did in chapters 7 and 8.

3

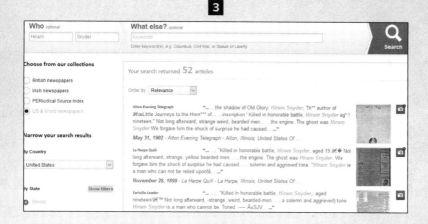

3 Select your results. Click either the title or the preview image to view a paper. Opening a record on FindMyPast saves it to your My Records file, which you can access at the top of any FindMyPast page. There, you can add notes about the record or view the image again. Note: If you have a per-credit subscription at FindMyPast, you'll need to consider whether or not viewing this result will cost you a credit. I chose the first result from the *Alton Evening Telegraph*.

4 View your results. Once the full-page image loads, you have options to "Download page" or "Print page." The first creates a PNG file, which you can save on your computer and either print, crop, or convert to another file type from your desktop. The latter sends the paper to the printer.

ACCESSIBLE ARCHIVES

Founded in 1990, Accessible Archives **<www.accessible-archives.com>** describes its mission as providing comprehensive collections of "diverse primary source materials reflecting broad views across American history and culture." Its non-newspaper collections include county histories, journals about women's suffrage and the Civil War, and books such as the memoir *Twelve Years a Slave*.

As far as newspapers, Accessible Archives' marquee collections have been several Colonial newspapers (such as the *Virginia Gazette* and Benjamin Franklin's *Pennsylvania Gazette*) as well as a superb collection of African-American newspapers such as the *Christian Defender* (more on these newspapers in chapter 11). Some of the newspapers are no longer unique assets, with other subscription sites such as Newspapers.com and GenealogyBank having at least a partial set. Accessible Archives has also added a collection of American Military Camp Newspapers from the WWI era, plus newspaper articles in its Civil War Collection (which also includes many other sources such as regimental histories and generals' memoirs).

At the time of publication, Accessible Archives is available to individuals for $29.95 a quarter or $89.95 for a year. Note the site's staff has to manually activate subscriptions once fees have been paid, so don't expect to be able to research immediately. Note too, that individual subscriptions do not allow the user unlimited printing from the site. Institutional subscriptions are also available, and are really the bread-and-butter for Accessible Archives, so it's not a bad idea to check with libraries and colleges in your area to see if you can access that way.

For many of its assets (both newspaper and non-newspaper), Accessible Archives has not only images of the original printed documents but also transcribed individual entries, complete with bibliographic citations, to help users. These transcriptions essentially function as text representation for the newspapers. You can also browse (rather than search) document sets such as newspapers.

LIBRARY-ONLY SUBSCRIPTION SERVICES

While it's natural to want all newspaper resources at your disposal all the time, take a step back and realize that having free and subscription websites with full-page and article images available for individual users is a concept but a dozen years old. That dozen years has been exciting, with exponentially more newspaper pages and titles available for individual desktop use.

However, newspaper resources sold only to institutions such as public libraries and colleges still have value for researchers. We'll look briefly at the assets of ProQuest, Readex, Gale, and EBSCO. To determine whether a library in your area has subscriptions to newspaper collections that interest you, go to the library's website. Often, you'll find a tab on the home page marked "Databases" or "Research Databases" that identifies what database access the library has purchased. Sometimes, you'll need to click on a home page tab such as "Services" to get to the menu identifying the databases.

PROQUEST HISTORICAL NEWSPAPERS

ProQuest <www.proquest.com> dates to the 1930s when it was founded as University Microfilms. As the name implies, the original company was a microfilm publisher. Since then, it has transitioned to offering products electronically, and ProQuest LLC has been involved in preserving information in everything from academic dissertations and theses to scholarly journals. Its ProQuest Historical Newspapers brand <www.proquest.com/products-services/pq-hist-news.html> has been a leader in bringing newspapers to libraries with some thirty-five million pages of searchable newspapers, including about two-dozen big-city titles from cities such as Atlanta, Chicago, Los Angeles, New York, and Philadelphia. Also available—either as part of the overall Historical Newspapers package or separately, depending on the institution's focus—are American Jewish Newspapers, Black Newspapers, and International Newspapers. It also has even more focused databases such as Chinese newspapers, and ProQuest is the vendor for library editions of both NewspaperArchive and Newspapers.com.

READEX

You may remember Readex <www.readex.com> being mentioned as part of NewsBank, the parent of newspaper-rich GenealogyBank. Just like ProQuest, Readex began as a provider of microfilmed primary sources and transitioned to searchable digital editions. In fact, Readex was the source of many newspapers for the GenealogyBank collections.

Readex has a bevy of products from which institutions can choose in response to the needs of their specific audiences. It has more general collections such as "Early American Newspapers, 1690–1922" (which can be sliced and diced further, too, by places, "eras," or decades of publication) as well as many specific ones, such as "American Ethnic Newspapers," "American Business: Agricultural Newspapers," "American Business: Mercantile Newspapers," "American Politics: Campaign Newspapers" and "American Religion: Denominational Newspapers."

GALE AND EBSCO

Gale <www.gale.com>, now owned by Cengage, is another educational publishing company with roots in the mid-twentieth century. In addition to many other products, it has many collections of British newspapers and "Nineteenth Century U.S. Newspapers," with many titles from both large and small American cities and towns. It also vends niche products such as "Confederate Newspapers: A Collection from Florida, Georgia, Tennessee, Virginia, and Alabama" and "Japanese-American Relocation Camp Newspapers Perspectives on Day-to-Day Life."

EBSCO Information Services <www.ebsco.com>, amidst many separate industries, includes a couple of newspaper-related collections, called "Newspaper Source" and "Newspaper Source Plus." Both these services mix newspaper and other media sources (much like GenealogyBank's NewsLibrary service) and include only the last decade or two in most cases. They are transcriptions, not newspaper images in any case.

KEYS TO SUCCESS

★ Several other individual subscription sites (as well as library-only subscription collections) are worth investigating.

★ NewspaperArchive is available as an individual subscription but also through FindMyPast and through libraries.

★ Accessible Archives has Colonial newspaper assets as well as other collections.

★ ProQuest, Readex (through NewsBank), Gale, and EBSCO all have library-only subscription products.

★ Access to library-only subscriptions depends on the particular library; some allow holders of library cards remote access.

10

Seeking Out Newspapers

After introducing you to the many media in which newspaper resources appear (chapter 5) and providing you with free and for-pay online newspaper services that bring newspapers to you (chapters 6–9), I now want to shift our focus to what you can do as a researcher to reach out and find more newspapers.

Trying to sort through all the possibilities is one of the greatest challenges in newspaper research, and we'll examine in detail two particularly powerful tools (Chronicling America's "US Newspaper Directory, 1690–Present" and WorldCat) while also talking about some of the best repositories for newspapers. In this chapter, we'll also zoom out and evaluate the holdings of the multiple digital newspaper repositories we discussed in chapter 6, including specialty guides and undigitized newspapers in addition to online holdings.

Whether you use newspapers that come to you by chance or that you found through diligent searches, you can't be sure where your journey will take you, only that it will be an interesting ride. This chapter covers the tools that will add the maximum number of newspaper "signposts" to your research highway.

EXTRA, EXTRA!
RESEARCHER CRACKS CLARK COUNTY COLD CASE

Terry Reigel from North Carolina reached out for further information about a relative and what he found after years of effort led him to say: "Sometimes a newspaper search takes you to a place you may end up not sure you wanted to be." The initial newspaper item in Reigel's story came courtesy of GenealogyBank <www.genealogybank.com>, with an item in the "Brevities" column of the *Olympia Daily Recorder* in Washington state that referred to her great-grandfather's twin brother William David Reigel as being extradited in 1911 to Missouri "on a charge of attempted statutory offense."

Reigel says this prompted a seven-year search of various sources for the story behind this brief item. "A request for further information in Washington archives produced no results. Searching for records in Missouri was difficult because I didn't then know where he had been living in Missouri," he said. "But I finally found his record from the Missouri State Penitentiary at the Missouri State Archives. From that I found he was incarcerated for assault, and the date."

The Missouri archives record helped redirect Reigel to Webster County, since the Washington state newspaper had indicated the extradition was at the request of Clark County, Missouri, officials—when, in reality, the "Clark County" being referenced was in Washington. (In total, twelve states have a Clark County.) "My initial effort to find him in Clark County, Missouri, of course, proved fruitless," Reigel said.

After learning the Missouri Historical Society had an extensive collection of newspapers on microfilm in addition to those it has online, Reigel joined the society at a level of membership that entitled him to borrow films. He then went to work reviewing films of local papers and finally uncovered the full story in an article from *The Marshfield Mail*, Marshfield, Missouri, headlined "Charged with Seduction." The "statutory offense" involved William David Reigel's thirteen-year-old daughter.

US NEWSPAPER DIRECTORY, 1690–PRESENT

We've already discussed Chronicling America website <chroniclingamerica.loc.gov> in its capacity as the leading free source of digitized newspaper images. But as we noted in passing in chapter 6, the same website run by the Library of Congress and National Endowment for the Humanities has another key feature worth exploring: "US Newspaper Directory, 1690–present." The database serves as a directory to the decades-long work of the US Newspaper Program, allowing you to explore the newspapers that might apply to your research goals.

The US Newspaper Program's goal was to preserve print newspapers that were in jeopardy of crumbling by microfilming them—officially, to "locate, describe [catalog], and selectively preserve [via treatment and microfilm] historic newspaper collections." However, the state-level groups that ran the projects methodically uncovered a larger number of papers than expected as it searched libraries small and large, private collectors' holdings, and publishers' attics.

The project turned up previously published catalogs that revealed thousands more newspapers than expected, with catalogs Clarence S. Brigham's *History and Bibliography of American Newspapers, 1690–1820* and Winifred Gregory's *American Newspapers, 1821–1936, A Union List of Files Available in the United States and Canada* providing a lot of new information. A fair number of the "new" titles had only a single surviving issue. In some cases, no issues of a paper survived, but instead the newspaper was described from accounts in books such as county histories. Still other "unique" newspapers were additions to already known "newspaper families," in which the new title was just a retitling of an existing newspaper.

Nevertheless, the ranks of known newspapers increased, and the microfilming portion of the state-level projects sometimes needed to set priorities and make decisions on which projects to spend money on microfilming. Single issues of a title were often not as highly valued as "runs" (consecutive issues of the newspaper) since the historical research value of any one particular edition is usually limited. Likewise, while the state-level projects tried to ensure that at least one newspaper from each county was microfilmed, you won't be surprised to learn this wasn't always executed. As a result, unmicrofilmed single-issue newspapers (along with their competing views of history and rich, irreplaceable accounts of contemporary American life) can either crumble away or be disposed of by someone unaware of their importance.

The upshot for researchers is that the directory on Chronicling America was developed from library catalog records created by the US Newspaper Program. The state-level projects contributed bibliographic descriptions and library holdings information to the Newspaper Union List, now hosted by the Online Computer Library Center (OCLC). This data includes approximately 150,000 bibliographic title entries and nearly a million separate library holdings records and continues to updated annually through OCLC which is discussed in depth later in this chapter.

SEARCHING THE US NEWSPAPER DIRECTORY ON CHRONICLING AMERICA

Users have access to versatile searching and browsing capabilities using the US Newspaper Directory <chroniclingamerica.loc.gov/search/titles>, which you can also access from the Chronicling America home page.

The first and most obvious way to seek information on the newspapers you want is to browse by title. Each letter of the alphabet (along with numbers zero through nine, since a handful of newspaper names begin with numbers) has a subdirectory you can browse.

DIGITAL NEWSPAPER ARCHIVES

Before delving into major tools, let's take a quick second to offer some pretty basic advice. Virtually all newspapers in existence today—even those that literally have gone all digital—will have their own websites. While this website primarily will be an echo of the same model as a print newspaper (i.e., news content and advertising), the beauty of digital is that it can preserve more than one day's content as well as contain "bonus features" for which there was no room in the print edition, such as additional photos of an event or even video clips of interview subjects.

As such, you'll likely find a ready-made archive of content from the point in time at which a newspaper began posting on that website. Of course, the key phrase is "from the point in time," and that may be a relatively short amount of time. However, if you remember the digitized morgues discussed in chapter 5, newspapers often have a considerably longer digital back file, some so substantial that the newspaper will charge a fee to access its in-house archive. (Usually searches are free but the fee comes into play if you want to access the actual items.) Also, as noted in chapter 5, some newspapers offer digitally archived versions of the print edition rather than just the headline, text, and photos of an item in a digital layout (which lacks, therefore, the context of the original such as where the item was "played" in relation to the other items that day).

As is standard in nearly all alphabetization schemes, the words *a, an,* and *the* are omitted from consideration in ordering newspaper titles.

But what if you're not sure of the first non-article word in the title? "Enter keywords" comes to the rescue. Without any further information, for example, simply enter *Hamilton* if you want to find any newspapers with titles (or place names) that include Hamilton. If you want to limit the search to only newspapers from Hamilton, Ohio, you can enter those two words (with or without any punctuation such as commas or quotation marks), and the search returns only those newspapers with both words in either the title or the place name.

Another way to limit searches is to "drill down" from those 150,000 total entries by state, county, and city using the "Select where the newspaper was published" section in the main search page. To select a city, you need to have at least a state from the search dropdown list (selecting both a state and county is OK, too). The "Select when the newspaper was published" range of dates can be used either in conjunction with the "where published" menu or independently. In any case, the "when published" menu will return all titles whose known years of publication "touch" within the beginning and ending ranges that are listed. In other words, if a range of 1850 to 1860 is specified, among the title entries retrieved are ones such as the *Weekly Standard* of Raleigh, North Carolina, published from 1858 to 1865. The search will also show titles whose beginning or ending years are either filled with question marks (????) or partially filled (for example, 18??) if the other known date of (beginning or ending) publication makes it possible that the newspaper existed in the time range specified. The "when published" menu is entered as a default.

You can also use several "More search items" in conjunction with or independently from other parameters to limit the titles found by a search. These include Frequency (on what cycle the newspaper was published); Language (including some obscure ones such as Chechen); Ethnicity Press (which may or may not match the Language menu); Labor Press (a list mostly of occupations but also including political search terms such as *Anarchism*, *Fascism*, and *Anti-fascist movements*); Material Type (including types of microfilm, originals, or "online resource," the latter of which only shows whether the newspaper has digitized images on Chronicling America or ProQuest); and LCCN (the Library of Congress Control Number, which is an eight-digit unique identifier preceded with the letters *sn* and then a space for each newspaper).

After filling in the search parameters, press the Search button in the lower right corner, and the search returns the titles that meet your criteria in a clickable list that shows only the titles, places of publication, and years of publication (as previously noted, some years contain question marks). From the list, click on any line in it to see the full bibliographic record. The default view for the menu is the About tab, which lists statistics about the newspaper—including whether it had a predecessor and successor in the same newspaper "family." (Note names of the newspapers often changed, not just with ownership but at the whims of editors, it seems!) The second tab, "Libraries that Have It," shows the places (identified during the US Newspaper Program) that had the newspaper in some format. The third and final tab, MARC Record, contains bibliographic information in a standardized format that librarians revel in but other mortals fear to tread.

Let's walk through a sample search of the US Newspaper Directory on Chronicling America:

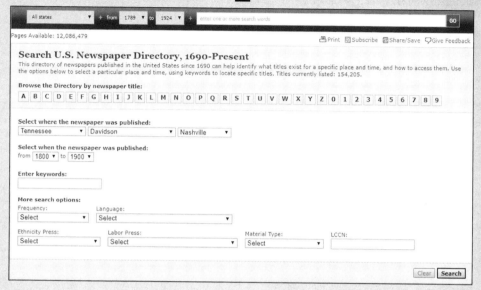

1 **Enter your search criteria**. Navigate to **<chroniclingamerica.loc.gov/search/titles>**, then select the state, county, and city from the respective dropdown menus. Also select a year range. For my search, I selected Tennessee, Davidson County, and Nashville as place, with 1800 to 1900 as date.

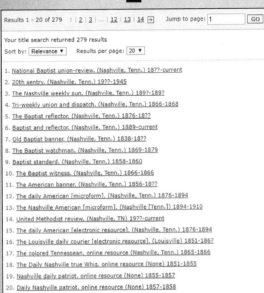

Results 1 - 20 of 279   1 | 2 | 3 | ... | 12 | 13 | 14 ▸   Jump to page: 1   GO

Your title search returned 279 results

Sort by: Relevance ▾   Results per page: 20 ▾

1. National Baptist union-review. (Nashville, Tenn.) 18??-current
2. 20th sentry. (Nashville, Tenn.) 19??-1945
3. The Nashville weekly sun. (Nashville, Tenn.) 189?-189?
4. Tri-weekly union and dispatch. (Nashville, Tenn.) 1866-1868
5. The Baptist reflector. (Nashville, Tenn.) 1876-18??
6. Baptist and reflector. (Nashville, Tenn.) 1889-current
7. Old Baptist banner. (Nashville, Tenn.) 1838-18??
8. The Baptist watchman. (Nashville, Tenn.) 1869-1879
9. Baptist standard. (Nashville, Tenn.) 1858-1860
10. The Baptist witness. (Nashville, Tenn.) 1866-1866
11. The American banner. (Nashville, Tenn.) 1856-18??
12. The daily American [microform]. (Nashville, Tenn.) 1876-1894
13. The Nashville American [microform]. (Nashville [Tenn.]) 1894-1910
14. United Methodist review. (Nashville, TN) 19??-current
15. The daily American [electronic resource]. (Nashville, Tenn.) 1876-1894
16. The Louisville daily courier [electronic resource]. (Louisville) 1851-186?
17. The colored Tennessean. online resource (Nashville, Tenn.) 1865-1866
18. The Daily Nashville true Whig. online resource (None) 1851-1855
19. Nashville daily patriot. online resource (None) 1855-1857
20. Daily Nashville patriot. online resource (None) 1857-1858

About Republican banner. (Nashville, Tenn.) 1837-1875
Nashville, Tenn. (1837-1875)

About | Libraries that Have It | MARC Record

Title:
Republican banner. : (Nashville, Tenn.) 1837-1875

Alternative Titles:
- Nashville weekly republican banner
- Republican banner and Whig
- Weekly banner

Place of publication:
Nashville, Tenn.

Geographic coverage:
- Nashville, Davidson, Tennessee | View more titles from this: City County, State

Publisher:
S. Nye & A.A. Hall

Dates of publication:
1837-1875

Description:
- Began Aug. 22, 1837; ceased Sept. 2, 1875. Cf. Tenn. newspapers.

Frequency:
Weekly (frequency varies during sessions of the legislature)

Language:
- English

Subjects:
- Davidson County (Tenn.)--Newspapers.
- Nashville (Tenn.)--Newspapers.
- Tennessee, Davidson County, fast (OCoLC)fst01205346

2 Evaluate your results. You'll see the name of the paper, along with the place of publication and a date range. Note that some papers have date ranges that include question marks, indicating the US Newspaper Directory is unsure of the paper's start or end date.

3 View newspapers. Click the hyperlink for a result to see alternative titles, places and dates of publication, publisher, description, frequency, language, notes, LCCN, OCLC, and preceding, succeeding, and related titles. Click "Libraries that Have It" to view where you can find an original copy.

Research Tip: RUN, RUN, RUN

Note that the listed date range ("run") of a particular newspaper may not be as unbroken as a catalog entry suggests. You may discover that newspaper collections are missing issues between the dates listed in the title or description. Be especially on the lookout for a note about "scattered issues wanting."

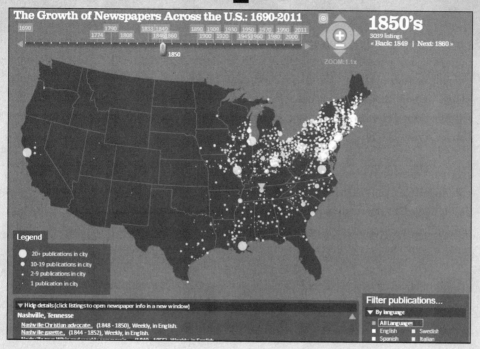

The Stanford Visualization has mapped out the publications in the US Newspaper Directory, allowing you to browse newspapers close to where your ancestor lived.

THE STANFORD VISUALIZATION

For those who like searching in a more visual way, the Bill Lane Center for the American West at Stanford University's Rural West Initiative has created a tool called Data Visualization: Journalism's Voyage West <**web.stanford.edu/group/ruralwest/cgi-bin/drupal/ visualizations/us_newspapers**>. This takes the data from the US Newspaper Directory and "plotted them [newspapers] over time and space" in an interactive map titled "The Growth of Newspapers Across the U.S.: 1690–2011" (image A). From a timeline at the top margin of the map, you can choose any year from 1690 to 2011. You can also filter newspapers by language and publication frequency. The map defaults to a view of the entire United States, but you can zoom in as far as you wish to home in on a group of states, the border area of several states, a single state, or even a single city. The map has dots representing the presence of a newspaper in a community, with each dot's relative size indicating the number of newspapers in that locality. Clicking on a city's dot brings up a list of the papers in the city at that time, including the titles, years of publication, frequency, and language.

The Stanford site is great for putting together a research plan to maximize newspapers because you can start by homing in on one particular town, then see on the map the

BOOKS ABOUT NEWSPAPERS

We've pretty much exclusively dealt with information from newspapers—either some media with the actual newspaper pages, today's online content, or what we've dubbed "newspaper resources," abstracts, scrapbooks, and the like. But it's also important to note that many books have been written about newspapers that may be relevant to researchers of historical papers.

They fall into two genres: histories of a particular newspaper, or a book or monograph devoted to a particular area or specialty of newspapers. Let's look at an example of each.

Robert W. Wells' *The Milwaukee Journal: An Informal Chronicle of Its First 100 Years* (Milwaukee Journal, 1981) recounts the first century (1882–1982) of a venerable Wisconsin institution. On the verge of failure just a few weeks after its founding, the newspaper was saved by an intrepid young newspaperman named Lucius Neiman, who gave it a reputation for rooting out government corruption as a public watchdog. The book covers the personalities who made up the paper as well as background on the events that it covered, providing a wealth of social history and a look through the lens that filtered the Journal's view of its circulation area.

The Newspapers of Lebanon County, Pennsylvania, by Robert A. Heilman and Gladys Bucher Sowers (Lebanon County Historical Society, 2011), on the other hand, brings to life the small county's hundred-plus publications in a two-century history. As much information as is known about the publishers of each newspaper appears in the spiral-bound volume. The authors trace how Lebanon County's early German-language dominance was gradually replaced by bilingual publications ,then finally by English-only newspapers.

These two types of books on newspapers are found across the country, so search for your ancestor's locality or local newspaper to see if such a volume was published. As was the case of the *Milwaukee Journal,* many of the books on specific newspapers are written in conjunction with some sort of anniversary of the paper's first publication.

towns with newspapers closest to it. The site is also excellent for conveying newspaper history at milestone years, such as the introduction of the Penny Press Era in 1833 or the 1950s and the effects of suburbanization. Clicking the individual paper listings opens up a new window with that title's About tab in the actual US Newspaper Directory on the Chronicling America site.

However, the tool isn't perfect. County lines are not shown, which would be nice to have since many publications in more rural areas were "county seat" papers. The Introduction text on the Stanford site also notes its coverage has both omissions and duplicates—but the same criticism can be said of the directory on Chronicling America, since that was the basis for the mapping. Some errors are unique to the Stanford map, however; for example, somehow Stanford lists "Bethania" as the place of publication for a single, short-lived 1830s paper, but the paper's dot on the map is actually Lancaster, Pennsylvania. Also, it appears that newspapers with question marks for beginning or ending dates in the directory have been omitted from the visualization.

Research Tip: KEEP AN EYE ON THE DIGITAL PUBLIC LIBRARY

The Digital Public Library of America **<dp.la>**, like WorldCat, contains holdings from more than 1,600 libraries, archives, and museums. Its collections may include newspapers in the future, so watch for future developments at this resource.

WORLDCAT

As good as the US Newspaper Directory is—and despite its mindful efforts to keep current its data that was first put together some thirty years ago—another big mega-database is worth newspaper researchers' while, especially when looking for modern-day newspapers and the holdings of them in paper form and microfilm. WorldCat **<www.worldcat.org>** is the ultimate "big dog" in library catalogs, a "union catalog" that itemizes the collections of more than seventy thousand libraries. The catalog also has large geographic spread, with information from the more than 150 countries that participate in a global cooperative called Online Computer Library Center (popularly known in librarian-speak as OCLC), operated by the OCLC Online Computer Library Center Inc.

WorldCat, however, does not show "real-time" changes to the libraries' holdings, so it can't indicate the status (borrowed, lost, being repaired) of an item or whether the library owns multiple copies. Fortunately, individual subscribing libraries can add links with real-time statuses and the particular library's call number for the item.

Rather than merely describing how to search WorldCat, let's look at an example:

1

1 **Enter your search terms**. Navigate to **<www.worldcat.org>** and enter your search terms. I typed in *Nashville, Tennessee*, but you can search for another locality or keyword. If you're looking for something besides newspapers, you can also search a different form of media by selecting a different tab.

2 Filter results. WorldCat returns what items are in its libraries' collections. Notice the column on the left, which allows you to select a resource type. Click the Newspaper box to limit your results. You may have to click "Show more" multiple times under the Format filter on the left side until you see it. (The database contains many kinds of research materials.)

3 View the newspaper. Click on a newspaper to view its detail page, including its place of publication and the publisher. Click on the subject links to view other items from those categories (in this case, other newspapers related to Nashville and/or Davidson County as well as materials related to Davidson County, Tennessee).

4 Discover where it's held. If you want to access this newspaper, scroll down to view what participating libraries have at least a partial run of the newspaper. Click on a specific library to see its holdings detail page for this entry.

COMPARING NEWSPAPER COLLECTIONS

The newspapers "arms race" has become less important with the proliferation of websites with digital newspaper images, which is why we've devoted such a large amount of space (chapters 6 to 9) to them. But evaluating major newspaper collections' holdings isn't enough if you want to exhaust all resources in your newspaper search. While they don't have the brand-name recognition of a Newspapers.com <www.newspaper.com> or GenealogyBank <www.genealogybank.com>, these four resources (in addition to both online and offline documents) have accumulated institutional expertise and targeted finding aids that remain useful for the individual interested in doing exhaustive and comprehensive research.

LIBRARY OF CONGRESS

For decades, the Library of Congress <www.loc.gov> (LOC) has been synonymous with historical newspapers and boasts "the nation's largest collection of newspapers." (Of course, collecting newspapers is just one of its many missions—the historical resources housed in its buildings could be a book by themselves!) You can access its many, many resources in person in The Newspaper & Current Periodical Reading Room of the James Madison Building in Washington, DC. The mammoth collection includes approximately a million

CYNDI'S LIST

In addition to just a simple Google search for a newspaper's name (and, yes, make it Google—not search engines such as Bing <www.bing.com> or Yahoo <www.yahoo.com> that heavily favor ads over information in their searches), you should make use of the hundreds of thousands of websites categorized by Cyndi's List of Genealogy Sites on the Internet <www.cyndislist.com>. This site is a standard starting point for any type of family history research. In the Newspapers category are links to sites ranging from individual newspapers to columnists to indexes and digitized collections. The site's Category Index includes subcategories titled: Genealogy Columns & Columnists, General Resources, History, How To, and Newspaper Directories, in addition to alphabetical listings for A through Y (apparently there are no Z links that are worthwhile!). All in all, Cyndi's List contains almost a thousand website links.

unbound issues, close to a hundred thousand bound volumes, and approximately three hundred thousand reels of microfilm.

Among its online assets, the LOC has a listing <www.loc.gov/rr/news/news_research_tools/ayersdirectory.html> of digital versions of the *Rowell's American Newspaper Directory* that started in 1869 and the *N.W. Ayer & Son's American Newspaper Annual* that started in 1880.

The LOC has subscriptions to many major online newspaper services such as Accessible Archives <www.accessible-archives.com>, ProQuest Historical Newspapers <www.proquest.com>, Gale NewsVault <www.gale.com/primary-sources/historical-newspapers>, and a couple of African American newspaper collections.

The LOC also has many specialized research and finding aids for newspapers, as well as books with newspaper abstracts. Notably, the Newspaper Reading Room is one of the few parts of the Library of Congress that allows remote users to "chat" online about questions <www.loc.gov/rr/askalib/ask-news.html>.

The LOC also has many foreign newspapers—some twenty-five thousand titles—but publications printed in a non-Roman typeface (such as Cyrillic or Arabic) are not housed in the Newspaper Reading Room but rather with the specific reading room for that part of the world (such as "European" or "African & Middle Eastern").

Research Tip: CHECK GROUPS OUT

Publisher associations, often organized on the state level, might be another place to learn where to find undigitized newspapers, so be sure to research any such groups in your ancestor's hometown.

WISCONSIN HISTORICAL SOCIETY

If the LOC is the greatest national collection of newspapers, then the Wisconsin Historical Society <www.wisconsinhistory.org> in Madison, Wisconsin, is a clear number-two. This is a result of a long-time collections policy that includes all North American newspapers, giving the society the largest collections of Native American, African American, and military-based newspapers. The library has some ten thousand bound volumes of newspapers, a substantial portion of which are also included on its 150,000 reels of microfilmed newspapers (including sixty thousand reels devoted solely to Wisconsin newspapers). In addition, the Wisconsin Historical Society has either published or has copies of hundreds of books outlining specialty newspaper collections, such as those appealing to Native Americans, African Americans and labor union members.

The Wisconsin Historical Society was a leader in the microfilming newspapers beginning in the 1940s, long before the US Newspaper Program. As noted in chapter 6, it has continued to be a newspaper leader in the digital age, putting together the Archive of Wisconsin Newspapers (funded by the Wisconsin Department of Public Instruction in collaboration with the Wisconsin Newspaper Association) for its BadgerLink website <badgerlink.dpi.wi.gov>, targeting its home-state residents.

At the time of publication, the Wisconsin Historical Society has also completed a test run of using Archive-It software to capture newspaper websites. The site might more fully deploy the software in the future, especially for newspapers that it does not have digital copies of.

AMERICAN ANTIQUARIAN SOCIETY

Headquartered in Worcester, Massachusetts, the American Antiquarian Society <www.americanantiquarian.org> was founded in 1812 by Revolutionary War patriot and printer Isaiah Thomas. The society bills itself as both a "learned society" and a major independent research library, with a library housing the largest and most accessible collection of pre-1876 books, pamphlets, broadsides, newspapers, periodicals, music, and graphic arts material printed. The newspaper portion of the society's collection contains newspapers published in the eighteenth and nineteenth centuries in the United States, Canada, and the West Indies. The society has accumulated more than eighteen thousand newspaper titles, including more than two million issues on five miles of shelving.

CENTER FOR RESEARCH LIBRARIES

The Center for Research Libraries <www.crl.edu> is based in Chicago and is a consortium of universities, colleges, and independent research libraries in North America that pools together its members' resources to acquire and preserve both traditional and digital resources for research and teachings. Items are made available to its member institutions through interlibrary loan and electronic delivery. Included in its collections are many microfilms of American ethnic newspapers as well as a huge collection of foreign newspapers, including a significant collection from Africa.

SUMMARY

Literally every public or university library—as well as your local or regional historical society—is a potential spot for you to find a newspaper that's not part of a major website's collection of digitized images. In some cases, a library may have received a grant to digitize a local newspaper, or it may still have microfilm or even bound paper copies of historical newspapers that came its way. While the convenience of digital makes a fine first option, do not ignore newspaper references you find in the US Newspaper Directory or through WorldCat. The effort you put forth is likely to return some type of reference (though, as Terry Reigel's anecdote at the beginning of this chapter proves, not all references will be pleasant).

Whether they are broad-sweeping national collections such as the LOC or small-town repositories like a local historical society (or so many other repositories that may have collections such as clipping scrapbooks or newspaper morgues), many repositories can contain valuable information about your ancestors—and it's up to you to sleuth out newspapers and the data they contain about your research subjects.

KEYS TO SUCCESS

★ You can't always count on newspapers or databases of digitized publications to "come to you"—you have to seek them.

★ The Chronicling America website, in addition to housing many digitized images, also has the "US Newspaper Directory, 1690–Present," the result of a decades-long project to categorize the country's newspapers.

★ WorldCat, a master catalog of subscribing libraries' holdings, can be searched for newspapers.

★ The Library of Congress and the Wisconsin Historical Society have the two largest collections of American newspapers.

★ Many other libraries have focused collections, often strongest to their service areas, and may have newspapers in any media.

PART 3

DIVING DEEPER INTO NEWSPAPERS

11

Ethnic-Focused Newspapers

Remember back in chapter 1 when we defined one of the characteristics of a newspaper as "intended for a 'general public' as opposed to only scholars in a certain field"? Well, this chapter gives life to the fact that newspapers serve *a* general public, rather than *the* public at large. Depending on its mission, a newspaper may only serve one particular ethnic or linguistic group. In fact, serving a general public is one of the ways in which a newspaper sets itself apart from other kinds of publications. By serving a narrower market, these niche newspapers often include more—and more accurate—details about the specialized audience than English-language newspapers aimed at a more general audience.

Newspapers focused on a particular ethnic group can provide new, enlightening information about a community and the individuals within it. For example, researcher Lisa Gorrell from California spotted an obituary in the Swedish-language newspaper *Vestkusten* (image **A**) mentioning her husband's great-grandmother's birthdate (August 14, 1868) and her place of birth in Sweden (Rappestad, Östergötland). This detailed obituary appears as part of *Vestkusten*'s digitized run on the California Digital Newspaper Collection

<cdnc.ucr.edu/cgi-bin/cdnc>, which is a site that generates optical character recognition (OCR) text representation (see chapter 6) and makes the task of translating the obituary for English-only speakers less onerous.

The payoff for finding this obituary in a newspaper geared toward the woman's fellow Swedish immigrants is immense. It traces her from her birth, mentions her two marriages, and discusses her immigration and work because of her second husband's travels as a minister. The detailed account of her life ends with her final days on earth: "For three months, she suspected her passing and announced it at the breakfast table when she said, 'I have been in heaven tonight. The Lord was fighting me. Oh, how bad is that!'"

While similar to ethnic-focused newspapers, African American newspapers outside the American South had a slightly different mission. These papers were keenly aware that much of their audience had kin in other areas of America and therefore tailored more of their "out-of-town" news to reporting on the people in places from which their closer geographic base had migrated. Timothy N. Pinnick, who has literally written the book on African American newspapers (see its full information in appendix B), notes that it was common for big-city newspapers such as the *Chicago Defender* to have social columns from all over the American landscape. He uses as an example a column in a 1923 issue of the *Defender* (datelined Rock Springs, Wyoming) that begins with the obituary of a well-traveled man named Tom Moore, who at different times had residences in Virginia, Tennessee, and Ohio on his way to Wyoming. The column continues with the comings and goings of several people from the area and ends with what can be hoped was a temporary but painful setback for an area woman: "Mrs. Mattie Brown slipped and fell on the ice and split her right arm open to the bone and has been confined to her home for several days."

Adding these foreign-language and ethnically specialized newspapers to your research brew—and spicing the pot further with papers serving religious, labor, and international communities (see chapter 12)—will give you a stew that's overflowing with richness on any topic or person you choose. And while these types of newspapers will be of

Stillahafskusten

CALIFORNIA.

Mrs N. M. Nilsen afliden. Mrs Hulda Nilsen (f. Anderson) i San Pedro afled i lördags å. d. Hon var född i Rappestad, Östergötland, den 14 aug. 1868. Hon tillbragte sin ungdomstid i St. Mellösa, Närike, tills han år 1893 kom till Amerika och ingick äktenskap med sin efterlämnade make, pastor N. M. Nilsen den 20 maj 1893.

Hon har varit medlem af Hilmarförsamlingen från d. 28 juni 1908 tills för fem år sedan när pastor Nilsén flyttade från Hilmar till San Pedroförsamlingen. För omkring 3 månader sedan började hon att lida af svår hufvudvärk och blifva nervös, hvilket tilltog ganska fort, så att i medio af sept. hennes tanke började blifva åtskilligt oredig. Hon fick stilla sluta sin jordevandring i sin makes och dotters närvaro den 15 nov. i en ålder af 56 år, 3 månader och 1 dag.

För tre månader sedan anade hon sin bortgång och meddelade den vid frukostbordet, då hon sade: "Jag har varit i himmelen i natt. Herren hämtade mig. O, hvad det var härligt!"

Hulda Nilsen's obituary appeared in the December 4, 1924, edition of *Vestkusten*, a Swedish-language newspaper that can be searched online as part of the California Digital Newspaper Collection.

primary importance when researching people from the specific target audience, you can also use them to see greater context by observing a nonmajority culture.

AFRICAN AMERICAN NEWSPAPERS

Those researching African American ancestors need to especially be in tune with specialized newspapers, as papers documenting the lives and experiences of the black community formed central parts of the black experience. These newspapers document the long and often bitter history of African Americans, from enslavement before and during the American Civil War to the systematic racism that has dogged the community in the century and a half since. Your African American ancestors may have been listed as "runaways" in antebellum advertisements, or as persons of interest from families using the black press to reunite their families after the war.

While African Americans can appear in newspapers in many different capacities, several projects are underway with the goal of making these items more accessible to researchers. Let's dive into some of the most common ways in which African American ancestors appear in specialized newspapers.

ADS SEEKING RUNAWAYS AND REUNIONS

Chronologically, the first widespread mentions of African Americans by name in newspapers were the pre-Civil War fugitive slave or "runaway" advertisements placed in the press (image **B**), many offering rewards for their return to enslavement. These often contain many details about the enslaved individuals, an especially useful trait since slaves were mostly anonymous in other records of the time, such as US federal censuses. Typical ads included a slave's name, age, height, build, complexion (e.g., "bright" indicating a person of lighter skin), and markings (many times the result of punishment and torture). Sometimes further details included personal and family history details, such as when and where they had been bought or sold. A few of the ads even ventured a guess about where the enslaved person might have been headed and why. It is estimated that upwards of one hundred thousand of these advertisements appeared in newspapers from the Colonial period through the end of the Civil War.

While many of these ads can be found in digitized newspapers by keyword searches (such as *fugitives*, *runaways*, and/or a slave's first name), Cornell University's Edward E. Baptist, an associate professor of history, began an ambitious project called Freedom on the Move: a database of fugitives from North American slavery **<freedomonthemove.org>**. When completed, the database will include scans of advertisements from all North American newspapers as well as search capabilities for names, locations, and characteristics (such as occupations).

A variety of "crowdsourcing" avenues are being used in the construction of the database. One, a "history lab" model, has professors and teachers entering data from ads as class assignments. Another, the "citizen historian" model, is encouraging individuals and historical or genealogical societies to contribute by checking and analyzing documents. In all cases, part of the process will be to correct errors made by OCR technology when ads were scanned. You can track the project's progress on its website.

Some abolitionist newspapers ran autobiographies of former enslaved people even before the Civil War, and these narratives

NEW ADVERTISEMENTS.

Runaway in Jail.

Was brought to the Jail of this Parish a runaway negro boy who calls his name MADISON, and says that he was on the steamer Luna, and belongs to a Mr. Powers, of New Orleans; said negro is about 37 years of age, 5 feet 10 inches high. The owner will please come forward, pay charges and take him away.
    no28   HENRY SULLIVAN, Jailor.

Marron en Prison.

Il a été amené à la geole de Plaquemine un nègre arrêté comme marron, nommé MADISON, et qui se dit appartenir à Mr. Powers, a Nlle. Orleans. Let dit nègre est agé d'environ 37 ans, 5 peids 10 pouces de taille.
    no28   HENRY SULLIVAN, Geolier.

Advertisements relating to runaway slaves in the *Southern Sentinel* of Iberville, Louisiana, were published in both English and French (November 28, 1849).

became more popular after the war (particularly in the black-owned press). These stories shared the personal reflections of people who had persevered through that dark era, giving hope to others still living in oppression. Joe Clovese, who at 105 was the last surviving African American member of the Grand Army of the Republic, told the story of his more-than-twenty-year search for his mother to both the *Indianapolis Times* and *Indianapolis News* in 1949. In it, he reveals that a chance conversation with another patron of the French Market in New Orleans led him to the home of his mother only a few blocks away.

But as compelling as the antebellum ads for runaways and postbellum reflections are to researchers today, they're not the only heartbreaking type of distinctly African American newspaper item. The end of enslavement brought with it notices of people looking for family members ripped from each other by slave transactions, with words equal parts hopeful and traumatized.

The various ways in which African American families were separated—sold away to new, distant enslavers or moved during the Civil War away from battle lines—led to an ironic use of the black-owned press that came into its own with the Civil War. For generations of captivity, enslaved people were denied the right to educate themselves, in particular the ability

LABOR, RELIGIOUS, SCHOOL, AND SHOPPERS NEWSPAPERS

Sometimes the historical communities for which we're searching aren't ethnic in nature, but come about instead from the bonds formed in a labor union, church organization, school, or college. These publications have even smaller "general publics," limited by the organizations' memberships. And since they cover news of a smaller group, they're often filled with more opinions than general interest newspapers.

That does not mean you should omit these newspapers from your research. Quite the opposite, in fact—given the role of religion in forming the primary community for many people, denominational newspapers can contain crucial information about people and their religious beliefs. Especially during the newspaper's golden age, these publications can give you much better historical context into someone's Methodist, Lutheran, or Catholic background. Some of these documents are being digitized as parts of the collections mentioned in previous chapters. Others will only be found the archives of the respective church groups—if they've been preserved at all.

In a similar way, labor newspapers, of which there have been more than thousand throughout American history, ranged from overly socialist publications to the mouthpieces of specific trade unions. As you learned in chapter 10, the Wisconsin Historical Society has a large collection of labor newspapers. These newspapers can hold everything from lists of members and officers to the comings and goings of these "brotherhoods."

School newspapers, especially of high schools, can present particular challenges. American education has gone through a couple waves of consolidation, first from the one-room schoolhouses popular until the Great Depression and again in the 1950s and 1960s. As a result, many schools are now part of larger units, making their student newspapers harder to find. Some combination of successor schools (schools into which the smaller schools were merged), local historical societies, and alumni can hold the newspaper's archives. As mentioned in passing earlier, one of the best current efforts to preserve college-level newspapers is the Historically Black Colleges and Universities (HBCU) Newspaper History Project <docs.google.com/document/d/1lYgrqT2ao-JV4-O1FLD16XfUYo1dda9wbewHyLCh784/edit>, which seeks to preserve newspapers published on the campuses of America's HBCU.

Finally, what to make of so-called "shoppers"—neighborhood publications heavy on advertisements but well-read by people in their communities? While these are a type of newspaper with little editorial content, they do generally have calendars of events. While such shoppers that are published as standalones might be difficult to find—a few have been considered historically valuable to be archived. A good number of them are owned and printed by general-interest newspaper companies, which may have back-issue stocks. Ignore any sort of newspaper content at your peril!

to read and write. Forming newspapers of their own—*The Black Republican*, *The Colored Tennessean*, and the *South Carolina Leader*, to name a few that began at the war's end in 1865—became a place for advertisements seeking reunions with family members.

One of the more prolific publishers of these ads was the *Christian Recorder*, the official paper of the African Methodist Episcopal (AME) Church. Published under a somewhat longer title in the 1850s, the *Recorder* gained celebrity during the Civil War by chronicling the movements and experiences of the United States Colored Troops, publishing letters from soldiers. It seemed a natural segue for the paper to become a prodigious publisher of these attempts to bring together families torn apart by slavery and war.

Generally fewer than a hundred words, the typical case describes a family member being sold away to an identified slaveholder:

> Information wanted of Moses Marlow or Howard, who belonged to John Howard in Leflore county, near Smith Mill, and about nine miles from Greenwood, Miss. His mother was Ersia Howard. His father was Matthew Howard. His mother had three sisters: Jane Pierson, Silva House, Clarenda Miller, and two brothers: Louis Moore and Robert Moore. Mrs. Clarenda Miller is the mother of the writer, Ersia Jurault, of Whaley, Miss. Ministers at Vicksburg please read to congregations. (*Christian Recorder*, August 3, 1899, page 4)

These advertisements are the subject of a project by Villanova University professor and director of the graduate program in history, Judith Giesberg. She launched a project in cooperation with Mother Bethel AME Church in Philadelphia to digitize and transcribe the *Christian Recorder* advertisements. Last Seen: Finding Family After Slavery <informationwanted.org/about> is a volunteer effort and has more than fifteen hundred entries at the time of this printing. The project has expanded to include ads from newspapers beyond the *Recorder*.

We can't definitively say how many advertisements resulted in a successful reunion, though researchers today still benefit from these families' efforts. Researcher Dionne Ford, for example, found references in a newspaper ad not just to a great-great-great-grandmother, but also to a reunion her ancestor had with a sister. The nineteenth-century newspaper record relates the overwhelming joy and excitement, made only better by twenty-first century descendant Ford being able to know about it. She shared her incredible story as an article on her blog, titled "Treasure Chest Thursday: Another Enslaved Ancestor Found!" <dionneford.com/treasure-chest-thursday-another-enslaved-ancestor-found>.

The bulk of the advertisements were taken out shortly after the war's end, but families continued to place ads for missing relatives, friends, and comrades during Reconstruction and beyond. Despite the low percentages of success, African Americans remained hopeful. This most likely was the mindset of Ellen Tate, a wife, mother, and AME church member. She placed this notice in the Information Wanted column of the *Cleveland Gazette* appearing March 26, 1887, as she searched for one of her sons, approximately twenty-eight years of age:

> Any information of the whereabouts of Fred Tate, who left his home in Zanesville, O., May, 1884, will be thankfully received by his mother, Mrs. Ellen Tate, No. 109 Muskingum avenue, Zanesville, Ohio.

As with any genealogical search that seeks context as well as names, researching these types of newspaper information can be helpful even if your ancestors are not named. A runaway from the same plantation as your ancestor might give some clue about your own ancestor's conditions of enslavement. Likewise, "reunion" blurbs also could reference other enslaved families on your ancestral plantation—or even give a time or place indication of when, where, or to whom your enslaved kin was sold.

WIDER GEOGRAPHY FOR AFRICAN AMERICAN NEWSPAPERS

As noted in Pinnick's example from the *Chicago Defender* earlier in this chapter, another distinguishing factor of the African American press was its large geographic reach in covering social news. Shamele Jordon, the New Jersey researcher whose use of Newspaper.com's collaboration tools we talked about in chapter 7, found this out first-hand. The minority-owned *Philadelphia Tribune* covered the town of Lawnside, New Jersey (the first independent, self-governing black municipality north of the Mason-Dixon Line), years before most non-African American big-city papers adopted a more metropolitan approach to newsgathering. Jordon found articles about murder, mayhem, smallpox quarantine, a duel, a jealous husband shooting his paramour, suspicious deaths, a church meeting on whether men were the cause of most marital strife, voodoo women, a Medal of Honor winner, a colored town fighting for survival, wedding pictures, and more.

While African American newspapers went in and out of business over time, many saw continued growth. According to the 1913 edition of the *Negro Year Book*, 288 newspapers were in operation at the time, and the US Newspaper Directory shows more than two thousand entries for African American papers throughout history. Simply because of the wide-ranging social columns, Pinnick recommends the following five papers that every researcher should become familiar with for their wide-ranging social columns: *The Pittsburgh Courier, Chicago Defender, The Freeman* (Indianapolis), *Norfolk Journal and Guide*, and *Cleveland Gazette*.

DIFFERENT ALPHABETS

Many of the languages in which newspapers have been printed have just a few characters of difference from standard English, such as umlauts (*ü* or *ö*) or the esset (*ß*) in German, the "slashed O" (*ø*) in some Scandinavian languages, or the "hook under the c" (*ç*) in Romance languages. Given the diversity, you won't be surprised to know that, while it has attempted to account for these foreign-language oddities, OCR technology sometimes misfires at higher rates when interpreting these letters.

Sites such as Chronicling America offer the "OCR text representation" discussed in chapter 6, and this is helpful when identifying problems with what has been "read" by the OCR software. Remember the tips on OCR mistakes in chapter 5 also apply to foreign languages (and see the German section in this chapter for a specific list of concerns when reading the Fraktur font).

Websites such as Fonts2U **<fonts2u.com>** offer free downloads of fonts with foreign character sets that might be helpful in further transcribing newspaper materials on your computer (usually the first step you want to do before translating).

If you're getting a "bad" translation from Google, turn it around. Put in the word you think might be in the text in the English to (insert other language here) box and see what comes up—what's in the newspaper is probably a spelling variant or typographical error. For character-based languages such as Chinese or Hebrew, special OCR conversions have been developed; the same "turn around" in Google translate can pay benefits if you have some idea of the wording.

In previous chapters, we've mentioned online databases of African American newspapers, but to recap: Chronicling America **<chroniclingamerica.loc.gov>** has digitized images of several dozen African American newspapers, as does Accessible Archives **<www.accessible-archives.com>** and GenealogyBank **<www.genealogybank.com>**. In addition, several organizations have created libraries-only databases, and other projects seek to make school newspapers from HBCUs more accessible.

FOREIGN-LANGUAGE AND ETHNIC NEWSPAPERS

The enduring mythology behind the American "melting pot" belies the foreign-language press that was vibrant throughout the centuries of US existence. The German press, reflective of that ethnicity's significant position in American demography, was the first foreign-language press to develop, and it wielded tremendous influence in the many cities and states with substantial German-born (or German-speaking) populations, sometimes even generations after the population immigrated. The number of newspapers in the languages of other ethnic groups often mirrored their respective shares of the ethnicity "melting pot."

Research Tip: GO (PENNSYLVANIA) DUTCH

The people of German descent labeled "Pennsylvania Dutch" used a spoken dialect of that name but, until the dialect began to die out after World War II, the language in print was high (i.e., standard) German.

Many of the foreign-language and ethnic newspapers tended to function in two complementary ways: On the one hand, they were a place for immigrant communities to find news of their homelands (as well as their particular New World enclaves) but equally important was their role in instilling a sense of what would make them "fit in" as successful Americans. For some immigrant communities, newspapers were second only to the churches they established in terms of institutions in the lives of the people. In the Old World, many newspapers were oriented more toward the elite or business classes (in addition to often being government controlled), while in America the newspapers were put into the hands of many common people.

GERMAN-LANGUAGE NEWSPAPERS

No foreign-language press was more vibrant than newspapers in German. The first American newspaper in German was published in 1732 in Philadelphia, and German-language newspapers remained a peculiarity of the Pennsylvania German culture—the single largest white ethnic minority not from the British Isles—until the early 1800s.

By the middle of the nineteenth century, however, German-language newspapers had spread throughout the mid-Atlantic region and into the Midwest. The failed revolutions of 1848 in Europe drove a huge number of Germans to emigrate—especially disgraced or politically exiled journalists who were interested in making their marks in the New World via the press. Many more German newspapers sprang up in the Northeast and Midwest, and German-language papers made their debut in California not long after the Gold Rush of 1849. The number of titles peaked just before the turn of the twentieth century, but overall circulation was setting records a few years into World War I (which heightened interest in new publications). With America's entry into the war, however, all things "German" became unpopular and unpatriotic—including German-language newspapers, which went into swift decline. More than 375 titles remained in 1920, dropping to 235 a decade later and barely more than a hundred by midcentury. A few dozen still exist today, most of them in larger metropolitan areas.

Similar to African American newspapers, German-language papers often had larger geographic areas of coverage. German newspapers, however, were less concerned with covering other regions of the United States and more interested in covering countries with large ethnic-German populations (Hungary, Romania, the Czech Republic, to name a few in addition to Germany, Austria, and Switzerland). Karl J.R. Arndt and May E. Olson's three-volume set *The German Language Press of the Americas* captures the dynamism of these German-language publications, giving state-by-state summaries of journalistic activity as well as some background about each newspaper.

Another distinction of German-language newspapers is that they used the Fraktur font, which can be hard for modern eyes to read. This antiquated typesetting lends itself to more OCR mistakes than do English-language newspapers. Some of the more common possibilities (in addition to the ones noted in chapter 5 for English-language fonts, some of which may also apply to Fraktur) are:

- For uppercase letters: *C*, *E*, and *G*; *S* and *G*; *B* and *V*; *I* and *J*; *N* and *R*
- For lowercase letters: *h*, *n* and *y*; *s* and *f*; *c* and *e*; *i* and *j*

NEWSPAPERS IN OTHER FOREIGN LANGUAGES

Many ethnic communities, from Poles to Italians to Native Americans, produced their own newspapers. The US Newspaper Directory and Chronicling America document some of these publications, as do state-specific sites and even some of the paid subscription services. While the coverage isn't as complete as it is for English-language, German-language, or African Americans, these sites can still provide valuable information about your ancestors from different ethnic groups.

As might seem obvious, the particular community's activity in the newspaper world was either helped or hindered by the group's literacy rate. In *Norwegian Newspapers in America*, author and historian Odd S. Lovoll notes most of the Norwegian immigrants landing in the United States beginning in the 1840s were literate, leading to a fairly quick blossoming of newspapers in the Norwegian language. Though a relatively tiny immigrant

---

Research Tip: LIMIT BY LANGUAGE

The US Newspaper Directory on the Chronicling America website can be drilled down by any language and/or ethnicity press. One option, the Stanford Visualization, can be broken down by certain languages, but many are put in an "other" bucket.

group compared to many others, Norwegian immigrants created more than two hundred newspapers over time!

In addition to its megacollection of English-language newspapers, the Wisconsin Historical Society has a number of book guides to various ethnic newspapers, many compiled by its legendary former newspapers and periodical librarian James P. Danky. Among the compilations he helmed were union lists of Native American, Hispanic, and African American newspapers (titles shown in the bibliography). Wisconsin also has guides to Polish newspapers as well as Susan Bryl's *Ethnic Newspapers: Guide to the Holdings of the State Historical Society of Wisconsin Library*.

One of largest collections of ethnic newspapers was that of the former Balch Institute for Ethnic Studies, which merged into the Historical Society of Pennsylvania in 2002. Many of its newspapers were scanned and digitized by NewsBank for its library subscription database "Ethnic American Newspapers from the Balch Collection, 1799–1971," including newspapers in Czech, French, German, Hungarian, Irish, Italian, Japanese, Jewish, Lithuanian, Polish, Slovak, and Welsh.

When you do find foreign-language newspapers, be sure to transcribe the document (that is, re-type the text or copy-and-paste into a word-processing program). Then you can turn your attention to translating the document. While online translation tools aren't perfect, they can help you get a general sense of what a document contains.

Here's a quick tutorial for using Google Translate **<translate.google.com>**, one of the most frequently used online translation services.

1

1 **Go to the Google Translate home page**. Note the "from" and "to" languages above the empty text boxes, along with a down arrow to find additional languages (you can also select "Detect language" if you are not sure). Adjust them to the language of the original (left-hand side) and the language you want it translated into.

2 Select your language and enter your text. In this case, I choose Swedish for the original language and English for the translation language. Then, either type in or cut-and-paste the original text in the box. Here, I pasted the text from the example of an obituary from the beginning of the chapter.

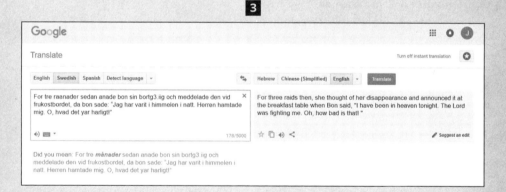

3 Review the translation. Notice the OCR misinterpreted the Swedish word for months (*månader*) but Google Translate flags it with a "Did you mean" notation that would be better than the literal translation. Clicking on and accepting *månader* corrects the translation. (Often Google Translate will not be this smart, and you'll need a foreign language dictionary to look up words to substitute.)

KEYS TO SUCCESS

★ Specialized newspapers appealed to a more narrow audience than did general-interest English-language newspapers, but the more niche publications often covered their audiences more deeply.

★ The United States' history of slavery and racism has resulted in many African Americans having a different presence in newspapers, both before and after the Civil War.

★ Foreign-language newspapers targeting national or ethnic groups served a dual purpose: keeping immigrants in touch with their homelands, and giving "rules of the road" toward Americanization.

★ Labor, religious, school, and other newspapers should not be neglected since they, too, may cover people who did not appear (or who were viewed quite differently) in general-interest newspapers.

SPECIALTY NEWSPAPERS CHECKLIST

Use this worksheet to list what newspapers you'd like to research. Download a printable, fill-able version online **<bit.ly/ft-newspapers-guide-downloads>**.

Ethnic

Ethnicity of person/family: _____

Language(s) spoken: _____

Name of newspaper	Language	Access notes

Religious

Religion of person/family: _____

Name of newspaper	Access notes

Occupational

Occupation of person/family: _____

Name of newspaper	Access notes

Educational

Educational institution(s) attended by person/family: _____

Name of newspaper	Access notes

International Newspapers

Having "spiced the stew" with foreign language, ethnic, and African American newspapers in chapter 11, it's time to go south of the border (so to speak) to add some tremendous flavor to your newspaper research—or north to Canada and its many digitized newspapers, or east to Europe where images of newspapers of the British Isles and Germany are popping up all over, or west to Asia and Australia where some rich databases exist. To put it another way: The web now hosts digitized newspapers from all around the world, and these resources are ripe for the picking.

While many of the same techniques and caveats that we've discussed in regards to US newspapers also apply to international publications, this chapter will discuss some of the special considerations you'll need to make when researching newspapers from various countries. For example, interlibrary loan is not normally a factor for international publications (as it is for US newspapers) so we'll be concentrating almost solely on online newspapers.

Between the holdings of some of the services already familiar to you from previous chapters—Newspapers.com **<www.newspapers.com>**, Google News Archive **<news.google. com/newspapers>** and NewspaperArchive **<www.newspaperarchive.com>**, for example, include some international newspapers, along with library-only subscription databases

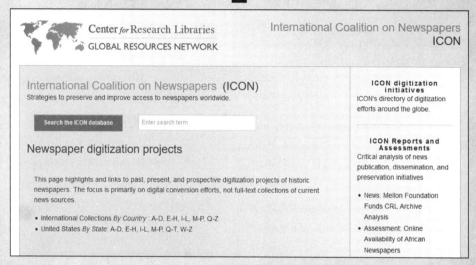

Center for Research Libraries
GLOBAL RESOURCES NETWORK

International Coalition on Newspapers
ICON

International Coalition on Newspapers (ICON)
Strategies to preserve and improve access to newspapers worldwide.

Search the ICON database | Enter search term

Newspaper digitization projects

This page highlights and links to past, present, and prospective digitization projects of historic newspapers. The focus is primarily on digital conversion efforts, not full-text collections of current news sources.

- International Collections *By Country* : A-D, E-H, I-L, M-P, Q-Z
- United States *By State*: A-D, E-H, I-L, M-P, Q-T, W-Z

ICON digitization initiatives
ICON's directory of digitization efforts around the globe.

ICON Reports and Assessments
Critical analysis of news publication, dissemination, and preservation initiatives

- News: Mellon Foundation Funds CRL Archive Analysis
- Assessment: Online Availability of African Newspapers

The website of the International Coalition on Newspapers gives a status report on digitization efforts around the world.

and a number of nation-specific caches of online newspapers (some by subscription and some that are free)—papers from the four corners of the world are represented online. Let's take a tour around the world to see how researchers can find what's out there.

AROUND THE WORLD LISTINGS

A number of websites will give you the lay of the land regarding digitized international newspapers. Note the sites in this section will not host digitized newspaper images themselves; rather, they are helpful aids that will lead you to the archives of currently published newspapers or to websites with such images. While, in a perfect world, we could hope for one "master catalog" like the US Newspaper Directory is for American historical newspapers, no "one-stop shop" has yet been created for international publications.

INTERNATIONAL COALITION ON NEWSPAPERS

You might recall we mentioned the International Coalition of Newspapers (ICON) in chapter 6, and from that you already know the site has a nifty rundown of digitization projects in the United States. But as its full name implies, ICON <icon.crl.edu> (image **A**) does far more than just keep track of American digitization. You also might recall the Center for Research Libraries that was mentioned in chapter 10 (a major player in the US newspaper repository universe). Well, the Center also administers ICON, which it describes as "a multi-institutional effort to promote the accessibility and preservation

EXTRA, EXTRA!
WOMAN TRACES ANCESTOR'S JOURNEY BACK TO ENGLAND

In her publication *One Leg of an Immigrant's Journey to Minnesota*, Ann C. Gilchrest shared what she found in English newspapers: descriptions of the weather from the day her immigrant ancestor Joseph Schindler left Liverpool. What's more, additional newspapers allowed her to follow Joseph's ship as it left the British Isles, and even more publications from the American side of the Atlantic provided her with several more "sightings" of the ship *Robert Morse* while at sea. With all that info, Ann was basically able to plot the course on which the ship sailed in 1852!

The details she obtained from newspapers—including some not as specific to her immigrant ancestor and his ship's passage—nonetheless allowed her to authentically recreate that pivotal voyage to America. She was able to use drawings run by *The Illustrated London News* to show the conditions at the port in England and aboard a typical ship. An advertisement in the *Sheffield & Rotherham (England) Independent* showed the scheduled departure dates for the *Robert Morse*. And an article that an Australian newspaper reprinted from a Liverpool publication gave her some emigration statistics for the year in question.

of international newspaper collections by gathering and providing data on physical and digital collections of newspapers from all world regions."

And that nifty rundown of digitization projects <icon.crl.edu/digitization.php> goes country-by-country around the world, listing digitization projects involving newspapers. The ICON listing is a great clearinghouse that, in some cases, reaches down to individual newspapers. Other times it gives listings for projects that a particular nation is doing (or are being done with a library or museum with an interest in that nation). It also helpfully includes digitized newspapers that are part of subscription collections (showing both those available for public purchase as well as those available to libraries through such vendors as Readex and ProQuest).

In most cases, the ICON site also gives a brief description of the newspaper or collection in question and, naturally, a link to the website with the digitized newspapers. The listings use a dollar sign in a circle to indicate services that require a subscription. A listing of what it calls "International Collections," such as the ones detailed in previous chapters, is shown before ICON's country-by-country roundup.

WIKIPEDIA NEWSPAPER ARCHIVES LIST

Wikipedia's "List of Online Newspaper Archives" <en.wikipedia.org/wiki/Wikipedia:List_of_online_newspaper_archives> contains a large number of country-by-country individual newspaper names, indicating whether each is "Free" or "Pay." However, unlike ICON, Wikipedia lists only the newspaper's name and not whether it's part of a library-only subscription collection such as Readex or ProQuest. Sometimes Wikipedia also includes lists of magazines and other periodicals.

INTERNATIONAL NEWS ARCHIVES

Normally, you'd give up on a webpage that hasn't been updated in some time, but the International News Archives on the Web <www.ibiblio.org/slanews/internet/intarchives.htm> merits a mention because, despite its inactivity, it lists some active links to newspapers that are not found on the ICON and Wikipedia lists. The main webpage to which the International News Archives links is <www.ibiblio.org>, where the site is described as a collaboration between the University of North Carolina at Chapel Hill's School of Information and Library Science, the School of Media and Journalism, and Information Technology Services.

This site only covers non-US newspapers and is organized by area of the world, divided by the following continents and subcontinents: Canada (the only nation to get its own section); Central America and the Caribbean; South America; United Kingdom and Ireland; Europe; Asia; Middle East; Africa; and Australia and New Zealand. Under each of its sections of the world, the newspapers are divided by nation (or, in the Canada section, by provinces and cities), then show the name of the newspaper along with a clickable link to the newspaper's main website; a clickable link to the paper's actual archive sites, which may differ from its main website; dates available in the archive (a feature neither ICON nor Wikipedia have); and notes about language or search capabilities in some cases.

CANADIAN NEWSPAPERS

Most researchers today can move past merely relying on clippings in family Bibles—although, as Stephen Young's example shows, some clippings may be all that remains—with a number of great collections of Canadian newspapers online, many of which are listed in the international standby lists of ICON and Wikipedia. The International News Archive also has a decent Canada section (despite not being updated recently).

You should, however, check out the numerous websites devoted solely to preserving Canadian newspapers. Many subscription services, especially ProQuest, have significant

No one needs to tell Stephen C. Young, a Canada native who now lives in Provo, Utah, about how much insight can be gained from newspapers of the land in which he was born. Stephen and his father visited a cousin, Frederick Paige Mitchell, in 1979 for Thanksgiving dinner. Frederick and his family were friendly as always, and Stephen (having researched Canadian census records at a local library and walking a local cemetery) mentioned his new interest in genealogy. Frederick's wife immediately showed him the mother lode of all genealogy home records: the family Bible.

The family Bible contained the usual birth, marriage, and death entries, but Stephen also found an old newspaper clipping that really intrigued him: the obituary of Nelson Mitchell, a brother to his great-great-grandfathers. The obituary was a clipping, likely from an April 1906 edition of the *Grand River Sachem*, the local newspaper for Caledonia, Ontario—a paper for which no archived copies survive for that time period.

Seeing the clipping further spurred on Stephen's interest in genealogy and lineage. "It was the first time I'd understood that I had United Empire Loyalist ancestry," referring to some of the "Loyalist" Americans who did not support the Revolutionary War and resettled in what was then called British North America (modern Canada).

Stephen also found another clipping, this one from *The Free Press* (London, Ontario), in his grandfather's effects that reported about Stephen's father's service in the Royal Canadian Navy during World War II. The photograph in the clipping bears the catch-line of "Back From a Risky Mine-Sweeping Tour," and you can almost feel the sigh of relief that must have accompanied the return of "Able Seaman C. Young, London" after perilous duty that included sweeping the seas of the English Channel in preparation for the D-Day invasion.

THE FREE PRESS, LONDON, ONTARIO, THURSDAY, OCTOBER 18,

BACK FROM A RISKY MINE-SWEEPING TOUR in British waters are these Canadian Navy personnel from London and Western Ontario. These tars, serving on Bangor sweepers, were a small part

Canada native Stephen C. Young found a report about his father's WWII activities in a clipping from the *The Free Press* (London, Ontario) in his grandfather's effects.

Canadian newspapers. And just like the many free US state sites, online sites at the provincial level can be helpful as well.

Dave Obee's CanGenealogy site has an excellent listing of back-issue Canadian newspapers **<cangenealogy.com/newspapers.html>**, broken down by province, then by city. Obee, a journalist as well as a genealogist, also lists the years available along with the names of the individual newspapers. He also identifies the digital collection to which they belong. All told, Obee has more than a thousand Canadian newspapers in his list. The Library and Archives Canada website **<www.bac-lac.gc.ca/eng/discover/newspapers/Pages/newspapers. aspx>** has a number of tools you can access by clicking Newspaper Collection under the Research Aids heading, including a national catalog search (which, unfortunately, does not have much functionality as of this writing) and a geographic microfilm list that is organized by province, then alphabetized by town name.

While no online site has an all-newspapers listing analogous to the US Newspaper Directory for Canada, the Union list of Canadian newspapers held by Canadian libraries (French title: *Liste collective des journaux canadiens disponibles dans les bibliothèques canadiennes*), published in the late 1970s, roughly parallels the approach of the US directory.

NEWSPAPERS FROM GREAT BRITAIN AND IRELAND

Newspaper research in the British Isles is a typical "good news, bad news" situation. Collectively, England, Wales, Scotland, and Ireland make up an extremely compact area compared to either the United States or Canada, and as such people and the newspapers they create have fewer nooks and crannies to fall into. As a result, a greater percentage of British Isles newspaper pages have been digitized as compared to US newspapers, many of which have yet to be made available online.

That, of course, is the good news. The flip side is that (with a few notable exceptions), you're going to either pay for these digitized pages or have to find a library subscribing to ProQuest databases.

Let's start with the two biggest kahunas with newspaper collections from this

This page on the FindMyPast site leads directly to its newspaper collections.

area, FindMyPast and the British Newspaper Archive. FindMyPast <www.findmypast.co.uk> (image **B**) is the leading paid subscription service for all types of records relating to the British Isles, from civil registrations to census to parish records. As we noted in chapter 9, the site offers a "backdoor" to access the US-rich resources of NewspaperArchive while avoiding directly dealing with the latter company. Similarly, FindMyPast has a partnership with the British Library to digitize its stock of newspapers.

Speaking of the British Library: It operates The British Newspaper Archive <www.britishnewspaperarchive.co.uk> a subscription service that (unlike FindMyPast) includes only newspapers. The library has an almost complete collection of British and Irish newspapers since 1840, partly because of the legal deposit legislation of 1869 that required newspapers to supply a copy of each edition of a newspaper to the library. In total, the British Library collection consists of 660,000 bound volumes and 370,000 reels of microfilm that all told have tens of millions of newspaper pages, with 52,000 titles represented.

As part of the licensing between FindMyPast and the British Library, all newly digitized newspaper titles added to The British Newspaper Archive website are exclusively on that site for six months before being added to FindMyPast. Deciding which of the two sites to use may be a matter of research focus: Genealogists looking for the widest breadth of British resources are likely to find value in FindMyPast's higher subscription cost, while historians who want only to look at newspapers might be better served by The British Newspaper Archive, especially with new titles going there first.

When you move beyond these behemoths, you'll find the same names you've heard before from the world of vendors peddling library-subscription plans: Gale (with its British Newspapers, 1600–1950) and ProQuest (with *The Scotsman*; *Irish Times*, 1859–2012; *The Guardian*, 1821–2003, and *The Observer*, 1791–2003). The National Library of Wales also sponsors the free Welsh Newspapers Online site <newspapers.library.wales>.

EUROPEAN NEWSPAPERS

While the digitization coverage for the continent of Europe is not as high percentage-wise as the British Isles—since, to return to our earlier metaphor, the continent does have a bunch of nooks and crannies—digitization projects in various stages of development and execution are working to make newspapers available online. Even better, most of the continent's digitized newspapers are free as part of public or university library websites. For example, the European University Institute runs one Europe-focused consortium of sorts called European History Primary Sources, and its website <primary-sources.eui.eu/type-source/newspapers> links to other European sites with newspapers.

Many of Germany's historical newspapers, including official state gazettes from the nineteenth century, are being digitized and placed online at a variety of websites. A guidebook to this digitization maze is Ernest Thode's *Historic German Newspapers Online*. While the book is designed somewhat backwards (the author places charts with newspapers' years of coverage and source information at the end of the book), it is useful for providing a list of German newspaper digitizers. The book begins with a section in chart form that lists the websites—starting with a code that Thode has assigned them, then listing only their names and URLs. A second section with a chart separates the newspapers by country of the repository hosting the website, then the repositories and finally the titles of the newspapers. Only in the third and final section does the book list the titles of the newspapers, then the "dates of coverage" and the code of the repository where its online issues are found.

Among the top sources for digitizing German newspapers are Google Books Germany **<books.google.de>**, ZEFYS **<zefys.staatsbibliothek-berlin.de/en>** (a joint project of the State Library in Berlin and the Prussian Cultural Heritage Foundation), and the Bavarian State Library's Bavarica **<www.bsb-muenchen.de/en/collections/newspapers>** (image **C**). Another

C

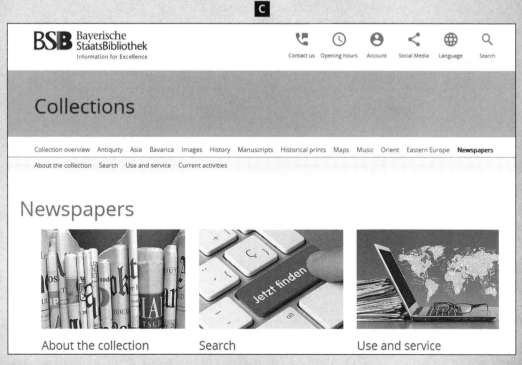

The Bavarian State Library in Germany has many digitized newspapers.

important book relating to newspapers for researchers with German forbears is Friedrich R. Wollmershäuser's *Passengers listed in the* Allgemeine Auswanderungs-Zeitung, *1848–1869*, which discussed immigrants from Germany and listed the names of many of them as they set off for America.

The national library of Germany's neighbor, the relatively small Netherlands, has similarly been digitizing its newspapers for more than a decade. The library's website, Delpher **<www.delpher.nl>**, is closing in on 100 million pages from about seven thousand titles. Significantly, the library is digitizing not just newspapers from the Netherlands but also former Dutch colonies around the world: Indonesia in southeast Asia, Suriname in South America, and the Dutch Antilles in the Caribbean.

Researchers with Italian heritage can access L'Emeroteca Digitale (Biblioteca Nazionale Braidense) **<emeroteca.braidense.it>**, which hosts an archive of about a thousand periodicals and newspapers from Italy.

Projects are afoot in many other European nations, too. Russia has archives online of the Soviet-era publications *Izvestia* **<www.eastview.com/Files/EVIzvestiiaDA.pdf>** and *Pravda* **<www.eastview.com/Files/EastViewPravdaDigitalArchive.pdf>**, as well as a selection of Siberian newspapers from the Novosibirsk State Regional Scientific Library **<rstlib.nsc.ru>**. In France, Gallica **<gallica.bnf.fr/accueil/>** is the digital project of the national library and includes newspapers, while Portugal's Hemeroteca Digital **<hemerotecadigital.cm-lisboa.pt>** also has publications. The ICON list mentioned earlier in the chapter has lists of digitization projects completed and ongoing for every country in Europe.

NEWSPAPERS IN AUSTRALIA, CHINA, LATIN AMERICA AND AFRICA

When we canvass newspaper offerings beyond North America, the British Isles, and continental Europe, there's little doubt that the National Library of Australia brings home the top prize. Its aptly named Trove website **<trove.nla.gov.au/newspaper>** (image **D**) has well over twenty million pages from more than a thousand Australian newspapers, representing every one of its states and territories from the first publication in 1803 through the middle of the 1900s. The digitization project under the Australian Newspaper Plan (ANPlan for short) has made its goal as nothing short of collecting and preserving every newspaper ever published in the country. And it's free, too.

For the world's largest nation in population, the Shanghai Library's National Index to Chinese Newspapers & Periodicals **<www.cnbksy.com/login>** contains more than thirty million entries from around eighteen thousand periodical and newspaper titles. The project adds millions of article entries each year, and the Shanghai Library provides access to articles on demand. For coverage of Japan and East Asia for more than a century, the

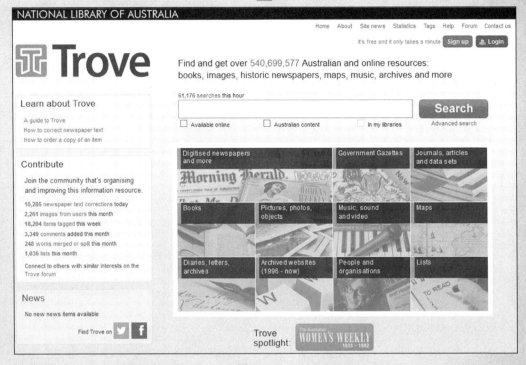

D

Australia's Trove website is literally a treasure trove of that nation's newspapers.

English-language *Japan Times* has an online digital archive of the newspaper from 1897 to 2013 that is available by annual subscription to institutions.

A leading site for newspapers in Latin American countries is Hemeroteca Nacional Digital de México (National Digital Library of Mexico") <www.hndm.unam.mx/index.php/es>, which has page images and full-text search of nearly six hundred titles ranging from 1722 to 1978.

In addition to some standalone newspaper sites you can find through ICON, Wikipedia, and the International News Archives (many of which, admittedly, are "archives" only built in the last few years and containing articles since their inception), you can search Readex library-subscription collections (which include papers from South Asia, Africa, the Caribbean, and Latin America) for a number of areas with little other access. The content of the Readex collections is found online <www.readex.com/collections>, with a list of all the Readex holdings. After clicking on a particular collection, you'll view an overview of that collection. You can access a link to the collection from a menu on the right-hand side.

KEYS TO SUCCESS

★ Several websites can give you helpful listings about newspapers from around the world.

★ Many of the big names in US historical newspapers, such as Newspapers.com and Google News Archive, also have international collections.

★ FindMyPast and the British Newspaper Archives both have a large collection of newspapers from the British Isles.

★ Collections of international newspapers from Latin America and Africa are part of the collections offered to subscribing libraries by ProQuest and Readex.

13

Preserving, Collecting, and Citing Newspapers

So you've made your way through this book and amassed great resources from across the country and the world—whole newspapers rescued from bound volumes, newspaper clippings via microfilm, digital publications, and images of all sorts of publications (from large databases or otherwise). But what do you do now?

This chapter will cover the back end of newspaper research, namely how to preserve and collect historical newspapers, plus how to correctly cite them in your research.

PRESERVING NEWSPAPERS

The examples from Sue Kellerman's fieldwork (see the Profiles in Preservation sidebar) illustrate the somewhat random nature by which a researcher may come across newspapers from years past. Suffice it to say that most instances would not involve locating large caches of old issues from former publishers. Rather, a few entire issues from important national or global events may have been saved by a family member (like my parents did with newspapers from the John F. Kennedy assassination), or perhaps a relative was someone who enjoyed clipping and scrapbooking stories related to his or her family or possessing

PROFILES IN PRESERVATION: L. SUZANNE KELLERMAN

In chapters 1 and 10, we discussed the US Newspaper Program and its impossible-to-overstate value in finding and cataloguing America's newspapers as well as preserving so many crumbling newspapers from practical extinction. But this project didn't just happen overnight—it required the dedication of "boots on the ground" to ferret out the whereabouts of those newspapers.

One of the most dedicated was L. Suzanne "Sue" Kellerman of Boalsburg, Pennsylvania. Kellerman is now the Judith O. Sieg Chair for Preservation and the head of preservation, conservation and digitization for the Penn State University Libraries. But during the heyday of the Pennsylvania Newspaper Project (a state affiliate of US Newspaper Program), Kellerman was a key figure traveling around the state to catalog newspapers during the project's run in the second half of the 1980s. She and others on her team were assigned thirty counties and visited almost five hundred repositories and individuals to assess holdings over a three-year period. Kellerman was hired full time by Penn State as a serials receipt librarian before the project ended, and she has been at the university ever since.

Kellerman's experiences during the project shine a bright light on the effort's importance to both academic and hobbyist researchers. During a break from cataloguing a couple of years into the project, she opened a "Help – Please Find" folder that the project kept with requests for newspapers "presumed lost." She looked at one from a professor of English who was an Edgar Allan Poe scholar. He was writing a paper (later turned into a book) and needed nine issues of the *Philadelphia Saturday News, and Literary Gazette* from the 1830s that were critical to his research. Because of the search capabilities created by what is now WorldCat (discussed in chapter 10), Kellerman was able to confirm the Library of Congress held the issues the professor sought.

The fieldwork of Kellerman and others also was responsible for preserving newspapers that were in private hands, often destined for destruction through intent or neglect. In one case, they found the only known issues of a German-language newspaper in a particular county being used as lining in an old truck at an antique dealer's shop. During a visit to another county, a private collector led the cataloguing team to a deserted building he owned and ripped away sections of paneling, behind which were stored a full century's worth of an important county newspaper that previously had not been microfilmed! A former publisher in a third county initially was not going to participate in the project—apparently because recalling his ownership of the newspaper brought back bad feelings—and was content for his back issues to rot in his attic. But the measured persistence of project staff led him to reconsider and donate the newspapers to a local historical society.

a common theme over many years. Either way, if you come across old newspapers, you'll want to know how to prevent them from being lost to history.

You can take some basic precautions when working with newspapers you want to preserve. It may seem obvious, but remove any food, drinks, or other unnecessary objects from the area being used for the preservation. Clean the area before opening a document, and carefully use a soft brush to remove surface dirt and dust from the newspapers.

One of the biggest threats to your old newspapers is acid—notably, the acid on your hands, acids in the wood-pulp paper used in the nineteenth and twentieth centuries, and

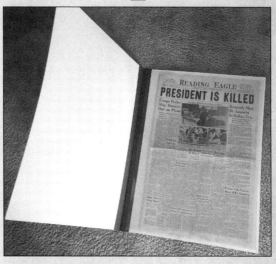

the ink used in printing. To avoid transferring acid from your skin to the newspaper, wear white cotton gloves when touching the paper, and take care that other papers (even from the same publication) don't touch the newspaper.

Two primary factors affect how valuable newspapers are—and how high a priority they are to preserve, as this will affect what methods you use to archive them. The first factor is the information contained within them, which is thoroughly discussed in chapters 2, 3, and 4. The second is their historical value as contemporary documents. If your main motivation for salvaging the newspaper is the information contained in it, it may be best to reproduce the

Placing newspapers in an acid-free folder and laying them flat are a couple of the preservation techniques needed for historical newspapers.

paper's contents onto acid-free paper instead of trying to preserve the original document.

In either case, follow the steps in this chapter to increase your chance of saving newspapers for years to come.

WHOLE NEWSPAPERS

To preserve full versions of original print newspapers, you'll need the proper equipment. Companies such as Gaylord Archival <www.gaylord.com> and Hollinger Metal Edge <www.hollingermetaledge.com> sell folders, envelopes, and boxes specifically designed to hold unfolded newspapers (image **A**). The box used to house the sleeves and folders should protect from dust, dirt, and light. The newspapers should be stored flat as opposed to upright due to their size and weight. If the newspapers will be handled or viewed frequently, clear newspaper sleeves can be used to prevent contact with skin, but newspapers should not be stored in them permanently, as research has shown that acidic paper deteriorates more rapidly when enclosed in a sleeve. Always use pencils when labeling folders, envelopes, or boxes as, like newsprint ink, pen ink contains acid.

Also be aware of how dry the paper is. If the paper is brittle or inflexible, you may need to humidify the paper before attempting to do any unfolding. If this is the case, hire a professional, as this procedure requires a delicate touch. In addition, since newsprint ink is so acidic, avoid allowing pages from different papers coming in contact with one another.

Many newspaper clippings have full date information, but researchers can use other knowledge about the individuals mentioned in the text to estimate the date.

Break up issues or even individual pages into folders or envelopes as much as possible. Always use acid- and lignin-free folders and envelopes, and be sure not to overfill them because this creates an opportunity for damage as the papers are removed and replaced.

When choosing an environment in which to store newspapers, consider the climate. The area should be cool and somewhat dry (between 68 and 72 degrees F and between 35 percent and 45 percent humidity), as high heat and moisture are catalysts for the physical processes that destroy newspapers over time. Also, large and frequent fluctuations in temperature cause the paper to expand and contract, which can cause the material to become mis-shapen. Try to find an environment that is protected from outside temperature fluctuations (avoid attics and base-ments that are not temperature-controlled) but also will not be subjected to large fluctuations that may naturally occur within a household. One example would be if the residents of a household were away for a week: Would the storage area be subjected to a large temperature fluctua-tion due to temperature-control devices like heating or air conditioning temporarily not being in operation?

CLIPPINGS FROM NEWSPAPERS

Many of the same principles apply to preserving newspaper clippings (image **B**), although their generally smaller size makes them easier to house. Place clippings in a polyester film folder with a sheet of alkaline buffered paper behind them (but do not fully encapsulate them because the acids will react even more quickly). In turn, put the polyester folders in file folders and boxes of high-quality (archival) acid-free alkaline buffered materials; store in cool, dry, and dark conditions.

Because of the document's smaller size, you might be able to simply scan the clippings and reprint them. (Note, if you have a high-resolution scanner, you have the capability to reduce "yellowing" and other legibility issues.) If you wish to use the clippings in a display, scan the original on acid-free paper because the original will deteriorate even under the best of conditions. If you feel that only the original will suit your purpose, have the clipping deacidified with chemical treatments such as sprays or baths—this is a job for a professional conservator! Be advised that even the best treatments will not undo damage already done, but instead slow further deterioration. In addition, the chemicals can react and make the paper darker.

For both whole newspapers and clippings, consult "The Family Curator" Denise May Levenick's book *How to Archive Family Keepsakes* (Family Tree Books, 2012) for tips for preserving family artifacts, especially in the context of photos and other memorabilia.

COLLECTING NEWSPAPERS

After taking the time to preserve your family's collection of newspapers and becoming adept with the preservation process, you may find that you have an interest in expanding your collection. Going back to our earlier discussion on a newspaper's value, collectors are drawn to newspapers for at least one of two reasons: to access information that isn't available on microfilm or in historical archives, and to obtain historically important documents as either novelties or artifacts.

Many readers of this book will fall into the first category. You may be looking for an obituary of a specific person or an individual birth or marriage announcement, but you find the publication you are looking for is not available in any archives or libraries on any medium for the time period. If this is the case, do as much research on the publication as possible. You would most likely not be the first person looking into the missing time period, and previous research efforts may lead you to possible private sources. Contacting the publisher (if the newspaper is still in print) or researching what happened to the publishing company (if the newspaper is out of print) may yield clues about where missing issues may have ended up.

If you fall into the second category, consider yourself a newspaper collector: someone who, perhaps, likes newspapers for aesthetic reasons or because they contain items that resonate with you (whether they relate to your ancestors or not). Collectors might consider contacting these private dealers of historically important newspaper issues:

- Steven A. Goldman Historical Newspapers: Oxford, MD
  <www.historicalnews.com>
- Timothy Hughes Rare & Early Newspapers: Williamsport, PA
  <www.rarenewspapers.com>

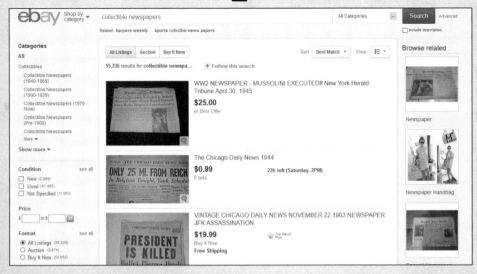

Online auction site eBay has a collectible newspapers category that can help you find old publications.

- Phil Barber's Historic Newspapers and Early Imprints: Cambridge, MA <www.historicpages.com>
- The Mitchell Archives: Bradenton, FL <www.mitchellarchives.com>
- Historical Newspapers & Journals: Skokie, IL
- MagazinesGalore.com: Phoenix, AZ <www.magazinesgalore.com>

The online auction website eBay also has an entire section of its website devoted to collectible newspapers, categorized by date (pre-1900, 1900–1939, 1940–1969, 1970–now) <www.ebay.com/sch/Collectible-Newspapers/13992/bn_2309720/i.html> (image **C**). A trade group for businesses whose goods may include old newspapers is the Antiquarian Booksellers' Association of America, and the organization's website has a membership directory you can use to find dealers with newspaper inventory <www.abaa.org>.

CITING NEWSPAPERS

As is the case with all sources in genealogy, newspaper sources need to be consistently and correctly cited in your research. Future readers of your family history (including viewers of your online family tree) need to be directed to your sources so they can independently verify your information. Without proper primary source citations and proof statements based on them, your compiled work could never be used as the basis for future research— and proper citations go a long way towards giving legitimacy to your work.

All source citations will tell the reader the who, what, when, and where about the source's creation. Each type of source has certain nuances, all of which are expertly laid out in Elizabeth Shown Mills' *Evidence Explained: History Sources from Artifacts to Cyberspace, 3rd Edition* (Genealogical Publishing Co., 2017). The source citations most related to newspapers are discussed in the sections that follow, organized (for the most part) by media type. Source list entries for bibliographies use a slightly different format than the first-reference citations, since they are generally noting an overall source for a work rather than a particular reference.

PRINT NEWSPAPERS AND NEWSPAPERS ON MICROFILM

For all but the most recent newspapers, you'll need to cite the original publication, plus whether you're accessing the original print edition or a microfilmed copy of that original print medium. Information required for most citations boils down to the following:

- Author (if stated/applicable)
- Article title
- Name of newspaper
- Issue date
- Page and column
- Film ID and roll number (for microfilms)
- Repository
- Repository location

Let's look at an example for a first-reference citation:

"Potter Wins Racquet Title," *Philadelphia Inquirer*, 10 February 1914, p. 13, col. 1; HSP microfilm 298, roll 7; The Historical Society of Pennsylvania, Philadelphia, Pennsylvania.

Research Tip: CHECK BOTH SIDES

If you have a newspaper clipping that doesn't include the date or name of the publication, remember to check the other side of the clip for any clue—including information you could put into a newspaper search engine to find the missing information.

And an example for source list entry:

Pennsylvania. Philadelphia. *Philadelphia Inquirer*, 1913–1915.

ONLINE AND DIGITIZED NEWSPAPERS

When you work with newspaper sources on the Internet, you may be looking at "born digital" articles that have never existed in print. In this case, some traditional citation elements—such as "column" and "page"—simply will not exist. Others, such as "edition," may be hard to find (since online newspapers update at irregular intervals and may or may not indicate whether an update has been made to a previously online "published" article).

However, digitized newspapers are overwhelmingly reproductions of previously micro-filmed print newspapers. These newspapers will include all the original citation material of offline sources plus the additional data needed to locate them on the web. Information required for these types of citations includes the following:

- Author (if stated/applicable)
- Article title
- Name of newspaper
- Issue date
- Page and column
- Edition
- URL
- Access date
- Credit line

Research Tip: FEED THE UNUSUAL

Undated newspapers clippings sometimes can be identified by using unusual words from the clipping in an online newspaper search—if the newspaper in question has been digitized. As a result, search for unusual words you find in a clipping to source the original.

The following is an example for first-reference citation:

"Potter Wins Racquet Title," *Philadelphia Inquirer*, 10 February 1914, GenealogyBank (http://www.genealogybank.com: accessed 10 December 2016); citing print edition, p. 13, col. 1.

Example for source list entry:

Pennsylvania. Philadelphia. *Philadelphia Inquirer*, 1913–1915.

NEWSPAPER CLIPPINGS

For newspaper clippings, get as much information as possible, as if you were citing the print newspaper as explained in the "Print Newspapers and Newspaper on Microfilm" section above. Some of the information may be missing if the person did not label the clipping when she cut it out, but do your best. In addition, record who has the source you consulted, as well as how he obtained it.

Example for first-reference citation:

"Potter Wins Racquet Title," undated clipping, ca. 1910s, from unidentified newspaper; Potter Family Papers, privately held by Virginia Potter, [Address for private use,] Ardmore, Pennsylvania, 2016. Given to her in 1965 by her grandmother Helen Potter, wife of Wilson Potter, subject of the article.

For a source list, a clipping might be listed by the collection (in this case, Potter Family Papers) or subject's name ("Wilson Potter").

KEYS TO SUCCESS

★ The steps for safely preserving newspapers depend on how much of the publication you're trying to archive, whether a whole newspaper or a clipping from one.

★ When preserving any newspaper document, the most important dangers to consider are the acids in the paper and ink of the newspaper or clipping.

★ Collecting newspapers can revolve around either seeking information or looking for an artifact/novelty with historical or aesthetic value.

★ Private dealers in newspapers and on eBay are two useful resources for tracking down privately held newspapers.

★ Citations are crucial for newspapers and vary based on the medium in which a newspaper is accessed.

CITATION ELEMENTS TEMPLATE

Use this worksheet to record the information you'll need to correctly cite newspapers in any format. Download a printable, fillable version online **<bit.ly/ft-newspapers-guide-downloads>**.

Format: Print   Microfilm   Digital   Online only

Author name: _____

Article title: _____

Name of newspaper: _____

Issue date: _____   Page and column: _____

Microfilm ID and roll number: _____

Repository: _____   Repository location: _____

URL: _____

Access date: _____

Credit line/source/provenance: _____

14

Putting It All Together

As you've learned about historical newspapers in this book, you've hopefully found some interesting and instructive samples in each chapter—examples and tidbits from other genealogists' and historians' work with newspapers. It seems fitting for the last chapter to include some more "industrial strength" examples: full-blown case studies that showcase how researchers have successfully used newspapers for various purposes. After all, while biographies or historical sketches rarely involved only newspapers, it's equally unusual for such studies to not be enriched by a variety of newspaper sources.

FONKERT FAMILY PHOTO FINDS

Several years ago, Minnesota genealogist J.H. "Jay" Fonkert wrote an article for the National Genealogical Society's Newsmagazine *titled "The threshing machine: Newspapers breathe life into a photo" (Vol. 38, no. 2, April–June 2012, pages 25–31). In it, he recounted how he used the newspapers of Sioux County, Iowa, to get a better sense of what his grandfather's life was like as a farmer in the heavily Dutch area. Fonkert's grandfather, Jan "John" Fonkert, died five years before the author was born, so he had to turn to a variety of resources to learn about him.*

After starting with US census schedules and various vital records, Fonkert was inspired by a family photo of a "weather-beaten harvesting crew with a large black monstrosity of a machine that looked like it could belch fire." From the "windows" afforded by those photos, Fonkert found that "newspapers brought him and the black monstrosity to life. A half-dozen small town weekly newspapers flourished in Sioux County during his lifetime. Hundreds of articles, most only a sentence or two in length, now give glimpses of [Jan] Fonkert's farm life."

As it turned out, Fonkert's grandfather was far from a common "dirt" farmer; he was a farm businessman whose ups and downs were chronicled in the pages of those weekly newspapers for close to half a century. Fonkert was able to estimate when his grandfather entered the threshing business from a 1934 "Thirty-five years ago" newspaper feature about the acquisition of a "threshing outfit" by Fonkert's grandfather and a partner in 1899. Contemporary news briefs talked about the transition to mechanized farming around the turn of the century, as well as pinpointing Fonkert's grandfather's earnings in a 1904 blurb in the *Alton Democrat*: "J. Fonkert averaged over $50 a day with his threshing outfit last week." Fonkert's grandfather also used advertising in the newspapers to sell or trade equipment as well as to find temporary help.

In addition to providing snapshots of Fonkert's grandfather's business life, the newspapers mentioned times when he fell ill, but (in a testament to how newspapers were the "social media of the day") also shared more pleasant descriptions of parties and picnics that were worthy of a Facebook post. Newspapers allowed the author to follow his grandfather to the end of his life—showing that the elder Fonkert was still threshing the year before his death, and had died just ten weeks after a spring 1944 advertisement for his "getting out of farming" sale.

Fonkert's article used a photo as a jumping-off point to document a huge chunk of his grandfather's life through many short mentions in newspapers, yielding a sense of social history he couldn't get elsewhere. Other newspaper case studies often hinge on a certain pivotal moment—sometimes recorded only in one publication while other times printed far and wide. Still others use newspapers to leverage additional information about people with a wandering foot.

FIRST NAME, LAST NAME, NEW NAME

Professional genealogist and Oakland, California, resident Linda Harms Okazaki had her research about ancestor Emerson Corville turn on a dime—and into a wonderful genealogical journal article—when a newspaper documented a name change. Other international newspaper articles added insight about Emerson.

As we'll see in a later case study, misspellings of the given and family names of a subject are common, as names can be spelled differently or Anglicized over the course of time and in different places, whether intentionally or unintentionally. But Linda Okazaki's "Who Was Emerson Corville?" (*California Nugget*, Spring 2012, pages 12–18) documents a different type of name change—when a person changed his or her legal name.

In the historically patriarchal societies of England and the United States, children generally take the surname of their fathers, and Okazaki was understandably befuddled by the fact that she couldn't find any other Corvilles in records when Emerson Corville "seemed to have mysteriously appeared in San Francisco one December day with a family and a booming oyster business." She even used the Corville name, which is an Anglicization of the French surname Courville, to theorize that she had French roots. But even with this theory in hand, this generation was a "proverbial brick wall" for her.

Newspapers to the rescue! The Family History Library in Salt Lake City had recently digitized issues of the *Evening Bulletin* (San Francisco, California) from the late 1800s, and a more-experienced genealogist with whom she was travelling suggested she search it and other newspapers for Emerson Corville. Sure enough, the newspaper reported on September 28, 1874, that "R.H. Emerson was permitted by Judge Stanly to-day to change his name to Emerson Corville." After finding her ancestor had changed his name, she was able to research his Emerson line back to the 1700s in Norfolk, England.

But Okazaki wasn't done with newspapers yet. She was curious about the circumstances that led up to Richard Harvey Emerson changing his name to Emerson Corville. Names, places, and dates are all necessary elements to further genealogical research, and our motivations for seeking these pieces of data are usually to try to better understand our ancestors' personalities and their reasons for doing what they did.

By now you know that newspapers are an incredible resource to do just that. Okazaki found an article in New Zealand from 1866 in which "Richard and his brother Albert each posted ... notices that they were severing ties with one another." She documented a near-miss for Richard's brother John, who was captain of his brother's oyster fishing ships, as he almost drowned when the ship sank according to the October 10, 1867, edition of *The Sydney Morning Herald*.

In a perfect example of the fact that our finds in genealogy will not always be glorious, Emerson had been arrested in Collinsville, Oregon, "for illegally operating a salmon cannery," as reported in the *Sacramento Daily Union* in the late 1870s as part of ongoing reporting on the topic of fish and game laws. Finally, Okazaki was able to find an article in *The Sonoma County Tribune* from December 15, 1892, that showed that he and his family had temporarily gone back to New Zealand. The newspaper said that they returned "because they had family members there."

"Since I wrote that article, I have been in contact with additional relatives in Australia, have traced the Cullum/Prosser line to north London, and found a treasure trove of photos and documents held in the home of Emerson Corville's youngest son," Okazaki notes. "Among those treasures were photos from the 1860s, with enough data to create a timeline of the family travels between Australia, England, and San Francisco. It's an ever-evolving story that really took off with one sentence in a newspaper."

Okazaki's case study shows us that we can use newspapers, not only to further our generational research, but also to bring interesting characters in our family histories to life. It also conveys the power of the digitization of newspapers; Okazaki never would have known to look in the September 28, 1874, issue of the *Evening Bulletin* (San Francisco, California), but a computer can search through millions of words for a specific string in seconds.

PINNING DOWN THE WANDERING SEA CAPTAIN

Longtime Virginia genealogist and US Fish and Wildlife Service retiree Sean Furniss hooked a big one when he was able to track down a sea captain's comings, goings, and demise through Colonial newspaper listings.

We often can learn more about our ancestors by first researching the records tied to their lives, then diving into the place in which they lived. But some of our ancestors had professions that required them to move around quite a bit, and this place-based research may not always be a possibility. One of those professions would certainly be someone involved in maritime industry. Someone who spent most of his time on a boat in an ocean may not show up very often in tax or census records—if at all.

After receiving a clue that his ancestor may have practiced a seafaring trade, Furniss devised a method for tracking his ancestor Isaac Hubber's comings and goings in the Americas, Europe, and Asia over the course of ten years.

First, Furniss searched for Isaac's name on Newspapers.com <www.newspapers.com>, and the results were a plethora of articles documenting departures and arrivals, with Isaac listed as the captain. However, Furniss saw some holes in the sequence of events during which Isaac seemed to have departed twice in a row without arriving. "When that happened, I was able to estimate his approximate date of arrival and search around specific dates until I could locate the missing record," Furniss said.

Even still, Furniss found the name of either the captain or the ship were misspelled in papers' text. As did Linda Okazaki's case study, this highlights one of the limitations of computer index searching: A computer will only look specifically for what it is prompted to by the user. Programmers have developed various methods of enhancing the computer's ability to search for words that are spelled similarly or sound close to the main search target, but they will not always be successful. Furniss' excellent deductive reasoning enabled him to locate articles that the computer was missing.

Using his newfound spelling flexibility, Furniss consulted no fewer than forty articles from 1794 to 1804, including: *Philadelphia Gazette*, the *American General Advertiser*, *Finlay's American Naval and Commercial Register*, *Poulson's American Daily Advertiser*, the *Morning Chronicle*, and the *Telegraphe and Daily Advertiser*. From all that research, he learned Isaac visited Jamaica and Haiti in the Caribbean; the Isle of Wight, Liverpool, and London in England; Hamburg and Cruxhaven in Germany; Canton in China; Batavia (now Jakarta, Indonesia); and Calcutta in India in his pursuit of maritime trading. He also learned that Isaac would have been aboard the ship *Camilla* when it battled French privateers at Batavia Roads on April 12, 1800. Throughout his research, Furniss traced his ancestor's comings and goings across the Atlantic and Indian Oceans aboard at least six different trading vessels.

But more research revealed why Isaac departed once more than he arrived: Furniss found an 1804 record for Isaac's vessel in Batavia, plus the vessel's arrival back in Philadelphia—with a new captain and no record of Isaac. He branched out his search and found mention of Isaac in a Baltimore paper: He died in the Sunda Strait, the dividing line between the modern-day Indonesian provinces of Lampung and Banten.

This squared with what Furniss already knew about Isaac's death. (From probate records in Philadelphia County, Furniss learned Isaac died around 1804.) But he was able to locate an exact place of his ancestor's death (and document a host of Isaac's exciting travels), all using newspapers.

ONE EVENT, MANY VERSIONS

Television researcher and Fairfield County, Connecticut, resident Janeen Bjork <www.janeenslist.com> has thrown herself into genealogy, including teaching and lecturing about genealogy and media at a variety of venues from local colleges to senior centers. Early in her research, she discovered a July 1894 murder-suicide story from Syracuse, New York, *involving her great-great-grandfather, who was shot and killed by his former best friend Henry Vogler. Using a variety of free and subscription sites, Bjork found the story in dozens of online newspapers.*

Newspaper reports differed in how they described the murder of William Strutz, but they agreed on the major details. Bjork's great-great-grandfather William Strutz died as he sat upon a pile of wood at a construction site across the street from the Vogler residence, hoping to get work from a passerby. Vogler, who had been fired from his job at the Greenway Brewery the night before for giving away beer to friends, arrived home. Vogler went into his house and deposited his lunch pail on the table. He returned to the street where he watched Strutz for as long as half an hour before approaching Strutz and telling him to get off the street.

Things were already tense between the two former best friends. Reports said they had a heated argument the year before after Vogler came home to find Strutz and Mrs. Vogler in a compromising position. Enraged, Vogler told people he intended to kill Strutz—and according to witnesses, Vogler did just that. Strutz said a few words from atop his pile of wood before Vogler shot him dead. Vogler then turned the revolver on himself and fired directly into his temple, dying at the hospital two hours later.

Henry Vogler couldn't have chosen a better day for researchers than Monday, July 2, 1894, to shoot his perceived rival and himself. All the important German-Americans in New York State had gathered in Syracuse for the twenty-fifth anniversary of that city's Turnverein Society, the most important German organization in the city. The violence was the talk of the town, and coverage spread far and wide. Both the gathering and the murder-suicide were noted in an 1894 year-end review that ran December 30 in *The Herald*, one of the leading Syracuse, New York, newspapers.

The *Syracuse Union*, a local German-language newspaper, was perhaps the most sympathetic to Vogler when it covered the story two days later. It portrayed Vogler as "honest and industrious and a family man," and claimed that Strutz had left his family many years before the incident and had struck up an affair with Mrs. Vogler. Police detectives found "the cheating wife" (as the paper referred to her) hunched over her husband's body trying to revive him.

The first thing Bjork noticed about the news' coverage of the dramatic murder-suicide was its inconsistencies—a theme that would occur time and again as the story made its way across the country.

It all started when one of the hometown papers, *The Journal*, published the wrong month and spelled Strutz incorrectly (no *r*). *The Journal* again spelled Strutz incorrectly when it interviewed Vogler's widow the following day and reported the funerals of the murderer and the victim three days later.

The errors continued as the wire services, United Press and Associated Press (AP), picked up the story. It appears the AP got the details right, as the first AP newspaper (the 2 p.m. edition of Joseph Pulitzer's *The World*) spelled both names correctly. Despite this, most publications misspelled one or both men's names (most often *Volger* for Vogler and *Stutz* for Strutz).

Those misspellings were minor compared to what some of the papers on the receiving ends of the wire stories did to compound the errors. *The Lowell (Massachusetts) Sun*'s 5 p.m. edition on the day of the murder transformed Henry into C.E., Greenway's Brewery into *Greenway's elevator*, and Strutz into *Frutz*. The following day, and just a column apart, the same paper repeated the previous day's error (printing *Stutz* rather than Strutz) and came up with another flawed story of its own: The semi-weekly edition of the *Cortland Standard* switched the two men's first names (image **A**). Although the newspaper got the first names correct in the *daily* edition (image **B**), it still misspelled both Vogler and Strutz. *The Weekly Town Talk* in Alexandria, Louisiana, reported that Henry Volger [sic] killed Henry [sic] Strutz. *The (Wheeling) Intelligencer* version ran with *Tolger*, rather than Vogler. Somehow, the *Omaha Daily Bee* looked at the wire story and printed *Helyea* rather than Henry (image **C**).

The (now butchered) story even made its way out west. An Oklahoma newspaper, *The Norman Transcript*, reported the story over a month later and stated that *Volger* [sic] shot and almost instantly killed Strutz on Thursday (in reality, the murder occurred on Monday, July 2).

How did these inaccuracies happen? Bjork researched how the different newspapers received stories, and what she found explained how one tiny mistake could be amplified. Most of the stories published in the first few days were transmitted via one of two wire services (each of which, as we noted earlier, were prone to errors), either by telegram or telephone.

In addition, many of the small-town weekly newspapers subscribed to "patent insides" or "patent outsides" (also known as "newspaper efficiencies"), and so carried abbreviated versions of the story on July 12/13, 1894. These "efficiencies" were services that sent three to six preprinted pages to small-town newspapers each week, and five of these "newspaper union" services supplied news to more than seven thousand weeklies in 1894. In fact, the leading newspaper unions provided copy to about three-fourths of the nation's weekly newspapers in the latter decades of the nineteenth century. In this case, the murder-suicide

A

SEMI-WEEKLY EDITION.

CORTLAND, N. Y.,
TUESDAY, JULY 10, 1894.

NEWS OF THE WEEK.
Monday, July 2.

—At Syracuse William Vogler kills
Henry Strutz, of whom he was jealous,
and then kills himself——

As the Strutz story made its way around the country, papers (such as the semi-weekly edition of the *Cortland Standard*) switched the men's names.

B

Cortland Standard.

CORTLAND, N. Y., MONDAY EVENING, JULY 2, 1891.

Murder and Suicide at Syracuse.

SYRACUSE, July 2.—At 7:45 this morning Henry Volger, aged 49, shot and instantly killed William Stutz, aged 50. Volger then fired a bullet into his own brain and died two hours later.

The daily edition of the *Cortland Standard* corrected the semi-weekly edition's switch of names ... but introduced spelling errors.

C

THE OMAHA DAILY BEE.

ESTABLISHED JUNE 19, 1871.   OMAHA, TUESDAY MORNING, JULY 3, 1894.   SINGLE COPY FIVE CENTS.

Double Tragedy Due to Jealousy.

SYRACUSE, N. Y., July 2.—Helyea Volger, a night watchman, shot and almost instantly killed William Strutz, a carpenter today. He then put a bullet into his own temple. He died two hours later. The cause was jealousy.

Who is "Helyea" Volger? *The Omaha Daily Bee* got some of the facts about this story wrong.

TIPS FOR USING NEWSPAPERS

The "Top Tips My Great-Great-Grandfather Taught Me" are the building blocks of the newspapers and genealogy programs Bjork has been presenting since 2014:

- Be aware of goofs, either from reporters (e.g., a last name listed as Stutz instead of Strutz) or typesetters (e.g., the murder being listed as June 2, 1894, rather than the correct date, July 2).

- Don't trust family stories. Family members often spin or "sanitize" details of scandalous stories, bending the truth.

- Look for coverage beyond local papers (e.g., stories distributed by wire services).

- Complete an exhaustive search. Use the Genealogical Proof Standard <bcgcertification.org/product/bcg-genealogy-standards> as a guide.

- Take notes to track your finds, including sources, name variations, and any conflicting data.

- Search for keywords and spelling variants, as names are often misspelled or misread by optical character recognition (OCR). Also search for initials and abbreviations in addition to names (e.g., Joseph William Smith may be Jos., Joseph W., or J.W.). Consider searching for syllables as well, as hyphens (which are used when a word extends across multiple lines of text) affect search results on most newspaper websites.

- Extend your records search for years after a person's death, as he may have been mentioned in documents after death (such as obituaries and real estate records).

- Handle any documents carefully, as newspapers and microfilm deteriorate and have limited lifespans.

- Keep looking! New newspapers are being digitized every day. For example, I researched this story in May 2017, and I found it covered in eleven different publications. By June 2017, that number had more than doubled to twenty-three.

was picked up in these newspaper efficiencies by publications in different states, sometimes in a column called "Sins and Sinners."

In addition, Bjork looked to journalism as a whole as she tried to describe the discrepancies between newspapers. She knew that journalism was still a trade and not a profession at the time, with the University of Missouri School of Journalism (the first formalized journalism program in the country) not opening until 1908. As was typical for local newspapers at the time, most of Syracuse's newspapers were understaffed and underfunded, leading to the wire service/newspaper union model and mergers between nearby publications.

If that wasn't bad enough, Syracuse newspapers faced a new, well-funded competitor in the weeks following the murder. A local political boss decided to solidify his base by

ONE LAST STORY

For a final snippet, we turn to Pat Richley-Erickson, who writes the DearMYRTLE genealogy blog <blog.dearmyrtle.com> for a short but incredibly touching outtake about her parents and grandparents (and herself as a child!) as found in newspapers. Titled "Treasures from Old Newspapers: What my Dad never knew about his mom," she found her grandmother (the namesake Myrtle of her nom de plume) leading a campaign to collect donations of footwear for needy people in the Great Depression. "My dad never knew about this until after Grandma passed away," Richley-Erickson said with a voice filled with a combination of excited and heavy emotion.

You can view the video here <spark.adobe.com/video/Syhca_MX>, which surely is an inspiration for historical newspaper users everywhere.

launching his own newspaper on July 10, 1894. *The Brooklyn Daily Eagle*'s June 24, 1894, assessment and prediction about the arrival of a new newspaper was prophetic: The first edition of the new paper (*The Post*) arrived a few weeks after its announcement, driving up salaries and driving down advertising rates. By October 1894, the boss' political hold on Syracuse would be complete, and he would begin belt tightening at *The Post*. At least two of the competing Syracuse newspapers fell on hard times, made worse by an 1893 recession. *The Evening News* went into receivership in 1897, and *The Journal* went the same route in 1898. *The Daily Standard* and *The Post* merged to form *The Post-Standard*, publishing the first issue of the newly merged paper on Jan. 1, 1899.

Despite some conflicting information, all this research provided Bjork with concrete tools and strategies for using newspapers; see the Tips for Using Newspapers sidebar for a list.

CONCLUSION

Jay Fonkert learned about his grandfather's business life, one sentence at a time. Linda Okazaki found the "big reveal" of her ancestor's name change. Sean Furniss filled in an ocean's worth of his sea captain forebear's biography and death half a world away. And Janeen Bjork doggedly pursued the expanded range of news about violent death through many (often erroneous) iterations. None of the people they researched were "exceptional people" (from the standpoint of being a household name then or today), proving the point that historical newspapers in all their various facets are better than ever as the building blocks for the biographies of the "Everyman" and "Everywoman" of the past.

The particular events may seem common. But when put together, they form a history that sparkles on forever, animated by the printers' ink and paper that first presented them as well as the articles, monographs, books, audio files, and videos for which they provide the material.

Newspaper Research Flowchart

Throughout this book, we've discussed why historical newspapers can be useful to your research and how to access them in various databases. But even with all these techniques and resources, you may still not know where to begin your newspaper research. The flow chart on the next two pages is here to help, with a series of questions that will set your research straight.

In addition to the tips in the flow chart, also keep the following in mind as you work with newspapers:

- Learn the pitfalls of OCR technology (chapters 5 and 6), as these may affect your searches.

- Consider looking for ethnic and/or foreign-language newspapers (chapter 11), as these publications that served more-specific communities can contain valuable details of your ancestors and their community. International newspapers (chapter 12) can similarly be helpful.

- Carefully preserve and cite your newspaper finds (chapter 13), as this will help both you and your descendants access these valuable historical documents.

- If you're stuck in your research, ask others for help and listen to genealogists' success stories (chapter 14).

STEP 1 : FORMULATE A RESEARCH GOAL

Use "time and place" (chapter 1) and knowledge of what newspapers covered (chapter 2) and when/where they were created (visualized in a chronology; see chapter 3 and appendix C).

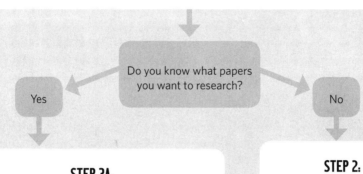

Do you know what papers you want to research?

Yes

No

STEP 3A: SEARCH FREE RESOURCES

Begin searching newspapers and newspaper records on websites that offer their services for free (chapter 6), including:
- ☛ Chronicling America
- ☛ State newspaper websites
- ☛ Local library sites
- ☛ Old Fulton NY Post Cards

STEP 2: FIND TITLES

Consult a list or catalog of newspapers to find publications in the time and place you're researching (chapter 10), such as:
- ☛ US Newspaper Directory
- ☛ Stanford Visualization
- ☛ WorldCat

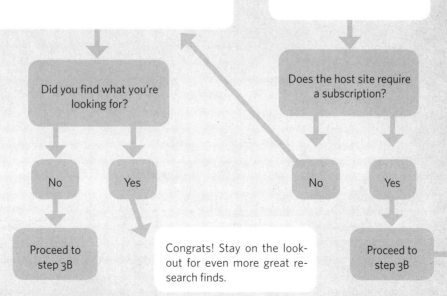

Did you find what you're looking for?

Does the host site require a subscription?

No

Yes

No

Yes

Proceed to step 3B

Congrats! Stay on the lookout for even more great research finds.

Proceed to step 3B

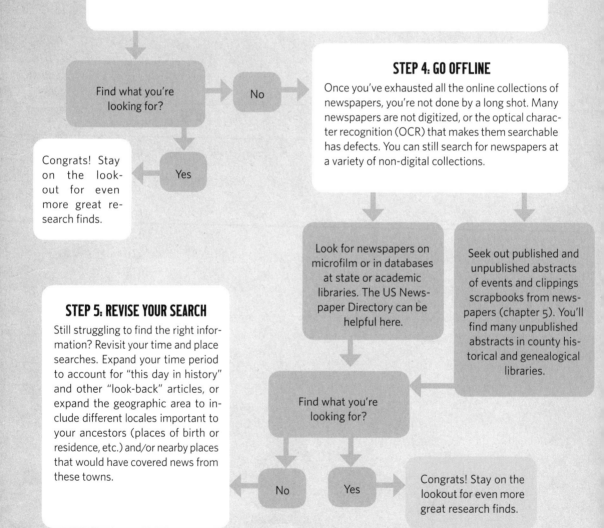

STEP 3B: SEARCH SUBSCRIPTION WEBSITES

If a newspaper you're looking for isn't available for research on a free website, consider consulting subscription digitized newspaper websites, such as:

☞ Newspapers.com (chapter 7)
☞ GenealogyBank (chapter 8)
☞ NewspaperArchive (chapter 9)
☞ Accessible Archives (chapter 9)

Before you sign up for a subscription, check if you can access these databases for free through your local library. Also bear in mind that most services offer free trial periods.

Find what you're looking for?

No

Yes

Congrats! Stay on the lookout for even more great research finds.

STEP 4: GO OFFLINE

Once you've exhausted all the online collections of newspapers, you're not done by a long shot. Many newspapers are not digitized, or the optical character recognition (OCR) that makes them searchable has defects. You can still search for newspapers at a variety of non-digital collections.

Look for newspapers on microfilm or in databases at state or academic libraries. The US Newspaper Directory can be helpful here.

Seek out published and unpublished abstracts of events and clippings scrapbooks from newspapers (chapter 5). You'll find many unpublished abstracts in county historical and genealogical libraries.

STEP 5: REVISE YOUR SEARCH

Still struggling to find the right information? Revisit your time and place searches. Expand your time period to account for "this day in history" and other "look-back" articles, or expand the geographic area to include different locales important to your ancestors (places of birth or residence, etc.) and/or nearby places that would have covered news from these towns.

Find what you're looking for?

No

Yes

Congrats! Stay on the lookout for even more great research finds.

Newspaper Resources

GENERAL RESOURCES

WEBSITES

Accessible Archives
<www.accessible.com/accessible/index.html>

The Ancestor Hunt
<www.theancestorhunt.com/newspaper-research-links.html>

Ancestry.com
<www.ancestry.com>

CanGenealogy
<cangenealogy.com/newspapers.html>

Chronicling America: Historic American Newspapers
<www.loc.gov/chroniclingamerica/index.html>

Cyndi's List of Genealogy Sites on the Internet
<www.cyndistlist.com>

Elephind.com
<www.elephind.com>

Find A Grave
<www.findagrave.com>

FindMyPast
<www.findmypast.com>

Fold3
<fold3.com>

Google News Archive
<news.google.com/newspapers>

Legacy.com

NewsBank Inc.—
"America's GenealogyBank"
<www.newsbank.com/Genealogists>

NewspaperArchive
<newspaperarchive.com>

Newspapers.com
<www.newspapers.com>

Obitfinder.com
<obitfinder.com>

Obitsarchive.com
<obitsarchive.com>

Old Fulton NY Postcards
<fultonhistory.com/Fulton.html>

The Online Historical Newspapers Site
<sites.google.com/site/
onlinenewspapersite>

ProQuest Historical Newspapers
<www.proquest.com/products-services/
pq-hist-news.html#accordionOne>

Small Town Newspapers
<www.smalltownpapers.com>

BOOKS

*African-American Newspapers and
Periodicals: A National Bibliography*
edited by James P. Danky and Maureen E.
Hady (Harvard University Press, 1999)

*American Newspapers, 1821–1936, A Union
List of Files Available in the United States
and Canada* by Winifred Gregory (H.W.
Wilson Company, 1937)

*Asian-American Periodicals and
Newspapers: A Union List of Holdings
in the Library of the State Historical
Society of Wisconsin and the Libraries
of the University of Wisconsin-Madison*
compiled by Maureen E. Hady and
James P. Danky (Wisconsin Historical
Society, 1979)

*Chronological Tables of American
Newspapers, 1690–1820* by Edward
Connery Lathem (American Antiquarian
Society, 1972)

Collecting America Newspapers by Jim
Lyons (self-published, 1989)

*Ethnic Newspapers: Guide to the Holdings
of the State Historical Society of Wisconsin
Library* by Susan Bryl (Wisconsin
Historical Society, 1975)

*Finding and Using African American
Newspapers* by Timothy N. Pinnick
(Gregarth Publishing Company, 2008)

"Foreign Affairs" by Rick Crume, *Family
Tree Magazine*, March/April 2016

*The German Language Press of the
Americas* (three volumes) by Karl J.R.
Arndt and Mary E. Olsen (K.G. Saur,
1976–1980)

*Guide to Collections Care: Paper,
Photographs, Textiles & Books* by Gaylord
Brothers (self-published, 2014)

A Guide to Labor Papers in the State Historical Society of Wisconsin by F. Gerald Ham and Margaret Hedstrom (State Historical Society of Wisconsin, 1978)

Hispanic Americans in the United States: A Union List of Periodicals and Newspapers Held by the Library of the State Historical Society of Wisconsin and the Libraries of the University of Wisconsin-Madison compiled by Neil E. Strache and James P. Danky (Wisconsin Historical Society, 1979)

Historic German Newspapers Online by Ernest Thode (Genealogical Publishing Co., 2014)

History and Bibliography of American Newspapers, 1690–1820 by Clarence S. Brigham (Greenwood Press, 1976)

How to Find Your Family History in Newspapers by Lisa Louise Cooke (Genealogy Gems Publications, 2012)

Native American Periodicals and Newspapers, 1828–1982: Bibliography, Publishing Record, and Holdings compiled James P. Danky, Maureen E. Hady, and Ann Bowles (Greenwood Press, 1984)

Newspaper Indexes: A Location and Subject Guide for Researchers by Anita Cheek Milner (Scarecrow Press, 1977)

"Newspapers" by Loretto Dennis Szucs and James L. Hansen, The Source: A Guidebook of American Genealogy (Third Edition) edited by Loretto Dennis Szucs and Sandra Hargreaves Luebking (Ancestry, 2006)

Norwegian Newspapers in America: Connecting Norway and the New Land by Odd S. Lovoll (Minnesota Historical Society Press, 2010)

"Obituaries in Genealogy: A Research Tool" by Cari A. Taplin (Legacy QuickGuide series, 2014)

Passengers listed in the Allgemeine Auswanderungs-Zeitung, 1848–1869 by Friedrich R. Wollmershäuser (Masthof Press, 2014)

Polish Newspapers in 1953, A Union List compiled by Jan Wepsiec (Mid-European Studies Center, 1955)

Searching for Your Ancestors in Historic Newspapers by Claudia C. Breland (self-published, 2014)

Trade Union Publications, 1850–1941 by Lloyd G. Reynolds and Charles C. Killingsworth (Johns Hopkins Press, 1944–1945)

Union List of Canadian Newspapers Held by Canadian Libraries (French title, Liste collective des journaux canadiens disponibles dans les bibliothèques cana-diennes) compiled by National Library of Canada, Newspaper Section (National Library of Canada, 1977)

"Using Historical Newspapers for Genealogy Research" by Julie Tarr (Legacy QuickGuide series, 2012)

STATE RESOURCES

ALABAMA

Alabama Department of Archives & History
<digital.archives.alabama.gov/cdm/landingpage/collection/cwnp>

Auburn University Library
<content.lib.auburn.edu/cdm/search/collection/agpapers>

Birmingham Public Library
<www.bplonline.org/resources/digital_project/IronAgeNews.asp>

Jacksonville State University <www.jsu.edu/library/collections/jacksonville_republican.html>

BOOKS

Abstracts from Alabama Newspapers by Larry E. Caver (self-published, 2006)

Alabama Records (several volumes) by Kathleen Paul Jones and Pauline Myra Jones Gandrud (various publishers, 1948–1996)

Allie Abernathy's Scrapbooks, 1893–1923: Marriages, Deaths, and Other Items from Chambers County, Alabama, Newspapers by Laura Alabama Floretta Abernathy (Family Tree, 1987)

By Murder, Accident, and Natural Causes: Death Notices from St. Clair County, Alabama, Newspapers, 1873–1910 by Joseph L. Whitten (Whitten, 2004)

Chilton County, Alabama: Index to Probate Court Records, Abstracts of County Newspapers, County Confederate Veterans by Cecil Little (Boyd Publications, 1999)

Cruising through the Coosa River News: Births, Deaths, Marriages and Other Items of Genealogical Interest Taken from the Coosa River News of Centre, Cherokee County, Alabama by John C. Awbey (self-published, 2007)

Death and Marriage Notices from Autauga County, Alabama Newspapers, 1853–1889 by Larry E. Caver (self-published, 2000)

Death and Marriage Notices from Jefferson County, Alabama Newspapers by Larry E. Caver (Pioneer Publishing Company, 2002)

Death and Marriage Notices from the Montgomery Advertiser (1881) by Larry E. Caver (self-published, 2006)

Death, Marriage and Legal Notices from Tallapoosa County, Alabama Newspapers: 1860–1890 by Larry E. Caver (self-published, 2005)

Death, Marriage and Probate Notices from Montgomery, Alabama Newspapers by Larry E. Caver (Pioneer Publishing Company, 2002)

Footprints in Time: Abstracts from Lawrence County Alabama Newspapers, 1891–1905 by Myra Thrasher Borden (Borden's Genealogical Books, 1993)

From Hollow Stump to Piedmont: Cross Plains, Alabama, 1857–1888: Newspaper Extracts by Josephine Rossiter Woolf (self-published, 2004)

Genealogical Abstracts from Chilton County Newspapers: Clanton, Alabama, 1898 through 1945 by Cecil Little (self-published, 1996)

Genealogical Abstracts from Dallas County, Alabama Newspapers (1823–1865) by Larry E. Caver (Pioneer Publishing Company, 2009)

Genealogical Abstracts from Marengo County, Alabama Newspapers (1840–1910) by Larry E. Caver (Pioneer Publishing Company, 2008)

Genealogical Abstracts from Shelby County, Alabama Newspapers (1868–1888) by Larry E. Caver (Pioneer Publishing Company, 2010)

Genealogical Abstracts from The Autauga Citizen, 1854 in Prattville, Autauga County, Alabama by Charlene Vinson (Heritage Books, 2000)

Genealogical Abstracts from The Banner, 1893 in Clanton, Chilton County, Alabama by Charlene Vinson (Heritage Books, 1999)

Index to Obituaries in the Mobile Register (Mobile Public Library, 1987)

Marriage & Death Notices from Barbour and Henry Counties, Alabama Newspapers, 1846–1890 by Helen S. Foley (Southern Historical Press, 1999)

Marriage Abstracts from Barbour County, Alabama, Newspapers, 1890–1905 by Helen S. Foley (self-published, 1976)

Marriage and Death Notices from Alabama Newspapers and Family Records, 1819–1890 by Helen S. Foley (Southern Historical Press, 2005)

Marriage and Death Notices from the South Western Baptist Newspaper by Michael Kelsey, Nancy Graff-Kelsey, and Ginny Guinn Parsons (Heritage Books, 2007)

Marriage, Death and Legal Notices from Early Alabama Newspapers, 1819–1893 by Pauline Jones Gandrud (Southern Historical Press, 2008)

Miscellaneous Alabama Newspaper Abstracts by Michael Kelsey, Nancy Graff-Kelsey, and Ginny Guinn Parsons (Heritage Books, 1995)

Newspaper Abstracts from Pike County, Alabama by Susie K. Senn (Southern Historical Press, 1999)

Obituaries from Barbour County, Alabama, Newspapers, 1890–1905 by Helen S. Foley (Southern Historical Press, 1992)

People and Things from the Blount County, Alabama News and News-dispatch by Robin Sterling (self-published, 2013)

Pike County, Alabama News, 1860–1864 by Susie K. Senn (self-published, 1995)

Russell County Then ... and Now: A Collection of Articles by John T. Smith (2002)

ALASKA

Alaska State Library
<library.alaska.gov/hist/newspaper/newspaper.html>

BOOKS

1898–1922 Vital Records of Alaska & Yukon (Marriage, Death, Birth, Divorce, Anniversary & Christening): As Reported in the weekly Douglas Island Newspaper, Douglas, Alaska by Betty J Miller (self-published, 1991)

Biographies of Alaska-Yukon Pioneers 1850–1950, Volumes 1-5 by Ed Ferrell (Heritage Books, 1994–2004)

Sitka Sentinel Obituaries by Robert N. DeArmond (self-published, 1992)

ARIZONA

Arizona Memory Project
<azmemory.azlibrary.gov/cdm/newspapers>

BOOKS

Abstract of Chronological Events, 1872–1893: Prescott Miner and Prescott Courier by Louise Polan Turk (self-published, 1990s)

Newspapers and Periodicals of Arizona, 1859–1911 by Estelle Lutrell (University of Arizona, 1950)

ARKANSAS

Arkansas State University
<www.astate.edu>

University of Arkansas
<uark.libguides.com/newspapers/historical>

BOOKS

A History of Batesville and Independence County, Arkansas: Excerpts from Local and Regional Newspapers by Gary Perkey (self-published, 2012)

Abstracts from Crawford County, Ark., Newspapers: Van Buren Press by Evelyn Sue Williams (self-published, 1994)

Abstracts from the Sharp County Record Newspaper: Published in Evening Shade, Arkansas (three volumes) by Desmond Walls Allen (Arkansas Research, 2000–2001)

Arkansas Newspaper Abstracts, 1819–1845 by James Logan Morgan (Arkansas Research, 1992)

Community News Northwest Johnson County, Arkansas, 1912–1923 by Jimmie and Doris Evans Dewberry (Arkansas Research, 2001)

Death Notices in Pocahontas, Randolph County, Arkansas Newspapers, 1873–1910 by Burton Ray Knotts (Arkansas Research, 2000)

Death Records from the Mena Star, 1896–1940 by Sondra R. Wood (Polk County Genealogical Society, 2000s)

Echoes from The Arkansas Unit Newspaper, 1926: Published in Morrilton, Arkansas by Cathy Barnes (Arkansas Research, 1999)

Extracts from the Pilot Newspaper: Morrilton, Conway County, Arkansas, November 14, 1890, through May 4, 1894 by Cathy Barnes (Arkansas Research, 1997)

The Grim Reaper's Footsteps Across the Nation as Mentioned in The Clay County Courier Newspaper, 1893–1925 by Cathy Barnes (Arkansas Research, 2002)

Historical and Genealogical Abstracts from Randolph County, Arkansas Newspapers by Burton Ray Knotts (Arkansas Research, 1999)

Life & Times from the Clay County Courier Newspaper Published in Corning, Arkansas by Cathy Barnes (Arkansas Research, 2000)

Madison County Arkansas Obituaries: An Ongoing Compilation Using Local Newspapers by Hope Hodgdon Creek (self-published, 1987)

Monette, Arkansas, Newspaper Obituaries & Death Notices 1920–1927: Including Formal Obituaries, Death Notices, Funerals Attended, Thank-you Notes for Condolences, Murders and Suicides by Joyce Hambleton Whitten (self-published, 2003)

Obituaries & Deaths from Scott County Newspapers by the Scott County Historical and Genealogical Society (self-published, 1999)

Obituaries of Benton County, Arkansas (nine volumes) by Barbara P. Easley and Verla P. McAnelly (Heritage Books, 1994–1996)

Polk County Newspaper Clips by Shirley Gypsie Cannon (self-published, 1987)

Pulaski County Wills and Administrations, 1820–1900 by Lucille R. Johnson (self-published, 1980)

Searcy County News by Geraldine Littelton et al. (Jim G. Ferguson Library, 2001)

Sherryl's Notes: Abstracts from Newspapers and County Records 1850–1899 by Sherryl Miller (2005)

Siftings from the Morrilton Democrat Newspaper: Published in Morrilton, Arkansas (multiple volumes) by Cathy Barnes (Arkansas Research, 1997–1998)

Vital Records Abstracts from Randolph County, Arkansas, Newspapers of 1928 through 1932 by Burton Ray Knotts (Arkansas Research, 2010)

Warren, Arkansas Newsbriefs: Extracts from the Arkansas Gazette, 1841–1900 by Jann W. Woodard (self-published, 1997)

Yell County, Arkansas, Newspaper Abstracts, 1875–1879 by Faye Greenwood Sandy (Arkansas Research, 1997)

Yell County, Arkansas, Newspaper Abstracts, 1880 by Faye Greenwood Sandy (Arkansas Research, 2000)

Yell County, Arkansas, Newspaper Abstracts, 1881 by Faye Greenwood Sandy (Arkansas Research, 2000)

CALIFORNIA

California Digital Newspaper Collection
<cdnc.ucr.edu/cgi-bin/cdnc>

BOOKS

Butte County, California Newspaper Vitals, 1880–1899 by Paradise Genealogical Society (self-published, 1992)

Gleanings from Alta California: Marriages and Deaths Reported in the First Newspapers Published in California, 1846 through 1850 by Mary Dean Alsworth (Dean Publications, 1980)

Index to Vital Data in Local Newspapers of Sonoma County, California (twelve volumes) by the Sonoma County Genealogical Society (Heritage Books, 2001–2012)

Newspaper Extracts from "The Marin Journal" "Marin County Tocsin": San Rafael, Marin County, California, 1889–1890 by Carolyn Schwab (Heritage Books, 2003)

Newspaper Extracts from Sausalito News, Sausalito, Marin County, California, 1885–1890 by Carolyn Schwab (Marin County Genealogical Society, 2007)

Newspaper Extracts from The Marin County Journal, Sausalito News, Marin County Tocsin, San Rafael, Marin County, California, 1895 to 1896 by Carolyn Schwab (Marin County Genealogical Society, 2007)

Newspaper Extracts from The Marin Journal, Marin County Tocsin San Rafael, Marin County, California, 1889–1890 by Carolyn Schwab (Heritage Books, 2003)

Newspaper Extracts from The Marin Journal, San Rafael, Marin County, California, 1885–1888 by Carolyn Schwab (Heritage Books, 2003)

Santa Cruz County California Marriages: From Early Newspapers (1856–1908) by Sara A. Bunnett (Genealogical Society of Santa Cruz County, 1989)

Santa Cruz County California Marriages: From Early Newspapers and Some Licenses (1909–1919) by Sara A. Bunnett (Genealogical Society of Santa Cruz County, 1991)

The Slav Community of Watsonville, California: As Reported in Old Newspapers (1881–1920) by Thomas Ninkovich (Reunion Research, 2011)

The Slav Community of Watsonville, California: As Reported in Old Newspapers (1920–1929) by Thomas Ninkovich (Reunion Research, 2017)

COLORADO

Colorado Historical Newspapers Collection
<www.coloradohistoricnewspapers.org>

Colorado State Library
<www.cde.state.co.us/cdelib>

BOOKS

Abstracts from Three Early Southern Colorado Newspapers: The Lamar Sparks (1896–1897), The Chronicle News (Oct–Dec 1899), and the Sierra Journal (1881–1883) (1995)

Boulder County, Colorado, Deaths and the Insane, 1859–1900 Newspaper Abstracts by Mary McRoberts (self-published, 1991)

Boulder County, Colorado Marriages, Anniversaries, Divorces, Births and Birthdays: Newspaper Abstracts by Mary Louise Pesek McRoberts (self-published, 1991)

CONNECTICUT

Connecticut State Library: Connecticut Digital Newspaper Project & Guide
<ctstatelibrary.org/collections/newspapers>

BOOKS

Abstracts from the New London Gazette: Covering Southeastern Connecticut (two volumes) 1763–1773 by Richard B. Marrin (Heritage Books, 2007-2008)

Abstracts from The Connecticut (formerly New London) Gazette: Covering Southeastern Connecticut (three volumes) 1774-1782 by Richard B. Marrin (Heritage Books, 2009–2012)

DELAWARE

University of Delaware Library, Delaware Newspapers
<guides.lib.udel.edu/delawarenewspapers>

BOOKS

Buried Genealogical Data: A Complete List of Addressed Letters Left in the Post Offices of Philadelphia, Chester, Lancaster, Trenton, New Castle & Wilmington between 1748 and 1780 by Kenneth Scott and Kenn Stryker-Rodda (Clearfield, 1998)

Delaware Advertiser, 1827–1831: Genealogical Extracts by Margaret M. Frazier (C. Boyer, 1987)

Delaware Genealogical Abstracts from Newspapers (five volumes) by Mary Fallon Richards and John C. Richards (Delaware Genealogical Society, 2000)

Delaware Newspaper Abstracts by F. Edward Wright (Family Line Publications, 1984)

Delaware Runaways, 1720–1783 by Joseph Lee Boyle (Clearfield, 2014)

DISTRICT OF COLUMBIA

Library of Congress
<www.loc.gov>

BOOKS

Abstracts of the Newspapers of Georgetown and the Federal City, 1789–1799 by F. Edward Wright (Willow Bend Books, 2000)

Georgetown, District of Columbia, Marriage and Death Notices, 1801–1838 by Wesley E. Pippenger (Willow Bend Books, 2008)

National Intelligencer & Washington Advertiser Newspaper Abstracts (forty volumes) by Joan M. Dixon (Heritage Books, 1996–2009)

FLORIDA

University of Florida Florida Digital Newspaper Library
<ufdc.ufl.edu/newspapers>

BOOKS

Madison County, Florida, Newspaper Clippings by Elizabeth Evans Kilbourne (Tad Evans, 2005)

GEORGIA

University System of Georgia Digital Library of Georgia
<dlg.galileo.usg.edu/Institutions/gnp.html?Welcome>

BOOKS

Clarke Co., GA, Newspaper Abstracts by Faye Stone Poss (self-published, 1998)

Dodge County Newspaper Clippings by Tad Evans (self-published, 1991)

Genealogical Material from Legal Notices in Early Georgia Newspapers by Folks Huxford (Southern Historical Press, 2007)

Georgia Newspaper Clippings, Dooly County Extracts by Tad Evans (self-published, 2003)

Georgia Newspaper Clippings, Montgomery County Extracts by Tad Evans (self-published, 1998)

Georgia Newspaper Clippings, Telfair County Extracts by Tad Evans (self-published, 1998)

Georgia Newspaper Clippings, Washington County Extracts by Tad Evans (self-published, 1998)

Georgia Newspaper Clippings, Wilcox County Extracts by Tad Evans (self-published, 2000)

Georgia Newspaper Clippings, Wilkinson County Extracts by Tad Evans (self-published, 2002)

Georgia Obituaries, 1740–1935 by Jeannette Holland Austin (self-published, 1993)

Hancock County, Georgia, Newspaper Abstracts, Hancock Advertiser, 1826–1830 by Faye Stone Poss (self-published, 2002)

Jackson County, Georgia Newspaper Clippings, Jackson Herald, February 1881 to December 1882 by Faye Stone Poss (self-published, 2007)

Jackson County, Georgia Newspaper Clippings, The Forest News, June 1875 to January 1881 by Faye Stone Poss (self-published, 2005)

Marriages and Deaths, 1763 to 1820; Abstracted from Extant Georgia Newspapers by Mary Bondurant Warren (Heritage Papers, 1968)

Marriages and Deaths, 1820 to 1830: Abstracted from Extant Georgia Newspapers by Mary Bondurant Warren (Heritage Papers, 1972)

Marriages and Deaths, Accidents, Duels and Runaways, etc.: Compiled from the Weekly Georgia Telegraph, Macon, Georgia by R. Newton Wilcox (Heritage Books, 2002)

Marriages and Obituaries from Early Georgia Newspapers by Folks Huxford (Southern Historical Press, 1989)

The News from Milan, Rhine and Old Telfair by Tad Evans (self-published, 2007)

Pulaski County, Georgia, Newspaper Clippings by Tad Evans (self-published, 2000)

Wilkes County, Georgia, Newspaper Abstracts by Faye Stone Poss (self-published, 2003)

HAWAII

Hawaii Digital Newspaper program

IDAHO

Bear Lake County Library Digital Archives (1880–2010)
<bearlake.advantage-preservation.com>

Blackfoot Newspapers (1880–1902)
<lib.byu.edu/collections/blackfoot-newspapers>

Council Valley Museum (including newspaper abstracts from 1877 to 1950)
<councilmuseum.com/Newspaper%20notes.htm>

East Bonner County Library Digital Archives (1969–1987)
<eastbonner.advantage-preservation.com>

Franklin County Library District Digital Archives (1832–1902, 1905–1961)
<franklincounty.advantage-preservation.com>

Idaho State Archives: Idaho's Digital Newspapers
<history.idaho.gov/digital-newspapers>

Minidoka Irrigator (1942–1945) published by Japanese-American inmates at the Minidoka concentration camp
<ddr.densho.org/?archive.densho.org=1&url=%2fResource%2fSearch.aspx>

Rexburg Newspapers (1909–1921)
<lib.byu.edu/collections/rexburg-newspapers>

Rigby Star (1906–1975)
<contentdm.lib.byu.edu/cdm/search/collection/RigbyStar>

Salmon Public Library Digital Archives (1867, 1886–1967)
<salmon.advantage-preservation.com>

Twin Falls Newspapers (1904–1922)
<abish.byui.edu/library/auth/info/twinFallsArchive.cfm>

Valley of the Tetons District Library Digital Archives (1909–2010)
<tetons.advantage-preservation.com>

ILLINOIS

University of Illinois, University Library
Illinois Digital Newspaper Collections
<idnc.library.illinois.edu>

BOOKS

Abstracts of the Oquawka Spectator by Virginia Ross (McDowell Publications, 1985)

Biographies & Genealogical Abstracts from Hardin County, Illinois, Newspapers, 1872–1938 by Ed Ferrell (Heritage Books, 1999)

Early Kaskaskia, Illinois newspapers, 1814–1832 by Lola Frazer Crowder (Frontier Press, 1994)

Early Marriages of Richland County, Illinois, 1840–1899 by Lola B. Taylor (Taylor Print Shop, 1970)

Early Newspaper Clippings of Hardin County, Illinois: From Uncle George Lavender's Scrapbooks by Marion Lavender Reynolds (self-published, 1994)

Gallatin County, Illinois Newspapers by Shirley Cummins Shewmake (self-published, 1994)

Genealogical Abstracts from Rock Island County, Illinois Newspapers by Janet Kathleen Pease (self-published, 1973)

Genealogical Data from the Monmouth Atlas, Warren County, Illinois, 1846–1855 by Marsha Hoffman Rising (self-published, 1980s)

Hardin County, Illinois Newspaper Abstracts (two volumes) by Marion Lavender Reynolds (self-published, 1992)

Hardin County's People: Miscellaneous Records from the 19th Century by Tony and Hannah Hays (Kitchen Table Press, 1985)

Montgomery County Newspaper Abstracts, 1891–1936 by Shirley Shewmake Manning (Alexander Printing, 2009)

Newspaper Abstracts from McDonough County, Illinois by Janet Kathleen Pease (self-published, 1975)

Pope County Illinois Herald-Enterprise Newspaper Abstracts by Bonnie Barton Skaggs (self-published, 1994)

River Roads to Freedom: Fugitive Slave Notices and Sheriff Notices Found in Illinois Sources by Helen C. Tregillis (Heritage Books, 2012)

INDIANA

Hoosier State Chronicles: Indiana's Digital Historic Newspaper Program
<newspapers.library.in.gov>

Indiana Memory
<digital.library.in.gov>

Indiana State Library
<www.in.gov/library/newspapers.htm>

BOOKS

Hinshaw's Historical Index of Winchester, Indiana, Newspapers, 1857–1984 by Gregory P. Hinshaw (Heritage Books, 2009)

Indiana Newspaper Bibliography: Historical Accounts of All Indiana Newspapers Published from 1804 to 1980 and Locational Information for All Available copies, Both Original and Microfilm by John W. Miller, Paul Brockman, and Patricia Lucken (Indiana Historical Society, 1982)

Local History and Genealogical Abstracts from Jonesboro and Gas City, Indiana Newspapers, 1889–1920 by Ralph D. Kirkpatrick (Heritage Books, 1996)

Local History and Genealogy Abstracts from Fairmount News, Fairmount, Indiana, 1888–1905 by Ralph D. Kirkpatrick (Heritage Books, 1997)

Local History and Genealogical Abstracts from Upland, Indiana Newspapers, 1891–1901 by Ralph D. Kirkpatrick (Heritage Books, 1999)

Local History and Genealogy Abstracts from Marion, Indiana Newspapers (four volumes) by Ralph D. Kirkpatrick (Heritage Books, 2001–2010)

Marriages and Deaths from Indianapolis Newspapers by Ronald L. Darrah (Circle City ComGen, 2002)

New Harmony, Indiana: Newspaper Gleanings by Carroll O. and Gloria M. Cox (Cook-McDowell Publications, 1992)

Newspaper Extracts from "The Hoosier State", Newport, Vermillion County, Indiana (ten volumes) by Carolyn Schwab (Heritage Books, 2005)

Porter County Obituaries and Death Notices by Steven Ross Shook (Northwest Indiana Genealogical Society, 2003)

Spencer County, Ind., Newspaper Abstracts by Sharon Patmore (self-published, 1988)

IOWA

Iowa Digital Newspaper Project
<iowaculture.gov/history/
research/collections/newspapers/
iowa-digital-newspaper-project>

BOOKS

A Bibliography of Iowa Newspapers, 1836–1976 by Alan Schroder (Iowa State Historical Department, 1979)

Warren County, Iowa, Newspapers: Deaths, Probates & Obituaries of Indianola Newspapers by the Warren County Genealogical Society (Iowa Genealogical Society, 1995)

KANSAS

Kansas Digital Newspapers
<www.kshs.org/p/
kansas-digital-newspaper-program/16126

Kansas Newspaper Database (Microfilm and Electronic)
<www.kshs.org/p/
newspapers-in-kansas/11528

BOOKS

The Corning Gazette of Nemaha County, Kansas, Sept. 1898 to Nov 1902: Births, Marriages, Deaths, Everyday Events by Enid Ostertag (Nemaha County Genealogical Society, 1995)

Crittenden Co., KY Newspaper Abstracts by Brenda Joyce Jerome (self-published, 1991)

Index to Births, Marriages, Deaths and Other Items Printed in the Alma Blade, Wabaunsee County News, Alta Vista Bugle, Alta Vista Record, and Progressive Patriot, Wabaunsee County, Kansas between the period of March 14, 1877 and November 22, 1888 by Sylvester C. Ekart (Riley County Genealogical Society, 2011)

KENTUCKY

The Kentucky Edition
<www.uky.edu/Libraries/NDNP/kycollections.html>

BOOKS

The Big Sandy News by Cora Meek Newman (Eastern Kentucky Genealogical Society, 2000)

Early Kentucky Newspapers. Volume IV, Statewide Deaths and Genealogical Abstracts from Clark County, Kentucky Newspapers, 1874–1923 by M.W. Elliston (self-published, 1990s)

Early Louisville, Kentucky Newspaper Abstracts, 1806–1828 by Lola Frazer Crowder (Frontier Press, 1995)

Estill County Kentucky Condensed Abstracts of Obituaries, Feuds, Local News by Ed Puckett (Estill County Historical and Genealogical Society, 1990s)

Excerpts from the Earliest Mason County, Kentucky Newspapers: The Mirror and The Maysville Eagle by Rachelle Winters-Ibrahim (Heritage Books, 2006)

Kentucky Obituaries, 1787–1854 by G. Glenn Clift (Genealogical Publishing Company, 2006)

Morgan County, Kentucky, Best Bits: A Genealogical Abstract Based on the Licking Valley Courier by Corbet Cochran (self-published, 2000)

Newspaper Excerpts from the Maysville Eagle, Mason County, Kentucky, 1827–1847 by Rachelle Winters-Ibrahim (Heritage Books, 2007)

Todd County, Kentucky Newspaper Abstracts by A.B. Willhite (self-published, 1980s)

LOUISIANA

Louisiana State University Louisiana Newspapers
<www.lib.lsu.edu/special/CC/louisiana-newspapers>

BOOKS

Marriages & Deaths from The Caucasian, Shreveport, Louisiana, 1903–1913 by Harry F. Dill (Heritage Books, 2012)

MAINE

Maine Newspaper Project/Digital Maine,
<digitalmaine.com/newspapers>

BOOKS

Grandpa's Scrapbook: His Genealogical Columns as Published in the Deering (Maine) News from 1894–1904 by Leonard Bond Chapman (Heritage Books, 2012)

Index to Portland Newspapers, 1785-1835 by William B. Jordan Jr. (Heritage Books, 1994)

Marriage Notices from the Maine Farmer 1833-1852 by Elizabeth Keene Young and Benjamin Lewis Keene (Heritage Books, 1995)

Vital Records from the Thomaston Recorder of Thomaston, Maine, 1837-1846 by Steven Edward Sullivan (Picton Press, 1995)

MARYLAND

Enoch Pratt Free Library
<www.prattlibrary.org/research/tools/index.aspx?cat=92&id=4885>

Maryland State Archives Online Digitized Newspapers <peccol.mdarchives.state.md.us/pages/newspaper/digitized.aspx>

University of Maryland, McKeldin Library Historic Maryland Newspapers Project <www.lib.umd.edu/digital/newspapers/home>

BOOKS

Abstracts from the Port Tobacco Times and Charles County Advertiser (five volumes) by Roberta J. Wearmouth (Heritage Books, 1990)

Abstracts of Carroll County, Maryland Newspapers, 1831-1846 by Marlene Bates and Martha Reamy (Family Line Publications, 1988)

Abstracts of Marriages and Deaths and Other Articles of Interest in the Newspapers of Frederick and Montgomery Counties, Maryland from 1831–1840 by Larry Tilden Moore (Heritage Books, 2008)

Abstracts of Marriages and Deaths in Harford County, Maryland Newspapers 1837–1871 by Henry C. Peden Jr. (Colonial Roots, 2005)

Abstracts of Marriages and Deaths in the American and Commercial Daily Advertiser, 1831–1836 by Lorrie A. E. Erdman (self-published, 2003)

Along the Potomac River: Extracts from the Maryland Gazette, 1728–1799 by Edith Moore Sprouse (Heritage Books, 2011)

Baltimore's Polish Language Newspapers: Historical & Genealogical Abstracts, 1891–1925 by Thomas L. Hollowak (History Press, 1992)

Caroline County Marriages-Births-Deaths, 1850–1880: Abstracts of Newspapers, Federal Mortality Schedules, and Court Records by F. Edward Wright (Anundsen Publishing Company, 1981)

Frederick County, Maryland Backgrounds by Steve Gilland (Heritage Books, 2012)

Genealogical Abstracts from Newspapers of Maryland's Eastern Shore, 1835–1850: Representing Papers Published in the Counties of Kent, Queen Anne's, Talbot and Caroline, Including News from

Other Maryland Counties and Adjoining States by Irma Sweitzer Harper (self-published, 1995)

The German Correspondent: Translation and Transcription of Marriages, Deaths and Selected Articles of Genealogical Interest by Gary B. Ruppert (Heritage Books, 2008)

Gleanings from Maryland Newspapers, 1786–1790 by Robert William Barnes (Heritage Books, 2011)

Index of Obituaries and Marriages of the [Baltimore] Sun (five volumes) by Joseph C. Maguire Jr. (Heritage Books, 2000–2011)

The King's Passengers to Maryland and Virginia by Peter Wilson Coldham (Heritage Books, 2006)

Marriages and Deaths from Baltimore Newspapers, 1796–1816 by Robert William Barnes (Clearfield, 2005)

Marriages and Deaths from Baltimore Newspapers, 1817–1824 by Henry C. Peden (Colonial Roots, 2011)

Marriages and Deaths from the Baltimore Patriot, 1820–1824 by Michael A. Ports (Genealogical Publishing Company, 2015)

Marriages and Deaths from the Newspapers of Allegany and Washington Counties, Maryland, 1820–1830 by F. Edward Wright (Family Line Publications, 1987)

Marriages and Deaths in the Newspapers of Frederick and Montgomery Counties, Maryland, 1820–1830 by F. Edward Wright (Heritage Books, 2007)

Marriages and Deaths of the Lower Delmarva, 1835–1840: From the Newspapers of Dorchester, Somerset and Worcester Counties, Maryland by F. Edward Wright (Family Line Publications, 1990s)

Maryland Eastern Shore Newspaper Abstracts (eight volumes) by F. Edward Wright (Willow Bend Books, 2000)

Newspaper Abstracts of Allegany and Washington Counties, 1811–1815 by F. Edward Wright (Heritage Books, 2008)

Newspaper Abstracts of Cecil & Harford Counties, 1822–1830 by F. Edward Wright (Heritage Books, 2008)

Newspaper Abstracts of Frederick County (two volumes) by F. Edward Wright (Family Line Publications, 1992)

The Omega Connections: Obituaries from Eastern Shore of Maryland Newspapers, 1850–1900: Over 10,000 Names by Irma Sweitzer Harper (self-published, 1995)

Prince George's County, Maryland, Marriages and Deaths in Nineteenth Century Newspapers (two volumes) by Shirley V. Baltz and George E. Baltz (Heritage Books, 2009)

"Sly Artful Rogues": Maryland Runaways, 1775–1781 by Joseph Lee Boyle (Clearfield, 2014)

Washington County, Maryland, Obituary Locator, 1790–1943 by C. William Ridenour (Willow Bend Books, 2001)

Western Maryland Newspaper Abstracts (three volumes) by F. Edward Wright (Family Line Publications, 1985–1987)

White Maryland Runaways by Joseph Lee Boyle (Clearfield, 2010)

MASSACHUSETTS

State Library of Massachusetts Historical Newspapers <**www.mass.gov/anf/research-and-tech/news-and-current-events/historical-newspapers.html**>

BOOKS

The 1848 Boston Cultivator: Marriages, Deaths and Miscellaneous Readings by Elaine Morrison Fitch (Willow Bend Books, 2003)

The Boston Recorder and Telegraph, 1825 by Elaine Morrison Fitch (Heritage Books, 2004)

Journal of Occurrences: Patriot Propaganda on the British Occupation of Boston, 1768–1769 by Armand Francis Lucier (Heritage Books, 1996)

MICHIGAN

Central Michigan University, Clarke Historical Library Digital Michigan Newspaper Portal <**www.cmich.edu/library/clarke/Pages/Michigan-Digital-Newspaper-Portal.asp**>

BOOK

Bay Breezes: Excerpts from the Traverse Bay Progress, a Newspaper Published in Elk Rapids, Michigan by Glenn Neumann (Elk Rapids Historical Society, 1996)

Eaton County Michigan Newspapers, Vol. 1, 1845–1867 by Joyce Marple Liepens (self-published, 1984)

Genealogical Abstracts from Reported Deaths, the Southwestern Christian Advocate, 1838–1846 by Jonathan Kennon Smith (self-published, 2003)

Kent County, Michigan: Marriage and Death Newspaper Notices: Newspaper Notices from Michigan Newspapers at the Michigan Historical Collections, Bentley Historical Library, University of Michigan by Marguerite Novy Lambert and James N. Jackson (Detroit Society for Genealogical Research, 2001)

Marriage and Death Newspaper Notices, Wayne County, Michigan, 1809–1868: Newspaper Notices from Michigan Newspapers at the Michigan Historical Collections, Bentley Historical Library, University of Michigan by Marguerite

Novy Lambert, James N. Jackson, and the Bentley Historical Library (Detroit Society for Genealogical Research, 2001)

Marshall Marriage and Death Newspaper Notices: Newspaper Notices from Michigan Newspapers at the Michigan Historical Collections, Bentley Historical Library, University of Michigan by Marguerite Novy Lambert and James N. Jackson (Detroit Society for Genealogical Research, 2001)

Ottawa County, Michigan, Newspaper Death Notices, 1851–1856; Newspaper Death & Marriage Notices, 1865–1867; Newspaper Marriage Notices, 1851–1856 by Marguerite Novy Lambert (Detroit Society for Genealogical Research, 1986)

MINNESOTA

Minnesota Historical Society Minnesota Digital Newspaper Hub
<www.mnhs.org/newspapers/hub

BOOKS

Newspaper Extracts from the Martin County Sentinel, Fairmont, Minnesota, 1 January 1879–27 September 1889 by Mary Lou Hackett-Magnuson (Park Genealogical Books, 1997)

Newspapers on the Minnesota Frontier, 1849–1860 by George Sigrud Hage (Minnesota Historical Society, 1967)

Pioneer Stories as Related by Minnesota Czech Residents, 1906–1930: Abstracted and Translated from Hospodář (Farmer) Periodical by Karleen Chott Sheppard and Margie Sobotka (1999)

MISSISSIPPI

Mississippi Department of Archives and History Search Mississippi Newspaper Holdings
<opac2.mdah.state.ms.us/msnews1.php>

BOOKS

Marriages and Deaths from Mississippi Newspapers (four volumes) by Betty Couch Wiltshire (Heritage Books, 1987–2002)

Mississippi Newspaper Obituaries, 1862–1875 by Betty Couch Wiltshire (Pioneer Publishing Company, 1994)

Mississippi Newspaper Obituaries, 1876–1885 by Betty Couch Wiltshire (Pioneer Publishing Company, 1998)

Spreading the Word: Mississippi Newspaper Abstracts of Genealogical Interest, 1825–1935 by Mary Lois S. Ragland (Heritage Books, 1991)

The Woodville Republican: Mississippi's Oldest Existing Newspaper (six volumes) by O'Levia Neil Wilson Wiese (Heritage Books, 1990–2007)

MISSOURI

State Historical Society of Missouri, Missouri Digital Newspaper Project
<shsmo.org/newspaper/mdnp>

BOOKS

Cedar County, Missouri, Death Notices, 1888–1900 and Cemetery Inscriptions: Abstracts from the Stockton Journal, Cedar County Republican, and Eldorado Sun by Marsha Hoffman Rising (Ozarks Genealogical Society, 1988)

Death Notices from Bolivar, Polk County, Missouri, 1870–1893: The Bolivar Free Press, the Bolivar Herald by Marsha Hoffman Rising (Ozarks Genealogical Society, 2002)

DeKalb County, Missouri, Death Notices from Area Newspapers (Northwest Missouri Genealogical Society, 1990s)

Genealogical Data from Southwest Missouri Newspapers, 1850–1860 by Martha Hoffman Rising (self-published, 1985)

Gleanings from the Daily Banner News of St. Charles County by the St. Charles County Genealogical Society (self-published, 2003)

Jefferson County Leader: Hillsboro, Jefferson County, Missouri by Charlotte M. Maness (self-published, 1992)

Missouri Marriages in the News by Lois Stanley et al. (Southern Historical Press, 1990)

Missouri Obituaries: Abstracts of Obituaries Published Weekly in the St. Louis Christian Advocate a Publication of the Methodist Episcopal Church, South by Mrs. Howard W. Woodruff (self-published, 1985)

Missourians in the Civil War: (Transcribed from Missouri Newspapers) by Kenneth Weant (self-published, 2012)

Obituaries: St. Charles, Missouri Newspapers by Gertrude Pfeiffer Johnson (St. Charles Genealogical Society, 1992)

Paper Pickin' by Twila Johnson Beck (self-published, 1989)

Pulaski County Obituaries, 1902–1952: Obituaries Taken from Pulaski County Newspapers Including Name, Birth, Death and Marriages: Includes Children, Parents, Number of Siblings, and Obituary Date by Chris Rowell (Genealogy Society of Pulaski County, Missouri, 1994)

Ripley County (Missouri) Records: Obituaries 1874–1910 by Thelma S. McManus (self-published, 1992)

Southwest Missouri Newspaper Abstracts by Ruth E. Browning (self-published)

Springfield, Greene County, Missouri Newspaper Abstracts by William Kearney Hall (Ozarks Genealogical Society, 1987)

Springfield, MO, Obituaries, 1932, with Other Items and Index by William Kearney Hall (self-published, 2001)

MONTANA

Montana Historical Society Montana Newspapers
<montananewspapers.org>

NEBRASKA

Nebraska State Historical Society Nebraska Newspaper Project
<www.nebraskahistory.org/lib-arch/whadoin/newspapr.htm>

BOOKS

Nebraska Newspaper Abstracts by the Nebraska State Genealogical Society (self-published, 1999)

Nova Doba (New Era): Abstractions & Translations, Deaths & Obits by Margie Sobotka (Eastern Nebraska Genealogical Society, 1984)

Wayne County, Nebraska, Newspaper Abstracts, 1876–1899 by Maureen M. Lee (Heritage Books, 2008)

NEVADA

University of Nevada, Las Vegas, University Libraries, Nevada Digital Newspaper Project
<nvdnp.wordpress.com>

BOOKS

Births, Marriages and Deaths, 1871–1879: (With Missing Dates) Published in the Nevada State Journal by Nona Parkin (1964)

The Newspapers of Nevada: A History and Bibliography, 1854–1979 by Richard E. Lingenfelter and Karen Rix Gash (University of Nevada Press, 1984)

NEW HAMPSHIRE

New Hampshire State Library, New Hampshire Newspaper Project
<www.nh.gov/nhsl/nhais/newspaper_project.html>

BOOKS

Genealogical Abstracts from Early New Hampshire Newspapers by Scott Lee Chipman (Heritage Books, 2000)

Manchester in the Mirror: Abstracts from The Mirror & Farmer Newspaper, Manchester, New Hampshire, 1865–1866 by Milli S. Kenney-Knudsen (Heritage Books, 2003)

New Hampshire Patriot and State Gazette 1824: Deaths, Marriages and Miscellaneous by Elaine Morrison Fitch (Heritage Books, 2007)

New Hampshire Patriot and State Gazette 1835, Deaths, Marriages and Miscellaneous by Elaine Morrison Fitch (Heritage Books, 2007)

NEW JERSEY

New Jersey State Archives, New Jersey Digital Newspaper Project
<blogs.libraries.rutgers.edu/njdnp>

BOOKS

Buried Genealogical Data: A Complete List of Addressed Letters Left in the Post Offices of Philadelphia, Chester, Lancaster, Trenton, New Castle & Wilmington between 1748 and 1780 by Kenneth Scott and Kenn Stryker-Rodda (Genealogical Publishing Co., 1977)

Notices from New Jersey Newspapers, 1781–1790 by Thomas B. Wilson (Hunterdon House, 1988)

Notices from New Jersey Newspapers, 1791–1795. Records of New Jersey, Volume III by Thomas B Wilson (Hunterdon House, 2002)

One Hundred Years of the "Sussex Register" and County of Sussex (New Jersey), 1813–1913: Record of Historical, Biographical, Industrial, and Statistical Events During a Century by Whitfield Gibbs (Heritage Books, 2007)

NEW MEXICO

University of New Mexico, University Libraries, New Mexico Digital Newspapers
<econtent.unm.edu/cdm/landingpage/collection/dignews>

BOOKS

The Santa Fe Trade: Selected Newspaper Articles, 1813–1846 by Gary D. Lenderman (self-published, 2011)

NEW YORK

NYS Historic Newspaper Project
<nyshistoricnewspapers.org>

BOOKS

Abstracts from Madison County, New York Newspapers in the Cazenovia Public Library by Mary Keysor Meyer et al. (Pipe Creek Publications, 1991)

Abstracts of Utica Sentinel & Gazette Newspapers: Oneida County, New York (Hanson Heritage Publications, 1980)

A Collection of Abstracts from Otsego County, New York, Newspaper Obituaries, 1808–1875 by Gertrude Audrey Barber (Heritage Books, 2008)

Death and Marriage Notices, Tompkins County, New York, 1870–1890 by Nancy E. Greene-Young (Heritage Books, 1996)

Deaths, Births and Marriages from Newspapers Published in Hamilton, Madison County, N.Y., 1818–1886 by Mrs. E.P. Smith et al. (Pipe Creek Publications, 1996)

Deaths, Marriages, and Miscellaneous from Hudson, New York, Newspapers: The Balance and Columbian Repository, 1802–1811 and the Rural Repository or Bower of Literature, 1824–1851 by Arthur C. M. Kelly (self-published, 1979)

Deaths Notices Copied from the "Cooperstown Federalist": From 1808–1809; Death Notices Copied from

"Watch Tower": From 1828–1831, Deaths pp. 1–11; Marriage Notices Copied from "Cooperstown Federalist": From 1808–1812; Marriage Notices Copied from "Watch Tower": From 1828–1831, Marriages pp. 12–26 by Gertrude A. Barber (1933)

Death Notices from Steuben County, New York Newspapers, 1797–1884 by Mary S. Jackson and Edward F. Jackson (Heritage Books, 2006)

Death Notices from Washington County, New York, Newspapers, 1799–1880 by Mary S. Jackson and Edward F. Jackson (Heritage Books, 1995)

Early Marriages from Newspapers Published in Central New York by William M. Beauchamp et al. (Heritage Books, 2007)

Genealogical Abstracts from Palmyra, Wayne County, New York, Newspapers 1810–1854 by S.D. Van Alstine and Harriet Wiles (Heritage Books, 2014)

Genealogical Gleanings Abstracted from the Early Newspapers of Penn Yan, Yates County, New York, 1823–1833 and 1841–1855 by Dianne Stenzel (Heritage Books, 1991)

In Remembrance II: Abstracts of Marriage & Death Notices, 1882 Brooklyn Daily Eagle Newspaper, Brooklyn, New York by Maggie Coletta (Heritage Books, 1999)

Irish Relatives and Friends: From "Information Wanted" Ads in the Irish-American, 1850–1871 by Laura Murphy DeGrazia & Diane Fitzpatrick Haberstroh (Genealogical Publishing Company, 2001)

Marriage and Death Notices from Schuyler County, New York Newspapers by Mary Smith Jackson and Edward F. Jackson (Heritage Books, 2006)

Marriage and Death Notices from Seneca County, New York Newspapers, 1817–1885 by Mary S. Jackson and Edward F. Jackson (Heritage Books, 2007)

Marriage and Death Notices from Tompkins County, New York, Newspapers by Mary Smith Jackson and Edward F. Jackson (Heritage Books, 2005)

Marriage and Death Records Abstracted from the Newark Weekly Courier, 1869–1873 by Harriet Wiles (Heritage Books, 2004)

Marriages and Deaths Reported in the Fishkill Standard, Fishkill Landing, New York, 1874–1877 by Katharine M. Chamberlain (Heritage Books, 2000)

Marriage Notices from Steuben County, New York, Newspapers, 1797–1884 by Mary S. Jackson and Edward F. Jackson (Heritage Books, 1998)

Marriage Notices from Washington County, New York, Newspapers, 1799–1880 by Mary S. Jackson and Edward F. Jackson (Heritage Books, 1995)

Marriages and Deaths from Steuben County, New York Newspapers, 1797–1868 by Yvonne E. Martin (Heritage Books, 1988)

Marriages from The Saugerties Telegraph 1846-1870 and Obituaries, Death Notices and Genealogical Gleanings from The Ulster Telegraph 1846–1848 by Audrey M. Klinkenberg. (Heritage Books, 2008)

Marriages from The Saugerties Telegraph, 1871–1884 by Audrey M. Klinkenberg (Heritage Books, 2012)

Marriages of Suffolk County, N.Y.: Taken from the "Republican Watchman", a Newspaper Published in Greenport, N.Y. by Gertrude A. Barber (1950)

Marriages Taken from the Otsego Herald & Western Advertiser and Freeman's Journal: Newspapers at the Cooperstown, N.Y. Library by Gertrude A. Barber (1932)

Notices of Marriages and Deaths, about 4,000 in Number, Published in Newspapers Printed at Poughkeepsie, New York, 1778–1825 by Helen Wilkinson Reynolds (Gateway Press, 1982)

Obituaries, Death Notices and Genealogical Gleanings from the Saugerties Telegraph (five volumes) by Audrey M. Klinkenberg (Heritage Books, 1989)

Orange County Patriot: a Newspaper Published at Goshen, N.Y. Marriages and Deaths from May 1828 to Dec. 1831 by Gertrude A. Barber (1935)

Sullivan County, N.Y.: Marriages, May 15, 1846–Nov. 15 1850: Deaths May 15, 1845–Aug. 4, 1848 by Joan Maynard (1934)

Town of Wilmington, Essex County, New York, Transcribed Serial Records by Harold E. Hinds Jr. and Tina M. Didreckson (Willow Bend Books, 2013)

Vital Statistics from Chittenango, New York, Newspapers, 1831–1854 by Clara Metcalf Houck et al. (Pipe Creek Publication, 1994)

NORTH CAROLINA

State Archives of North Carolina North Carolina Newspaper Digitization Project **<exhibits.archives.ncdcr.gov/newspaper/index.html>**

BOOKS

Abstracts of Vital Records from Raleigh, North Carolina, Newspapers by Lois S. Neal et al. (Reprint Company, 1979)

Deaths and Marriages from Tarboro, North Carolina, Newspapers, 1824–1865 by Hugh Buckner Johnston (Southern Historical Press, 1985)

Marriage and Death Notices from Extant Asheville, N.C., Newspapers, 1840–1870: An Index by Robert M. Topkins (North Carolina Genealogical Society, 1977)

The True Republican, or American Whig: "The Truth Our Guide—The Public Good Our End." 1809, Wilmington, North Carolina by Joseph E. Waters Sheppard (Heritage Books, 2008)

NORTH DAKOTA

State Historical Society of North Dakota, North Dakota Newspaper Index
<history.nd.gov/archives/whatnewspapers.htm>

OHIO

Ohio History Connection/State Library of Ohio, Ohio's Digitized Newspapers
<www.ohiohistoryhost.org/ohiomemory/newspapers>

BOOKS

Abstracts and Extracts from Athens County, Ohio Newspapers, 1890: Part I, The Athens Herald and the Athens Journal by Mary L. Bowman (Athens County Genealogical Society and Athens County Historical Society and Museum, 1992)

Clark County, Ohio Newspaper Abstracts, 1829–1832: Obituaries-marriages and Selected Genealogical Notes by Anne Burgstaller Snodgrass (Clark County Genealogical Society, 1991)

Clinton County, Ohio Newspapers, Death and Obituary Abstracts: 1838 to 1867 by Larry D. Mart (1973)

Clinton County Newspaper Abstracts by Joyce Hopkins Pinkerton et al. (Clinton County Genealogical Society, 2000)

Columbiana County, Ohio, Newspaper Abstracts by Carol Willsey Bell (Heritage Books, 1987)

Columbiana Ledger: Newspaper Abstracts from the Village of Columbiana, Ohio by Dorothy Yakubek and DeWayne C. McCarty (Closson Press, 2009)

Genealogical Abstracts from Loudonville, Ashland County, Ohio Newspapers: March 20, 1873 to Sept. 1, 1892 by Thelma S. Ungerer (self-published, 1970s)

Guide to Ohio Newspapers, 1793–1973: Union Bibliography of Ohio Newspapers Available in Ohio Libraries by Stephen Gutgesell (Ohio Historical Society, 1976)

Index of Death and Other Notices Appearing in the Cincinnati Free Presse, 1874–1920 by Jeffrey G. Herbert. (Heritage Books, 2011)

Index of Death Lists Appearing in the Cincinnatier Zeitung, 1887–1901 by Jeffrey G. Herbert (Hamilton County Chapter Ohio Genealogical Society, 2010)

Index of Death Notices and Marriages Notices Appearing in the Cincinnati Daily Gazette, 1827–1881 by Jeffrey G. Herbert (Heritage Books, 2007)

Index of Death Notices Appearing in the Cincinnati Commercial, 1858–1899 by Jeffrey G. Herbert (Ohio Genealogical Society, 1996)

Index of Death Notices Appearing in the Cincinnati Daily Times, 1840–1879 by Jeffrey G. Herbert (Heritage Books, 1994)

Index of Death Notices Appearing in the Cincinnati Volksblatt, 1846–1918 by Jeffrey G. Herbert (Heritage Books, 1998)

Marietta, Ohio Genealogy Notes by Paul Immel (Carol Montrose, 2004)

News from Marion: Marion County, Ohio, 1844–1861 by Sharon Moore (Heritage Books, 1995)

Newspaper Abstracts, Huron County, Ohio, 1822–1835 by Henry R. Timman (self-published, 1974)

Obituary Abstracts 1850–1890 from Eaton Register & Eaton Democrat Newspapers in Eaton, Preble County, Ohio by Audrey Gilbert (McDowell Publications, 1981)

Obituary Abstracts from the Ashland Times and Gazette Newspapers, Ashland, Ashland County, Ohio by Rita Bone Kopp (Ashland County Chapter of the Ohio Genealogical Society, 1991)

Ohio Patriot Abstracts: June 16, 1810 to December 27, 1866 by Carol W. Bell et al. (Columbiana County Chapter of the Ohio Genealogical Society, 2010)

Pioneer Ohio Newspapers, 1793–1810: Genealogical and Historical Abstracts by Karen Mauer Green (Frontier Press, 1986)

Pioneer Ohio Newspapers, 1802–1818: Genealogical and Historical Abstracts by Karen Mauer Green (Frontier Press, 1988)

Scioto County, Ohio, Newspaper Abstracts and Historical Reminiscences, 1866–1869 by Barbara Keyser Gargiulo (Little Miami Publishing Company, 2006)

Trumbull County, Ohio, Newspaper Obituary Extracts, 1812–1870 by Michael Barren Clegg (self-published, 1981)

The Willshire Herald: Newspaper Extractions of Births, Marriages, Deaths, Divorces, and Military Service of Citizens Living in and around Willshire, Van Wert County, Ohio by Kathryn Case Moore and Carol Montrose (self-published, 2005)

OKLAHOMA

Oklahoma Historical Society, Oklahoma Digital Newspaper Program <gateway.okhistory.org/explore/collections/ODNP>

BOOKS

Births and Deaths, 1874–1944, from Bryan County, OK Newspapers by Marion Downs (Bryan County Heritage Association, 2000)

Gardens of Stone, Harper County, Oklahoma: Cemetery, Funeral Home, and Newspaper Accounts by Deone K. Pearcy (T. P. Productions, 1995)

Jefferson County, OK, Personals: Abstracts from Various County Newspapers, 1893–1944 by Linda Norman Garrison (Southwest Oklahoma Genealogical Society, 2010)

Kiowa County, OK, Personals by Linda Norman Garrison (Southwest Oklahoma Genealogical Society, 2010)

Obituaries, Death Notices and News Items Extracted from the Vian Press by Fran Alverson Warren (2001)

Obituaries, Yukon Oklahoma: Copied from Canadian County, Oklahoma Newspapers, 1908–1949 by the Yukon Chapter of the Daughters of the American Revolution (self-published, 1990s)

Tillman County Personals: Abstracts from Frederick, OK Newspapers, May 1902–June 1911 by Linda Norman Garrison (Southwest Oklahoma Genealogical Society, 2009)

OREGON

University of Oregon Libraries, Oregon Digital Newspaper Project
<oregonnews.uoregon.edu>

BOOKS

Marion County, Oregon, Newspaper Abstracts: The Stayton Mail, December 1896 thru June 1908 by Daraleen Phillips Wade (self-published, 1988)

The Medford Mail Newspaper Abstracts by Ruby Lacy and Lida Childers (self-published, 1993)

The Medford Sun: Newspaper Abstracts by Ruby Lacy and Lida Childers (self-published, 1991)

Southern Oregonian Newspaper Abstracts by Lida Childers and Ruby Sullivan Lacy (self-published, 1988)

PENNSYLVANIA

Lancaster County Digitization Project
<lcdp.wikifoundry.com>

Penn State University Libraries, Civil War Newspaper Collection
<digitalnewspapers.libraries.psu.edu/Olive/APA/CivilWar/?skin=civilwar#panel=home>

Pennsylvania Digital Newspaper Project,
<libraries.psu.edu/about/departments/preservation-conservation-and-digitization/pa-newspaper-project/pennsylvania>

State Library of Pennsylvania, Pennsylvania Historical Newspapers
<digitalcollections.powerlibrary.org/cdm/landingpage/collection/sstlp-newsp>

BOOKS

8736 Marriages, 1866–1900, Old Newspapers, Westmoreland County, Pennsylvania by Della Reagan Fischer (self-published, 1970)

Abstracts from Ben Franklin's Pennsylvania Gazette, 1728–1748 by Kenneth Scott (Genealogical Publishing Company, 1975)

Abstracts (Mainly Deaths) from the Pennsylvania gazette, 1775–1783 by Kenneth Scott (Genealogical Publishing Co., 1976)

Abstracts of South Central Pennsylvania Newspapers, 1785–1800 (three volumes) by F. Edward Wright and Martha Reamy (Family Line Publications, 1988)

Abstracts of the Christian Herald: February 23, 1844–November 6, 1846 by Paul Keith Heckethorn (Closson Press, 2011)

Buried Genealogical Data: A Complete List of Addressed Letters Left in the Post Offices of Philadelphia, Chester, Lancaster, Trenton, New Castle & Wilmington between 1748 and 1780 by Kenneth Scott and Kenn Stryker-Rodda (Genealogical Publishing Co., 1977)

Deaths Reported by Der Libanon Demokrat: A German Language Newspaper Published at Lebanon, Pennsylvania, 1832–1864 by Robert A. Heilman (Heritage Books, 1990)

Early Deaths and Marriages in Armstrong County, Pennsylvania from Kitanning Area Newspapers by Constance Louise Leinweber Mateer (Closson Press, 1996)

Extracts from the Bedford Gazette, Bedford County, Pennsylvania, September 7, 1832– September 9, 1836 by Caryl A. Mitchell (Willow Bend Books, 2001)

Genealogical Data Relating to the German Settlers of Pennsylvania and Adjacent Territory: From Advertisements in German Newspapers Published in Philadelphia and Germantown, 1743–1800 by Edward W. Hocker (Genealogical Pub. Co., 1980)

Hollidaysburg Records: Marriages, Deaths & Partitions from Weekly Newspapers of Hollidaysburg, Huntingdon/Clair Cos., Pa., 1836–1852 by K. T. H. McFarland (Closson Press, 1994)

Marriage and Death Notices Extracted from the Genius of Liberty and Fayette Advertiser of Uniontown, Pennsylvania, 1805–1854 by Jean R. Rentmeister (Closson Press, 1981)

Marriage and Death Notices Transcribed from the Pages of the Lebanon Valley Standard, 1871–1879 by Robert A. Heilman (Heritage Books, 2009)

Marriages and Deaths from the Newspapers of Lancaster County, Pennsylvania by F. Edward Wright (Willow Bend Books, 2000)

Marriages and Deaths of Cumberland County, 1821–1830 by F. Edward Wright (Heritage Books, 2008)

Marriages and Deaths Reported by Der Pennsylvanier, a German Language Newspaper Published at Lebanon, Pennsylvania by Robert A. Heilman (self-published, 1991)

Newspaper Abstracts from the Philadelphia Repository, 1803 by Elaine Morrison Fitch (Willow Bend Books, 2005)

Newspaper Accounts of Births, Marriages, and Deaths: 1808–1929 (Not All Inclusive) Westmoreland County, Pennsylvania by Mary Jane Mains (Westmoreland County Historical Society, 1994)

Runaways, Rascals, and Rogues: Missing Spouses, Servants, and Slaves: Abstracts from Lancaster County, Pennsylvania, Newspapers by Gary T. Hawbaker (self-published, 1987)

White Pennsylvania Runaways by Joseph Lee Boyle (Clearfield, 2015)

Written in Stone: Obituary Abstracts from Indiana County Newspapers 1894 thru 1900 by D. S. Leathers (WordWorks Publishing, 2011)

RHODE ISLAND

Rhode Island Historical Society, Rhode Island Newspaper Project
<www.rihs.org/newspapers-and-periodicals>

BOOKS

Runaways, Deserters, and Notorious Villains from Rhode Island Newspapers (two volumes) by Maureen Alice Taylor (Picton Press, 2001)

Vital Record of Rhode Island: 1636–1850. First series: Births, Marriages and Deaths: A Family Register for the People by James N. Arnold (Narragansett Historical Publishing Company, 1990s)

SOUTH CAROLINA

University of South Carolina, University Libraries, South Carolina Digital Newspaper Program
<library.sc.edu/digital/newspaper>

BOOKS

Abstracts from The Pickens Sentinel, Pickens, South Carolina, 1875–1915 by Judy Chandler Ballard (Southern Historical Press, 2003)

Early Anderson County, S. C. Newspapers, Marriages and Obituaries, 1841–1882 by Tom C. Wilkinson (Southern Historical Press, 1978)

Marriage and Death Notices from Baptist Newspapers of South Carolina by Brent H. Holcomb (Reprint Company, 1981)

Marriage and Death Notices from Camden, South Carolina Newspapers, 1816–1865 by Brent H. Holcomb (Southern Historical Press, 2006)

Marriage and Death Notices from the Charleston Observer, 1827–1845 by Brent H. Holcomb (Heritage Books, 2008)

Marriage and Death Notices from Columbia, South Carolina, Newspapers, 1792–1839 by Brent H. Holcomb (Southern Historical Press, 1982)

Marriage and Death Notices from the Up-country of South Carolina as Taken from Greenville Newspapers, 1826–1863 by Brent H. Holcomb (self-published, 1983)

Marriage and Death Notices from Upper S.C. Newspapers, 1843–1865: Abstracts from Newspapers of Laurens, Spartanburg, Newberry, and Lexington Districts by Brent H. Holcomb (Southern Historical Press, 1977)

Marriages from the Carolina Spartan Newspapers, 1866–1869 by Faye Berry Emory (Piedmont Historical Society, 1983)

Miscellaneous Abstracts from Pre-Civil War Cheraw, South Carolina Newspapers by James C. Pigg (self-published, 1996)

The People's Journal: Pickens, South Carolina, 1894–1903: Historical and Genealogical Abstracts by Peggy Burton Rich (Heritage Books, 2010)

The Pickens Sentinel: Favorite Newspaper of Pickens County: Pickens Court House, South Carolina, 1872–1893: Historical and Genealogical Abstracts by Peggy Burton Rich and Marion Ard Whitehurst (Heritage Books, 1994)

Some South Carolina Marriages & Obituaries and Miscellaneous Information 1826–1854 by Robert F. Simpson Jr. and Mrs. Charles R. Barham Jr. (self-published, 1978)

York, South Carolina, Newspapers: Marriage, and Death notices, 1823–1865 by Brent H. Holcomb (Reprint Company, 2010)

SOUTH DAKOTA

BOOKS

Extractions of Vital Statistics and Interesting Articles from the Black Hills Area by the Rapid City Society for Genealogical Research (1987)

Newspaper Extracts from Java, South Dakota 1903–1918 by Linda Johnson (self-published, 1991)

Newspaper Extracts from the Pioneer Press Miller, SD 1899–1903 by Maurice Krueger (South Dakota Genealogical Society, 1992)

TENNESSEE

University of Tennessee Libraries, Tennessee State Library and Archives, Tennessee Newspaper Digitization Project <www.lib.utk.edu/tndp>

BOOKS

Genealogical Abstracts from Tennessee Newspapers, 1791–1808 by Sherida K. Eddlemon (Heritage Books, 1998)

Genealogical Abstracts from Tennessee Newspapers, 1803–1812 by Sherida K. Eddlemon (Heritage Books, 1989)

Genealogical Abstracts from Tennessee Newspapers, 1821–1828 by Sherida K. Eddlemon (Heritage Books, 1998)

Genealogical and Historical Notes from Crossville, Tennessee Newspapers by Michael W. Boniol (self-published, 1995)

Hardin County's People: Miscellaneous Records from the 19th Century by Tony and Hannah Hays (Kitchen Table Press, 1986)

Marriages from Early Tennessee Newspapers, 1794–1851 by S. Emmett Lucas (Southern Historical Press, 1978)

Maury County, Tennessee Newspapers, Abstracts, 1810–1844 by Jill Knight Garrett (1965)

Obituaries from Early Tennessee Newspapers, 1794–1851 by S. Emmett Lucas (Southern Historical Press, 1978)

Obituaries from Tennessee Newspapers by Jill L. Garrett (Southern Historical Press, 1995)

Shelby County, Tennessee, Newspaper Abstracts through 1859 by Helen Rowland (Mountain Press, 2002)

TEXAS

University of North Texas, Texas Digital Newspaper Program
<texashistory.unt.edu/explore/collections/TDNP>

BOOKS

Abstracts from the Northern Standard and the Red River District (seven volumes) by Richard B. Marrin and Lorna Geer Sheppard (Heritage Books, 2006–2010)

Abstracts of Early East Texas Newspapers, 1839–1856 by Linda Cheves Nicklas (Southern Historical Press, 1994)

Births, Deaths & Marriages from El Paso Newspapers … for Arizona, Texas, New Mexico, Oklahoma, and Indian Territory by Jane Beard and the El Paso Genealogical Society (Southern Historical Press, 1982)

Early Texas News, 1831–1848: Abstracts from Early Texas Newspapers by Helen Smothers Swenson (self-published, 1984)

Genealogical Abstracts of Wood County, Texas, Newspapers Before 1920 by the Wood County Genealogical Society (Heritage Books, 2012)

Kerrville Daily Times Obituary Index, 1925 to April 30, 1979 by Gloria C. Dozier (Willow Bend Books, 2004)

Miscellaneous Texas Newspaper Abstracts: Deaths (two volumes) by Michael Kelsey et al. (Heritage Books, 1997–2007)

Rains County Leader, 1912 by Elaine Nall Bay (Heritage Books, 1998)

San Antonio, Texas, Newspapers: Abstractions Nov. 17, 1848–Nov. 11, 1865 by Janey Eaves Joyce (San Antonio Genealogical & Historical Society, 2001)

Texas Baptist Newspaper Abstracts: 7 March 1855–21 February 1884 by Helen M Lu (Dallas Genealogical Society, 1992)

Texas Methodist Newspaper Abstracts by Helen M. Lu (self-published, 1997)

UTAH

University of Utah, J. Willard Marriott Library, Utah Digital Newspapers
<digitalnewspapers.org>

BOOKS

Salt Lake City Old Newspaper Clippings by Louise Kimball Clark (1989)

VERMONT

Vermont Department of Libraries, Vermont State Archives and Records Administration, Vermont Digital Newspaper Project
<libraries.vermont.gov/online_library/digital_newspapers>

BOOKS

Vermont Newspaper Abstracts, 1783–1816 by Marsha Hoffman Rising (New England Historic Genealogical Society, 2001)

VIRGINIA

Library of Virginia, Virginia Chronicle
<www.virginiachronicle.com>

BOOKS

Caroline County, Virginia Death Records, (1919–1994) from the Caroline Progress, a Weekly Newspaper Published in Bowling Green, Virginia by Herbert Ridgeway Collins (Heritage Books, 1995)

Genealogical Abstracts from 18th-Century Virginia Newspapers by Robert K. Headley Jr. (Genealogical Publishing Company, 1987)

Genealogical Abstracts from The Democratic Mirror and The Mirror, Loudoun County, Virginia by Patricia B. Duncan (Heritage Books, 2008)

Genealogical Abstracts from The Telephone, Loudoun County, Virginia by Patricia B. Duncan (Heritage Books, 2008)

Index to Marriage Notices in The Religious Herald, Richmond, Virginia, 1828–1938 by the Historical Records Survey of Virginia (Works Progress Administration, 1941)

Marriage and Death Notices from Alexandria, Virginia Newspapers, 1784–1852 by Wesley E. Pippenger (self-published, 2005)

Marriages and Deaths from Lynchburg, Virginia Newspapers, 1794–1836 by Lucy Harrison Miller Baber, Louise A. Blunt, and Marion Armistead Lewis Collins (Genealogical Publishing Company, 1980)

Marriages and Deaths from Richmond, Virginia Newspapers, 1780–1820 by the Virginia Genealogical Society (self-published, 1983)

Obituary Notices from the Alexandria Gazette, 1784–1915 by Lloyd House (Willow Bend Books, 1997)

The Virginia Journal and Alexandria Advertiser (four volumes) by Wesley E. Pippenger and James D. Munson (Family Line Publications, 1998–2001)

WASHINGTON

Washington State Library, Historical Newspapers in Washington
<www.sos.wa.gov/library/newspapers/newspapers.aspx>

BOOKS

50 Years of Vital Records Extracted from Bellevue, Washington, Newspapers, 1918–1967: "Lake Washington Reflector, Bellevue American" by Eastside Genealogical Society and Melissa Hanson Clausen (self-published, 1989)

Kent Area Marriages Extracted from Early Kent, Washington Newspapers by South King County Genealogical Society (self-published, 1991)

Kent Area Obituaries Extracted from Early Kent, Washington Newspapers by South King County Genealogical Society (self-published, 1988–1991)

Lewis County, Washington, Newspaper Abstracts by Ruby Simonson McNeill and Sharon Hunt Lyden (1978)

Newspaper Genealogical Abstracts, The Morning/Daily Olympian: Thurston County, Washington, 1891–1907 by Esther Raymond Knox (Olympia Genealogical Society, 1988)

Obituaries Extracted from Renton Record Chronicle Newspaper by the South King Genealogical Society (self-published, 1991)

WEST VIRGINIA

West Virginia University Libraries
<lib.wvu.edu/collections/collection.php?id=48>

BOOKS

Abstracts of Early Monongalia County, Virginia Newspapers 1816–1842 by Joy L. Gilchrist (Hacker's Creek Pioneer Descendants, 1997)

WISCONSIN

Wisconsin Historical Society, BadgerLink Archive of Wisconsin Newspapers
<badgerlink.dpi.wi.gov/resource/archive-wisconsin-newspapers> (Note: Wisconsin residents only)

BOOKS

Births, Deaths, Marriages and Other Genealogical Gleanings from Newspapers for Crawford, Vernon and Richland Counties, Wisconsin, 1873–1910 by Vernon D. Erickson (Heritage Books, 1997)

Genealogical Gleanings from Early Newspapers for Residents in and Near Crawford County, Wisconsin, 1897–1902 by Vernon D. Erickson (Heritage Books, 1999)

WYOMING

Wyoming State Library, Wyoming Newspapers

Creating a Newspaper Chronology

You may want to create a historical timeline to document a newspaper history if your research concerns a particular area throughout several years. This will help you track all the newspapers in an area during a given time, allowing you to keep titles and time periods straight as you view (at a glance) what publications your ancestors may have been mentioned in. While you may find many sets of variables for creating your own, this appendix has some guidelines that may be helpful, along with links to Excel templates to get you started.

Before you go through the instructions and call up the templates, you'll first need to do your homework on Chronicling America's "US Newspaper Directory" **<chroniclingamerica. loc.gov/search/titles>** to get the full list of newspapers in an area for which you want to build the timeline. You'll primarily be looking for the titles and year of publication start and stop dates. See chapter 10 for more in-depth coverage of this resource.

1

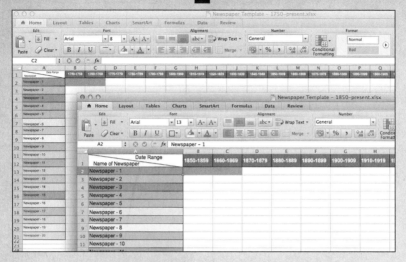

1 **Select your spreadsheet template**. Once you have your list of newspapers in front of you—either cut-and-pasted from the US Newspaper Directory or recorded in your own written compilation—use the templates found at **<bit.ly/ft-newspapers-guide-downloads>** to put that data into a spreadsheet. Select either the "1850-present" or "1750-present" template, based on the time period you're researching.

2

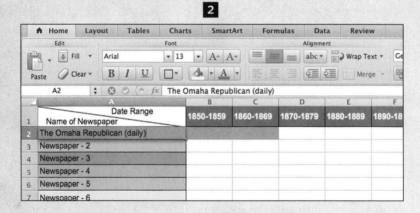

2 **Add titles**. Type in the newspaper names in chronological order in column A by typing over each cell. Be specific with these, as newspaper titles can sometimes have similar names.

Name of Newspaper / Date Range	1850-1859	1860-1869	1870-1879	1880-1889	1890-1899	190
The Omaha Republican (daily)		1864			1890	
Newspaper - 2						
Newspaper - 3						
Newspaper - 4						
Newspaper - 5						

 Add dates. In the appropriate column, type the actual years of publication into the cells for the beginning and ending of the publication's life cycles. For example, if the *Omaha Republican* ran from 1864 to 1890, you would type 1864 in the 1860–1869 column and 1890 in the 1890–1889 column.

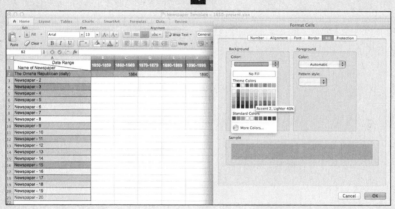

Add colors. Highlight the applicable date range to the right of each newspaper with the same color that appears in column A. You can ensure you have the same color by right-clicking on the column A cell, then clicking Format Cells. Select the Fill tab from the pop-up menu and note which color is being used. Hit cancel and select the cells you want to highlight by left-clicking and dragging. Right-click the outlined cells and follow the same instructions as before, then select the same color that appears in column A. Click OK, and the selected cells will have the same background color.

| | 825 | | | | fx | | | | | |

	A	B	C	D	E	F	G	H	I	
	Date Range / Name of Newspaper	1850-1859	1860-1869	1870-1879	1880-1889	1890-1899	1900-1909	1910-1919	1920-1929	
2	The Omaha Republican (daily)		1864			1890				
3	Western Bugle	1852–53								
4	Omaha Arrow	1854								
5	Papillion Times			1874				1912		
6	Omaha Daily News					1899			1927	
7	Omaha Daily Herald (evening)				1885–1889					
8	Examiner						1900		1924	
9	Newspaper - 8									
10	Newspaper - 9									
11	Newspaper - 10									

5 Repeat, and compare timelines. Keep adding newspapers until you have them all. Now, when you're looking for information about an ancestor in a particular locale, you'll have a quick way of determining what publications you might find him in.

These timelines will be helpful for you in determining how many potential newspapers a geographic area hosts. Remember that this is a starting point; you will likely find that the full runs of some of the newspapers are not preserved. But even if certain titles do not appear to have survived, knowing that they existed helps you focus on newspapers that still may be discovered or available in the collectors market outlined in chapter 13.

INDEX

PHOTO CREDITS

COVER AND INTRODUCTION

Left: Newspapers.com, *Weekly Gazette* (Fort Wayne, Indiana), 1 April 1895, p. 1.

Center: Newspapers.com, *The Daily Special* (McComb City, Mississippi), 29 March 1899, p. 1.

Right/Introduction: Newspapers.com, *The State Sentinel* (Decatur, Illinois), 19 September 1888, p. 1.

Title page: Newspapers.com, *Daily American Telegraph* (Washington, D.C.), 24 March 1851, p. 1.

CHAPTER 1

A: Chronicling America, *Gazette of the United States, & Philadelphia Daily Advertiser* (Philadelphia, Pennsylvania) 1796–1800, 15 November 1798, image 1. Image provided by Library of Congress, Washington, DC.

B: Newspapers.com, *The Leon Journal-Reporter* (Leon, Iowa), 14 July 1938, p. 1.

C: Courtesy <mlive.com>.

CHAPTER 2

A: GenealogyBank, "New Store Opens Today," *Kalamazoo Gazette* (Kalamazoo, Michigan), 28 May 1910, p. 12, col. 4.

B: GenealogyBank, "Son Finds Body of Murdered Mother," *St. Louis Palladium* (St. Louis, Missouri), 17 October 1903, p. 2, col. 5.

C: GenealogyBank, "Three Local Boys on Casualty List," *Trenton Evening Times* (Trenton, New Jersey), 19 October 1918, p. 7, col. 7.

D: GenealogyBank, "Flu Cases Total 81 in City; Four Deaths," *Wilkes-Barre Times* (Wilkes-Barre, Pennsylvania), 7 October 1918, p. 1, col. 3.

E: GenealogyBank, "A Tribute—To Our Policeman!" *Arkansas Democrat* (Little Rock, Arkansas), 31 December 1950, citing print edition, p. 17, col. 4.

F: GenealogyBank, Untitled advertisement, *Tucson Citizen* (Tucson, Arizona), 1 January 1920, p. 2, col. 5.

G: GenealogyBank, *Pennsylvania Gazette* (Philadelphia, Pennsylvania), 30 May 1754, p. 3.

H: GenealogyBank, "To the Citizens of the Borough of Wilmington," *Mirror of the Times, and General Advertiser* (Wilmington, Delaware), 18 January 1800, p. 4, col. 1.

I: GenealogyBank, "Gossip – No. 12," *Daily Alabama Journal* (Montgomery, Alabama), 14 April 1849, p. 2, col. 2.

J: Newspapers.com, "Letters to the Editor," *Fairbanks Daily News-Miner* (Fairbanks, Alaska), 9 January 1960, p. 3, col. 5.

K: GenealogyBank, "Local Church Matters," *Springfield Republican* (Springfield, Massachusetts), 21 June 1904, p. 5, col. 4.

L: GenealogyBank, "Handsome Painting of Hughy Glancy," *Pawtucket Times* (Pawtucket, Rhode Island), 4 June 1903, p. 2, col. 8.

M: GenealogyBank, "Xmas Cantata by L. Rowland", *Grand Forks Daily Herald* (Grand Forks, North Dakota), 10 December 1911, p. 6, col. 4.

N: GenealogyBank, "Remarkable Lineage," *Morning Herald* (Lexington, Kentucky), 6 May 1901, p. 2, col. 3.

O: GenealogyBank, "History of 'The Courant' During 150 Years Since It was Established by Thomas Green," *Hartford Daily Courant* (Hartford, Connecticut), 25 October 1914, p. 2, col. 1.

P: GenealogyBank, "Celebration of Golden Wedding," *Hobart Daily Republican* (Hobart, Oklahoma), 3 March 1915, HTML edition.

Q: GenealogyBank, "Germans Naturalized in Providence Today," *Pawtucket Times* (Pawutcket, Rhode Island), 26 May 1917, p. 12, col. 6.

R: GenealogyBank, "Real Estate Transfers," *Philadelphia Inquirer* (Philadelphia, Pennsylvania), 8 November 1891, p. 6, col. 1.

S: GenealogyBank, "Probate News," *Daily Inter Ocean* (Chicago, Illinois), 28 May 1892, p. 20, col. 1.

CHAPTER 3

A: Chronicling America, "City News: Births at Bismarck Hospital," *Bismarck Daily Tribune* (Bismarck, North Dakota), 24 April 1919, p. 5, col. 1.

B: Chronicling America, *Daily Evening Bulletin* (Maysville, Kentucky), 2 June 1887, p. 3, col. 2.

C: Chronicling America, "Marriage Licenses," *The Topeka State Journal* (Topeka, Kansas), 26 March 1920, p. 7, col. 2.

D: Chronicling America, "Says Wife Kissed Him Only Once During 13 Years," *The Topeka State Journal* (Topeka, Kansas), 26 March 1920, p. 7, col. 5.

E: Chronicling America, "Married Fifty Years," *Polk County Observer* (Dallas, Oregon), p. 1, col. 4.

F: Chronicling America, *The Denison Review* (Denison, Iowa), 21 May 1913, p. 5.

CHAPTER 4

A: Chronicling America, *The daily comet* (Baton Rouge, Louisiana), 6 November 1855, p. 3, col. 1.

B: Chronicling America, "George E. Hiersemann" (obituary), *Rock Island Argus* (Rock Island, Illinois), 29 September 1916, p. 10, col. 3.

C: Courtesy <legacy.com>.

D: Genealogy Bank, "Will of the Late Ananias P. Luse Presented to the Probate Court," *Daily Inter Ocean* (Chicago, Illinois), 29 January 1891, p. 11.

E: Courtesy <findagrave.com>.

CHAPTER 5, ALL ABOUT OCR SIDEBAR

Top: Chronicling America, *Omaha Daily Bee* (Omaha, Nebraska), 5 July 1910, p. 2, image 2. Image provided by: University of Nebraska-Lincoln Libraries, Lincoln, Nebraska.

Middle: Chronicling America, *Tägliches Cincinnatier Volksblatt*, 2 March 1914, p. 4, image 4. Image provided by: Ohio Historical Society.

Bottom: Chronicling America, *De Soto County News* (De Soto, Florida), 8 April 1915, p. 9, image 9. Image provided by: University of Florida.

CHAPTER 6

A, B, C: Courtesy <chroniclingamerica.loc.gov>.

D: Courtesy <news.google.com/newspapers>.

CHAPTER 7

All images courtesy <newspapers.com>.

CHAPTER 8

All images courtesy <genealogybank.com>.

CHAPTER 9

A: Courtesy <newspaperarchive.com>.

1, 2, 3, 4: Courtesy <findmypast.com>.

CHAPTER 10

1, 2, 3: Courtesy <chroniclingamerica.loc.gov>.

A: Courtesy <stanford.edu>.

1, 2, 3, 4: Courtesy <worldcat.org>.

CHAPTER 11

A: California Digital Newspaper Collection, "Stillahatskusten," *Verkusten*, 4 December 1924, p. 5, col. 1.

B: Chronicling America, "New Advertisements," *Southern Sentinel*, 28 November 1849, image 2. Image provided by: Louisiana State University; Baton Rouge, Louisiana.

1, 2, 3: Courtesy <translate.google.com>

CHAPTER 12

A: Courtesy <icon.crl.edu>

Extra, Extra! sidebar: *The Free Press* of London, Ontario, clipping courtesy of Stephen C. Young.

B: Courtesy <findmypast.com>.

C: Courtesy <bsb-muenchen.de/en/collections/newspapers>.

D: Courtesy <trove.nla.gov.au/newspaper>.

CHAPTER 13

A, B: Courtesy the author, James M. Beidler.

C: Courtesy <ebay.com>.

CHAPTER 14

A, B, C: Courtesy Janeen Bjork.

ACKNOWLEDGMENTS

Perhaps fiction authors can pull off working alone, but writing on a nonfiction book without lots of help from many people is impossible.

You will have found many samples from genealogists and historians—both professionals and hobbyists—around the world in this book, and I thank them all profusely for having contributed to this project. To those folks and others listed here, I'd like to express particular appreciation:

Pamela Pracser Anderson, Eric Bender, Janeen Bjork (with special thanks for sharing her lengthy case study), John Boeren, Claudie Breland, Terri Jo Bridgwater, Helen Brieske, Lisa Louise Cooke, Amy Johnson Crow, André Dominguez, Kathryn Doyle, Peter Drinkwater, Dick Eastman, J.H. "Jay" Fonkert, Sean Furniss, Ann C. Gilchrest, Lisa Gorrell, Martha Grenzeback, Rachel Hall Gutzler, Brian Hartzell, Bob Heisse, Patricia Hobbs, Debra A. Hoffman, Marilyn Holt, the late John T. Humphrey, Cyndi Ingle, Margaret Jerrido, Shamele Jordon, L. Suzanne Kellerman, Thomas J. Kemp, Bonnie Kohler, Ronald Larson, Denise Levenick, Alice Lubrecht, Annette Burke Lyttle, Jason Malcolm, Dave McDonald, Jill Morelli, Karen Morrow, Michael John Neill (source of many good newspaper tips), Trish Nicola, Dave Obee, Linda Okazaki, Timothy N. Pinnick, Elissa Powell, Terry Reigel, Pat Richley-Erickson. Judy G. Russell, Laurel Sanders, Kerry Scott, Jonathan Stayer, Carol Singer, Cari Taplin, Julie Tarr, Ernie Thode, Becky Thornton, Karen and Terry Tippets, Travis Westly and Stephen C. Young.

This book also would not have happened without the attention of the F+W team led by publisher Allison Dolan and editor Andrew Koch. Their gifts have enhanced this work from the initial idea to finished manuscript.

Finally, my special thanks go to Sean Kessler, an associate in James M. Beidler Research, for his assistance in the production of this volume.

ABOUT THE AUTHOR

James M. Beidler, a first-career newspaper copy editor, previously authored *The Family Tree German Genealogy Guide* and *Trace Your German Roots Online*, and has written "Roots & Branches," an award-winning weekly newspaper column on genealogy for nearly twenty years. He is also a columnist for *German Life* magazine, edits *Der Kurier* (the quarterly journal of the Mid-Atlantic Germanic Society), and has written for other periodicals, including scholarly journals such as *The Pennsylvania Genealogical Magazine*. He is also an instructor for the online Family Tree University and a contributor to *Family Tree Magazine*.

In addition to his writing, Beidler was president of the International Society of Family History Writers and Editors from 2010 to 2012, and is the former executive director for the Genealogical Society of Pennsylvania. He also served as national co-chairman for the 2008 Federation of Genealogical Societies conference in Philadelphia and sits on the selection committee for the Pennsylvania Digital Newspaper Project and Pennsylvania's State Historic Records Advisory Board.

He is an Enrolled Agent tax preparer and was a copy editor for *The Patriot-News* newspaper in Harrisburg, Pennsylvania, for fifteen years.

Beidler was born and raised in Berks County, Pennsylvania, where he currently resides. He graduated Phi Beta Kappa from Hofstra University in Long Island, New York, with a BA in political science in 1982.

DEDICATION

The late Richard C. "Old Pete" Peters, who as managing editor of the (now defunct) *Reading (PA) Times* hired me for my first newspaper job as a copy boy, also gave me a bit of enduring advice upon leaving for college: "Take as few journalism courses as possible—they can't teach you to write. Take classes to learn what you're writing about." I became a political science major and economics minor, and it's always served me well.

THE FAMILY TREE HISTORICAL NEWSPAPERS GUIDE: HOW TO FIND YOUR ANCESTORS IN ARCHIVED NEWSPA-PERS. Copyright © 2018 by James M. Beidler. Manufactured in the United States of America. All rights reserved. No part of this book may be reproduced in any form or by any electronic or mechanical means including information storage and retrieval systems without permission in writing from the publisher, except by a reviewer, who may quote brief passages in a review. The content of this book has been thoroughly reviewed for accuracy; however, the author and the publisher disclaim any liability for any damages or losses that may result from the misuse of any product or information presented herein. Readers should note that websites featured in this work may have changed between when the book was written and when it was read; always verify with the most recent information. Published by Family Tree Books, an imprint of F+W Media, Inc., 10151 Carver Road, Suite 300, Blue Ash, Ohio 45242. (800) 289-0963. First edition.

4 FREE

FAMILY TREE templates

929.1072 BEIDL
Beidler, James M.
The Family tree historical
newspapers guide : how to
find your ancestors in
archived newspapers   7/18
Neva Lomason
31057014247384

WEST GA REGIONAL LIBRARY SYS

31057014247384

- decorative family tree posters
- five-generation ancestor chart
- family group sheet
- bonus relationship chart
- type and save, or print and fill out

Download at <www.familytreemagazine.com/familytreefreebies>

MORE GREAT GENEALOGY RESOURCES

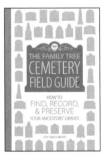

THE FAMILY TREE CEMETERY FIELD GUIDE

By Joy Neighbors

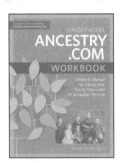

UNOFFICIAL ANCESTRY.COM WORKBOOK

By Nancy Hendrickson

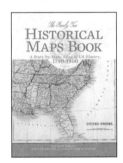

THE FAMILY TREE HISTORICAL MAPS

By Allison Dolan

Available from your favorite bookstore, online booksellers and **<familytreemagazine.com>**, or by calling (855) 278-040

 Join our community! <facebook.com/familytreemagazine>